PRAGMATICS OF DEMOCRACY

Pragmatics of Democracy

A POLITICAL THEORY OF
AFRICAN AMERICAN LITERATURE
BEFORE EMANCIPATION

Douglas A. Jones

The University of Chicago Press   CHICAGO AND LONDON

The University of Chicago Press, Chicago 60637
The University of Chicago Press, Ltd., London
© 2025 by The University of Chicago
All rights reserved. No part of this book may be used or reproduced in any manner whatsoever without written permission, except in the case of brief quotations in critical articles and reviews. For more information, contact the University of Chicago Press, 1427 East 60th Street, Chicago, IL 60637.
Published 2025

34 33 32 31 30 29 28 27 26 25   1 2 3 4 5

ISBN-13: 978-0-226-84511-1 (cloth)
ISBN-13: 978-0-226-84512-8 (paper)
ISBN-13: 978-0-226-84513-5 (ebook)
DOI: https://doi.org/10.7208/chicago/9780226845135.001.0001

Library of Congress Cataloging-in-Publication Data

Names: Jones, Douglas A., author.
Title: Pragmatics of democracy : a political theory of African American literature before emancipation / Douglas A. Jones.
Description: Chicago : The University of Chicago Press, 2025. | Includes bibliographical references and index.
Identifiers: LCCN 2025013544 | ISBN 9780226845111 (cloth) | ISBN 9780226845128 (paperback) | ISBN 9780226845135 (ebook)
Subjects: LCSH: American literature—African American authors—History and criticism. | American literature—African American authors—Political aspects.
Classification: LCC PS153.B53 J67 2025
LC record available at https://lccn.loc.gov/2025013544

Authorized Representative for EU General Product Safety Regulation (GPSR) queries: **Easy Access System Europe**—Mustamäe tee 50, 10621 Tallinn, Estonia, gpsr.requests@easproject.com
Any other queries: https://press.uchicago.edu/press/contact.html

FOR MY JONES GIRLS,
WHO I ALWAYS RUN TO . . .

Contents

Introduction 1

1 · Ecstasy 21

2 · Impersonality 45

3 · Violence 67

4 · Respectability 91

5 · Care 125

Epilogue: "We're Not a Democracy" 151

Acknowledgments 157

Notes 159

Index 187

Introduction

A few months before the Second Continental Congress unanimously declared the thirteen colonies independent from Great Britain, the Welsh pamphleteer Richard Price published *Observations on the Nature of Civil Liberty, the Principles of Government, and the Justice and Policy of the War with America* (1776).[1] *Observations on Civil Liberty* clarified the political-philosophical irony that motivated congressional delegates to constitute themselves as a new polity: only as a people free of the Crown and Parliament could they restore the rights they once enjoyed as Englishmen. Price singled out the Declaratory Act of 1766, which granted Parliament "full power and authority" over American colonists "in all cases whatsoever," as the death blow to their liberties.[2] He rebuked it as a "dreadful power indeed!" and claimed one could not "express slavery in stronger language."[3] The act codified what radicals on both sides of the Atlantic understood as *civil slavery*, which Price deemed the most wretched "state of slavery" possible. He writes: "Such a slavery is worse, on several accounts, than any slavery of private men to one another" because "between one state and another, there is none of that fellow-feeling that takes place between persons in private life."[4] American radicals embraced Price's polemic for the rhetorical force it gave their crusade against the metropole; they had been at war for nearly a year and skeptics throughout the colonies still questioned whether the conflict was necessary and just. The discourse of civil slavery that Price's pamphleteering fueled also solved the moral quandary that racialized chattel slavery posed for the revolutionaries: political freedom did not require the emancipation of Africans and African-descended persons because the African never held the lost liberties the revolution sought to restore.

Narratives of American exceptionalism have obscured the significance of the hierarchization of civil slavery over chattel slavery to the founding of the United States. How the concept of natural rights has evolved discursively—most famously encapsulated in the dictum "all men are created equal, endowed by their Creator with certain unalienable rights" from the Declaration of Independence—has made that story even hazier. The ahistorical reading, which is the reading most familiar to us, regards the founders as progenitors of the idea that a person has natural rights for no other reason than that he is a person; hence, they have become demigods in the American cultural imaginary. Yet the founders were quite clear that the natural rights they were fighting for and entitled to, the rights they had lost when Parliament "enslaved" them, derived from them having held them previously as Englishmen. It took black persons' activism and political-philosophical elaborations for America to begin to grapple seriously with the notion that God or nature confers unalienable rights upon a person simply because he is born. Their efforts were critical to the formation of an American body politic in which persons have rights grounded in their personhood rather than their ancestral or historical lineage—efforts that ushered in our ongoing commitment to egalitarianism as a structure of public life and of modernity itself.

A petition to the Massachusetts legislature in 1777 from eight black men demanding the abolition of chattel slavery in the state instantiates the canniness of their interventions. The petitioners were swept up in the same fervor that animated white revolutionaries but rejected the claim that civil slavery was worse than the enslavement they, their family members, and other black persons suffered. They said there were no caring intimacies, no "fellow-feeling," in being the human property of another person, as Price and pro-slavery apologists such as Thomas Jefferson claimed. Instead, the petitioners declared chattel slavery was "far worse than non-existence" precisely because the institution violated the laws of nature, and it was the legislature's duty to enact an emancipation statute so that enslaved persons "may be Restored to the Enjoyments of that Which is the [Natural] Right of all men."[5] By framing their demand as a *restoration* of rights, they subsumed their arguments under the broader revolutionary discourse that legitimated armed struggle against the metropole. By their lights, the revolution itself would be incomplete, if not nugatory, without abolition: "Every principle from which America has acted in the course of her difficulties with Great-Britain, pleads stronger than a thousand arguments in favor of your petitioners."[6] These men and other revolutionary-era black thinkers and writers insisted on a more expansive form of democracy than what white colonists imagined for America, a conception of being with others in public that emerged from black life in and with chattel slavery.

What interests me is why these eight petitioners, several of whom were then enslaved or had been previously, would ground their appeals in the discourse and procedures of their enslavers. How did they come to develop a plain reading of natural rights that fleshed out the founders' more conservative view, a reading that anticipated the animating logic of the French Declaration of the Rights of Man and of the Citizen (1789) by more than a decade? I take the petitioners' appeals to be more conceptually substantive than politically strategic, that they viewed themselves as co-producers of the revolution's most excellent aims and the new polity's most robust freedoms. Yet what convinced them that speaking to power from the margins could be not only comprehensible but also compelling? Was it the ubiquity of slavery talk in revolutionary discourse? Or was there something about their lives as black persons that disposed them to believe that the truly liberatory implications of the revolution were unattainable without their input? At stake here is the prioritization of the body in the formation of political thought: what inclines persons to deduce from their life experiences critical and normative claims about a political community and one's place in it? How African Americans from the eighteenth century through the national abolition of chattel slavery in the mid-nineteenth century conceived the relationship between bodily knowledge and democratic subjectivization is the subject of this book.

African American political thought before the Thirteenth Amendment to the US Constitution (1865), or what I will call Emancipation, centers principally on self-ownership as the natural or pre-political right upon which to develop any worthwhile political aim.[7] Black thinkers championed democracy as the only way to ensure that a polity maintains self-ownership as its organizing tenet because of democracy's commitment to the equal standing of persons and its mechanisms for the distribution of power across the many, especially among those at the bottom. Given the acts of domination and forms of exclusion they endured in the era, African Americans' trust in democracy might seem puzzling. One way to explain that trust is to say they yielded to the political allure manifested in the wave of democratic revolutions that swept the Atlantic world. The ascendancy of practices in modern politics, economics, and religions that diffuse authority among individuals and blocs of everyday people has made democracy seem like a mode of political organization that humans desire instinctively. But it is not. Ontologies of human nature neither sustain nor correlate absolutely to historically determined manners of political life. Conditions of existence and modalities of participation therein generate democratic and all other forms of political subjectivization. African Americans looked for a politics that would get them out of the horrors they lived as black persons; in democracy, they believed they had found that. "Democracy is the attempt of the many to reverse the natural cycle of power," Sheldon Wolin writes, "to translate social weakness into political power in order to alleviate the consequences of what is not so much their condition as their lottery."[8] This way of life requires intersubjectivities and public associations that are apart from, and not reliant on, governmental institutions for sanction or enforcement. It strives for a polity that safeguards the equality of personhood and standing without judicial fiat, legislative force, or state violence, but as the fruit of an always negotiated shared public culture.[9]

The literature African Americans produced before Emancipation reveals that they came to believe such political communities were attainable because, above all, they felt them to be so. That literature archives a world-historical reordering of what Jacques Rancière calls the "distribution of the sensible," those affective and embodied perceptions with which a person understands where and how his place and his voice fit within a polity. As Rancière puts it: "The distribution of the sensible reveals who can have a share in what is common to the community based on what they do and on the time and space in which this activity is performed. Having a particular 'occupation' thereby determines the ability or inability to take charge of what is common to the community; it defines what is visible or not in a common space, endowed with a common language, etc."[10] With the advent of democratic modalities of dissent as structuring forces in the late colonies and newly formed states, particularly against ecclesiastical and civil officials, enslaved Africans and their descendants laid claim to a set of political commitments that authorized them to *redistribute* the sensible in terms that emerged from their lives as enslaved chattel and the descendants of enslaved chattel. They sensed, and made sensible for others, that the *demos* in "democracy" denotes the "surplus community made up of those who have no qualification to rule, which means at once everybody and anyone at all."[11] *Pragmatics of Democracy* examines their literary productions to detail bodily events, from the ecstasies of religious worship to the brutalities of racial violence and the tenderness of acts of care, that oriented and habituated enslaved and free black persons to render this political judgment. In fact, they came to understand the epistemic frameworks they forged out of their "occupations" as human chattel and former human chattel as the best conceptual groundwork for the development of the most flourishing forms of democratic life.

WHAT WAS AFRICAN AMERICAN LITERATURE BEFORE EMANCIPATION? AN INDEX AND AN INSTRUMENT

A well-connected London merchant wanted to behold the enslaved eighteen-year-old poet who had bewitched the Anglo-American literary world with her verse. In October 1772, he went to her owners' home, where she also lived, on King Street in Boston; he requested that she write a poem before him. Phyllis Wheatley agreed to the request and asked him for a subject. With his own financial and political ambitions in mind, he told her to write about William Legge, Earl of Dartmouth, who had just been appointed Secretary of State for the Colonies. The Americans had long regarded Dartmouth as one of their greatest allies in Parliament because of his advocacy on behalf of the repeal of the Stamp Act in 1766. Wheatley knew this was an opportunity not only to endear herself with British authorities but also to thrust enslaved persons' political claims into the highest reaches of colonial discourse. The result became the poetic encomium "To the Right Honorable William, Earl of Dartmouth," which she composed in front of her visitor in a bravura performance that quelled any doubts he had about her talents.[12]

The first half of the four-stanza poem cheers Dartmouth's appointment as colonial secretary. Its gush of commendations culminates in a prophecy of a new day for the Americans, a day when "Freedom's charms" will "unfold" because Dartmouth now holds "the silken reins."

> No more, *America*, in mournful strain
> Of wrongs, and grievance unredress'd complain,
> No longer shalt thou dread the iron chain,
> Which wanton Tyranny with lawless hand
> Had made, and with it meant t' enslave the land.[13]

Wheatley evokes the colonists' so-called civil slavery ("wanton Tyranny") to transition to the meat of the poem's intervention: the explication of a political morality grounded in her life in chattel slavery. She marks that move with a volta at the start of the third stanza that shifts the poem's geography, temporality, and mode of address into a more informal intimacy:

> Should you, my lord, while you peruse my song,
> Wonder from whence my love of *Freedom* sprung,
> Whence flow these wishes for the common good,
> By feeling hearts alone best understood,
> I, young in life, by seeming cruel fate
> Was snatch'd from *Afric's* fancy'd happy seat:
> What pangs excruciating must molest,
> What sorrows labour in my parent's breast?
> Steel'd was that soul and by no misery mov'd
> That from a father seiz'd his babe belov'd:
> Such, such my case. And can I then but pray
> Others may never feel tyrannic sway?[14]

If American revolutionary politics emerged vis-à-vis political tyranny, Wheatley's did out of the existential tyrannies of capture and enslavement. Despite its decided lyricization, the poem homes in on the shared significance of her condition. Her "case," out of which "flows" her "wishes for the common good," instantiates the source of African American political thought. The formal constraints (e.g., Augustan poetics, neoclassicism) and lack of overt radicalism in Wheatley's poetry that so many critics have decried should not obscure the centrality of her work to what Paul Gilroy describes as an "anti-hierarchical tradition of thought that probably culminates in [the] idea that ordinary people do not need an intellectual vanguard to help them to speak or tell them what to say."[15] That ordinary people have authorized themselves to think and act politically in their own terms, based on their own lifeworlds and toward their own ends, is the bedrock of democracy.

Early black thinkers and writers like Wheatley regularly eschewed traditional forms of political philosophy. Their reasons range from the lack of training in formal disciplinarity to efforts to seize a broad readership via popular genres and formats. In any case, the generic and textual heterogeneity of early African American political thought requires attention to how the literary allows for dimensions of expressive clarity and resonance that conventionally philosophical discourse might not. Does the predominance of experience in autobiography and other genres of life-writing elucidate aspects of political striving in ways rationalist texts cannot? How might these differences reveal attributes of epistemic authority that would otherwise remain obscure(d)? Does the literary sketch's prioritization of character focalize capacities and virtues of personhood that other types of writing obfuscate or minimize? Might poetry and poetics' embrace of ineffability yield more compelling renderings of the grandeur of human dignity than do the analytical ruminations that philosophers since at least Immanuel Kant have offered? This book takes up these questions through a sustained scrutiny of how literary writing might enable particular features of political philosophizing.

I argue that African American literature before Emancipation serves the very basic, though overlooked, function of establishing a historicity of democratic theory: these are texts about persons coming into democratic personality that are missing from, or lacking parallels in, other Anglo-American literary traditions. However (auto)biographical or evidential of the so-called black experience, such stories "need not collapse into essence or epistemic closure" vis-à-vis black life, as Lewis Gordon writes of the "problem of biography in Africana thought."[16] Rather, their most abiding significance is found in their potential to broaden conceptual horizons beyond, and at times despite, the biographical event. To that effect, early African American narratives offer speculations, categories, and hermeneutics concerning democracy grounded in black life amid chattel slavery in the New World that sometimes contradict, sometimes complement those that prevailed in early American political thought.

Like any literature, what early black writers produced is a considered curation of those features of the world its writers, readers, editors, and critics found most meaningful. Their work offers what Jacques Rancière would call "a partition of the visible and the sayable, [an] intertwining of being, doing, saying that frames a polemical common world." Such framings—or, better, the motivations and interests that determine what is worthy to be framed at all—are "the politics of literature."[17] Emergent approaches in (African) American literary studies have established new critical agendas and priorities that move beyond critique to parse other aspects of the frames of black writing before Emancipation, such as its political aesthetics and normative claims. Spearheaded by Derrick Spires's scholarship in *The Practice Citizenship: Black Politics and Print Culture in the Early United States* (2019) and elsewhere, the dominant trend in the field is to explicate black writers' notions of citizenship. Spires hails citizenship as the watchword of early African American literary discourse and print cultures. The concept of citizenship is "capacious" in his work, moving beyond state-based protections, rights, and privileges to encompass "less structured acts, such as greeting others on the street."[18] There are two far-reaching problematics with so sweeping a definition: (1) It renders all uses of citizenship as a term effectually defunct; if something as mundane as greeting others connotes citizenship, what acts of interpersonal public exchange do not? (2) It obscures early African American literary writers' chief political-philosophical concern: the rudiments of democracy. As a corpus, their writing revolves around the matter of "self-ownership: he [who] must not be a slave," which is the *precondition* of citizenship, not citizenship per se.[19]

What I want to posit for the writings I explore in the chapters that follow is that they (and contemporaneous black-authored texts) constitute a "distinct literature" that measures and enacts democracy as a form of life. My argument responds to Kenneth Warren's field-stirring contention that black American writers only created African American literature as such in the era of segregation because of the "imperative demands" of Jim Crow laws and sociality. It was in this era, Warren says, that they self-consciously produced a literature that was "indexical" of the status of the race and "instrumental" in the effort to topple Jim Crow. Warren claims earlier works by black Americans were folded into this literature "only retroactively," but submits that he is "willing to concede in the face of textual evidence that some black writing before the Civil

War was understood by its practitioners and readers as something like a distinct literature."[20] *Pragmatics of Democracy* offer such evidence. From the lyricizations of enslaved poets in the eighteenth century to the black nationalist narratives of the 1850s, African Americans regarded their writing as *indexical* of the production of individual and collective democratic arousal. Black literary accomplishment was their "metric for assessing" the state of democracy in America—rather than "the progress of the race" in the face of a regime such as Jim Crow segregation, as it later would.[21] Early black readers and writers also understood their literary efforts as *instrumental* in the dissemination of democratic principles, especially self-ownership, as the normative regulatory codes for the polity. Their discourses, figures, and perspectives contributed to a range of affective and intellectual structures that organized discourse, public culture, and personal habits. Such efforts revolutionized American "doxa," or what Pierre Bourdieu defines as "that which is beyond question and which each agent tacitly accords by the mere fact of acting in accord with social convention."[22] The steady integration of the significations of early African American literature into doxa expanded the limits of democratic praxis in the era and beyond.

One of the most tangible effects of this integration was the redemption of the language of democracy in American literary and political lexicons, even though black writers rarely used the word or its permutations. Before the late 1820s, "democracy" was mostly a pejorative because it evoked social chaos and political disarray. Thomas Paine, in *The Rights of Man* (1791), wrote that the "simple democracy" of classical Athens would not work for a polity as complex as the United States because it does not allow for the kinds of civic restrictions (e.g., the vote) and safeguards the founders favored.[23] Paine and his contemporaries viewed democracies as unmanageable and overly excitable, but championed republics as practical and inherently prudential.[24] They espoused republicanism as the way to contain the bottom-up disruptions (e.g., mob rule or self-defeating policy ambitions) they associated with democracy. It was not until the Age of Jackson that democratic discourses came to be seen as positive goods in American literary and political cultures. (The Democratic Party was founded in 1828, for example.) The most familiar story we tell about the rise of chants democratic across the US credits white working-class persons, the so-called "common man," for this development. But it was the work African Americans began in the second half of the eighteenth century that initiated that phenomenon and established its discursive groundwork. Their efforts, literary and otherwise, affirmed a robust democratic culture as the engine of our ongoing pursuit of the country's finest aims and ideals.

DEMOCRACY AS SLAVE MORALITY

The best framework for understanding how (black) persons arrived at such commitments to democracy comes from Friedrich Nietzsche's moral philosophy. The Eurocentric aristocratism that organizes Nietzschean morality suggests it has nothing to offer black political thought other than a catalogue of racist logics and affronts that African American thinkers have had to navigate and rebut. William A. Preston's summary dismissal is instructive: "In the most profound sense, Nietzsche's whole philosophy—and not just his view of blacks—is racist. Blacks to Nietzsche are at a lower stage of evolution than whites, and as such are generally of marginal consideration."[25] Despite such judgments (which are ubiquitous), recent efforts to reclaim features of Nietzsche's thought as a positive resource for Black Studies have been generative.[26] I am not interested in doing so here because I find his deeply illiberal moral philosophy to be made in good faith and thus quite clarifying of the ideas he disdained. When one takes Nietzsche's moral philosophy as it is, a rather coherent schema of democracy and its historicity comes into view. That schema unfolds in his vehement and precise attack on what he called slave morality.

Slave morality rests on the repudiation of what Nietzsche calls "the aristocratic value equation (good = noble = powerful = beautiful = happy = blessed)."[27] It empowers the weak, the downtrodden, the outcast, and even the enslaved to make demands on the masters and the powerful that other political moralities preclude. Nietzsche develops his notion of slave morality out of his famously anti-Semitic genealogy of human valuation, at the top of which stands Jesus of Nazareth "as the embodiment of the gospel of love, this 'redeemer' bringing salvation and victory to the poor, the sick, to sinners—was he not seduction in its most sinister and irresistible form, seduction and the circuitous route to just those very *Jewish* values and innovative ideals?"[28] Nietzsche scorned the loving compassion of the Golden Rule, which Jesus preached in the Sermon on the Mount (Matthew 7:12), as a most disastrous development in the history of morals and the certain downfall of any society that adopts it as a credo.

In the eighteenth and early nineteenth centuries, black persons first came to adopt these new "values and innovative ideals" by way of the affective and intellectual revolutions of the First and Second Great Awakenings. They emerged from the awakenings with the belief that the "classical ideal, of the noble method of valuing everything," contravened God's word (*Logos*) because all persons, regardless of race or condition, are God's children (*imago dei*) and are therefore equally "good."[29] The political import of evangelical theology was obvious and monumental, and it quickly became the ideological foundation for abolitionism and black civil rights. If "[d]emocracy is the culmination of radical [P]rotestantism," as George Kateb writes, its most pervasive functionality is as slave morality.[30]

Lemuel Haynes's 1776 sermon "Liberty Further Extended" exemplifies the ways African American thinkers formulated democratic politics out of their evangelicalism. Haynes was one of the first black ordained ministers in America. He was indentured as an infant and became free when he turned twenty-one in 1774. Shortly after being released from his contract, Haynes joined a patriot militia, then moved on to study formal theology. His revolutionary bona fides and belief in the American project define his corpus. "Liberty Further Extended" epitomizes those commitments; its epigraph, for example, is the "unalienable rights" dictum from the Declaration of Independence. Yet Haynes's chief aim is to close the gap between the "good" (white, free, European) and the "bad" (black, enslaved, African). He writes: "To affirm, that an Englishman has a right to his Liberty, is a truth which has Been so clearly Evinced, Especially of Late, that to spend time in illustrating this, would be But Superfluous tautology. But I query, whether Liberty is so contracted a principle as to be Confin'd to any nation under Heaven; nay, I think it not hyperbolical to affirm, that Even an affrican [sic], has Equally as good a right to his Liberty in common with Englishmen."[31] Haynes calls liberty and freedom "innate principle[s]," and argues that to violate them is to do the work of the devil: "As *tyrony* had its Origin from the infernal regions: so it is the Deuty, and honner of Every son of freedom to repel her first motions. But while we are Engaged in the important struggle, it cannot Be tho't impertinent for us to turn one Eye into our own Breast, for a little moment, and See . . . we Do not find the monster Lurking in our Bosom." Haynes wrote the sermon so that its audiences and readers would purge themselves of this evil because, as he puts it, "Liberty is a Jewel which was handed Down to man from the cabinet of heaven, and is Coæval with his Existance."[32]

Haynes's judgment of individuals who violate another person's liberty or freedom as *evil* is the very axiological transposal on which Nietzsche's moral philosophy pivots. The "bad" in the "good/bad" binary comes to rechristen himself as "good," and he condemns the erstwhile "good" as "evil." Nietzsche writes: "Exactly the opposite is true of the noble one who conceives of the basic idea 'good' by himself, in advance and spontaneously, and only then creates a notion of 'bad'! This 'bad' of noble origin and that 'evil' from the cauldron of unassuaged hatred—the first is an afterthought, an aside, a complementary color, whilst the other is the original, the beginning, the actual deed in the conception of slave morality—how different are the two words 'bad' and 'evil,' although both seem to be the opposite for the same concept, 'good'!"[33] Slave morality, which underlies Haynes's sermon and African American democratic thought generally, comes into being precisely when those at the bottom begin to view their oppression as evil and formulate a politics based on that epiphany and reversal. Nietzsche disdained such politics as cynical, enervating value systems that enfeeble society and preclude human greatness. But for black thinkers in the eighteenth and nineteenth centuries, a politics founded on slave morality was precisely what was necessary for the most equitable and thriving society: it diffuses power and mitigates suffering for the broadest segment of the populace, especially for those who are literally enslaved.

To be sure, the belief in human equality in the eyes of one's God(s) and within religious milieux had long been established in Western history.[34] The political-philosophical upheaval that reoriented the course of human events, however, was African Americans' translation of that belief into secular politics. The Christian formats, lexicons, and religiosity that overdetermined early black rhetoric should not obfuscate just how transformative the interventions of black persons' slave morality were to the advent of egalitarian secularity in the West. The *fin-de-siècle* philosopher Anna Julia Cooper called their political ethos "the cause of the weak." Writing in the context of black feminist philosophy, itself a slave morality *par excellence*, Cooper argues that "when all the weak shall have received their due consideration," all persons will have their "rights"; at that point, "all the strong will have learned at last to deal justly, to love mercy, and to walk humbly; and our fair land will have been taught the secret of universal courtesy which is after all nothing but the art, the science, and the religion of regarding one's neighbor as one's self, and to do for him as we would, were conditions swapped, that he do for us."[35] Cooper renders democracy the secularization of what Jesus named as one of the two great commandments (Mark 12:31). The cause of the weak gives democracy its distinctive power to honor the sanctity and standing of all persons. Cooper's political vision derived from the conceptual interventions and interpretative protocols inaugurated by the African American thinkers I examine in this book.

PROCEDURES OF HABITUATION: A TYPOLOGY OF DEMOCRATIC SUBJECTIVIZATION

Melvin Rogers has recently explored the question of why African Americans maintained "faith" in democracy despite "the persistence of racial violence, exclusion, and domination" in American life.[36] He argues that they held an "aspirational view of the people" that hinged on two interrelated political-philosophical tenets: naturalism and perfectionism. Naturalism, he writes, is "the basic claim that society's norms emerged from our interactions with each other and the wider world to which we belong." Our worldly embeddedness thus authorizes the perfectionist aims that regulate African Americans' commitment to democracy. Perfectionism here means "a way of thinking about the *existing* features of democratic life (e.g., norms, beliefs, and social practices) and the cognitive-affective dimensions of human beings that make possible imagined futures," not "some static vision of the good or human excellence."[37] In Rogers's reading of black thinkers and artists from the early nineteenth through the mid-twentieth centuries, African Americans' faith in democracy rests on their belief that, contrary to what history might otherwise suggest, we can fashion a polity dedicated to "freedom and equal ethical standing [that] shows care and concern" for others because human actors are capable of creating it simply by virtue of being situated in the natural world.[38] Rogers details a perfectionist strain in African American political thought that is prophetic and notional: democracy's appeal is the promise of a better future to come.[39]

The reading of that tradition that I offer in *Pragmatics of Democracy*, albeit using an earlier epoch of black political thought than Rogers does, traces the more immediate contexts and bodily events that cultivate democratic habits of mind and action as productive of the most excellent forms of life.[40] These pragmatics are embodied, iterative, and normative procedures of habituation that discipline persons to internalize externalities and transform historical contingency (e.g., democratic personality) into our second nature. The body functions as habitus in these procedures, constituting a personal disposition that changes in relation to one's own actions, the actions of others, and nonhuman effects. As Pierre Bourdieu explains, the "objective structures" of one's world determine how he comes to understand himself and to act accordingly within that and other worlds. This "dialectical relationship" or habitus becomes the constitutional framework out of which subjecthood, political or otherwise, emerges.[41] One of the major lessons for political philosophy of Bourdieu's sociology is its insistence on attending to the historicity of a normative concept's provenance and the material instruments (e.g., the body) of its establishment across time and space. Such focus reveals not only the practical corruptions and epistemological blind spots of ideas like citizenship or liberty, but also how those ideas are negotiated and (re)imagined on the ground via the messiness of human interaction, exchange, and desire. In short, African Americans developed a *visceral* faith in democracy by means of bodily matters.

Concretized, historically situated variants of concepts amount to much firmer bases upon which to pursue political projects than do those borne of the *a priori* ratiocinations of ideal theory. Among the "vices of ideal theory," Charles Mills writes, is "the reliance on idealization to the exclusion, or at least marginalization, of the actual.... [Thus, it] is no accident that historically subordinated groups have always been deeply skeptical of ideal theory, generally see its glittering ideals as remote and unhelpful, and are attracted to nonideal theory."[42] This book examines what the experiences of one of these groups—enslaved black persons and their descendants in the slaveholding US—reveal about democratic subjectification as a mode of personhood that is achieved, conscious, and agential. It details how procedures of habituation within particular settings of black life create habitus inclined toward democratic forms of life.

The first chapter, "Ecstasy," examines how spiritual ravishment of bodies was paramount to enslaved and free black persons' adoption of evangelical theology's democratic elaborations. Religionists drew on

African traditions of full-bodied religious worship such as spirit possession to make Christianity appealing to downtrodden populations throughout British North America. Enslaved Africans largely rejected the proselytizing efforts of the Anglican Church because its doctrine and approaches were too noetic. But the evangelical call to be seized by God through the Holy Spirit evoked repertories of African religionism and refashioned Christianity as something far different from a pro-slavery, antiblack theology: that any person could be possessed by the Holy Spirit and achieve such direct intimacy with God was proof of the equality of personhood. I am interested in how these beliefs disposed black evangelical poets such as Phyllis Wheatley, Richard Allen, and Jupiter Hammon to initiate and contribute to Anglo-American literary cultures as forms of democratic dissent and personal fulfillment. They recognized how central literary discourse was to American political culture, and they regarded themselves as worthy contributors with the same authority as their white counterparts. Like slave spirituals and black folk tales, their poetry portrayed evangelical ecstasy and Jesus as close friend and guarantor of their deliverance as evidence of the sanctity of democracy.

The propinquity of God and man in early black theology found a powerful analogue in Emersonian Transcendentalism. Ralph Waldo Emerson's aphorism in "Circles" (1841)—"I am God in nature; I am a weed by the wall"—captures the notion of the divinity of human lowliness so fundamental to African American democratic thought.[43] Chapter 2, "Impersonality," explains how Frederick Douglass teased out the political implications of a shared divinity across persons—that is, impersonality—to refute racial biologism and the regimes of race-based subjugation it justified. Douglass's elaborations of Transcendentalist impersonality became his most potent condemnation of the highly influential pro-slavery science of the American School of Ethnology. At the core of his metaphysics is an understanding of the impersonal that spurns racial ontologies and their sociopolitical ascriptions. Through an extended reading of "Claims of the Negro, Ethnologically Considered" (1854), which Douglass first delivered at Western Reserve College and then circulated as a pamphlet, I describe how he repudiated antebellum ethnology to contend that all anyone can know about persons, black or otherwise, is that they are persons and therefore possess the same divinity as all other persons. Although "Claims" is Douglass's most scientific piece of writing, it ultimately lands upon Transcendentalism as the ground upon which to assert the shared political promise of impersonality: "Human rights stand upon a common basis ... all mankind have the same wants, arising out of a common nature ... God has no children whose rights may be safely trampled upon."[44] Perhaps paradoxically, the impersonal relies on the materiality of the body where, like the phantom limb, one feels its facticity.

If the body *qua* body affirms that persons have the "same wants" and a "common nature," physical violations of bodies do the same. The ubiquity of violence in early America gave rise to the notion of bodily integrity as a verity and a structure of modern democracy. Hannah Arendt has argued famously that violence is a speechless instrumentality that inhibits speech and thus politics itself. While violence might be "exclusively bent upon the destruction of the old" and aims to annihilate its victim(s), it regularly leaves some form of life in its wake from which something new can arise.[45] *Pragmatics of Democracy* explicates how democratic subjectivization emerges from the wreckage of violence, especially when jumbled with domestic intimacies. I argue that violence is not democracy's "greatest enemy," but one of its main catalysts.[46]

The history of bonded servitude in early colonial Virginia offers an excellent case in point. Virginians disciplined indentured white men and women with a cruelty that was rare in England. These laborers were subject to violent punishments that resulted in maiming and even death. But the colony's material conditions regularly forced them to live side by side with their masters. The entanglements between domesticity and brutal labor regimes, coupled with the lack of awe that buttressed the nobility and clergy in England, fostered structures of grievance and resentment that convinced white laborers that their masters were not their natural or ancestral betters. (The implicit force in the growing numbers of post-indenture free men with longer life expectancies, particularly in the aftermath of Bacon's Rebellion [1676], strengthened their resolve.) One might tease out facets of this history in the emphasis on bodily integrity in the first principles of American jurisprudence, republicanism, and liberalism, but the absence of experiential accounts from colonial white laborers means we must look elsewhere to discover how violent domestic subjection and labor exploitation readies persons for democratic self-(re)creation and frames democracy's tenets as axiomatic boons.

Chapter 3, "Violence," reads Harriet E. Wilson's semi-autobiographical novel *Our Nig* (1859) as a seminal text by which to grasp these dynamics.⁴⁷ A sort of bildungsroman of an African American girl called Frado abandoned in antebellum New Hampshire, *Our Nig* illustrates (domestic) violence's ability to foster democratic subjectivization irrespective of one's racial or gender identities. Frado endures incredible physical and psychic injury at the hands of several members of the Bellmont family, with whom she lives after her mother abandons her. She immediately becomes a menial in her foster home, and the nature of her labor and maltreatment belies the fact that she is neither enslaved nor indentured. The novel is nothing if not a catalogue of the torture Frado endures, brutality that worsens over the course of her childhood and adolescent years. After more than a decade of abuse, and under threat of attack with a stave, she commands her tormentors to stop the persecution: "Strike me, and I'll never work a mite more for you" (p. 58). Frado's speech act, which Arendt would deem a political response to violence's anti-politics, upends her relationship with the Bellmonts, compelling her to leave their home, follow her conscience, and deem her own intuitions and thoughts worthy of a full hearing. In the wake of domestic violence, she seizes a liberating power with which to pursue a life that comports with her own desires and intellection. The ambiguity of Frado's status redoubles the novel's force as political philosophy by framing cultures of violence as central to the establishment of bodily integrity as a credo of modern democracy.

Pain implicates the utter commonness of human bodies. Early black writers' assertions of bodily commonality bear on the vexed philosophical matter of the place of honor in a democracy. In fine, their narratives posit that honor is inimical to democracy because the cultivation of honor depends on interpersonal power relations fully at odds with the democratic tenets of equal human value, self-ownership, and civil parity. Orlando Patterson has elucidated the inextricability of honor and slavery, and pre-Emancipation Americans would have been keenly aware of their interrelation. "[T]he honor of the master was enhanced by the subjugation of his slave," Patterson writes, and "wherever slavery became structurally very important, the whole tone of the slaveholders' culture tended to be honorific."⁴⁸ Chattel slavery was structurally determinative to what became the US; thus, slave ownership was the most readily available way to attain honor therein. What's more, the slaveholder's honor did not rub off on his human chattel: they were always and remained fully degraded despite whatever material or psychological benefit their proximity to slaveholding power might have conferred. Such hierarchies violate the ethic of radical commonness of persons in its theological (e.g., evangelical) or philosophical (e.g., Transcendental) formulations.

The rejection of honor in early African American literary discourse in favor of something more basic, more attainable for all persons—namely, respectability—is the subject of the fourth chapter, "Respectability." Unlike honor, one achieves respectability through acts of self-imposition that do not degrade others or profane their dignity; the oppressive and self-defeating excesses of the non-respectable clarify its probity. Poor and working-class black persons embodied this form of respectability to great effect in how they navigated a polity that denigrated their race and labor. For them, respectability "was not based in a defense of extant social relations," as Tavia Nyong'o writes, "but enacted through a mimetic performative intervention into those relations, upon terms they well knew white supremacy might find unacceptable." They "claimed respect in the face of its quotidian denial."[49] This bottom-up form of respectability is at odds with the more familiar (and derided) form of respectability politics that capitulates to bourgeois norms to curry favor with majoritarian institutions and other social hegemons. It calls on others to recognize that society's lowliest are as good as, and thus equal to, all others in the polity. The labor activist Peter Paul Simons and the abolitionist-intellectual James McCune Smith, leading advocates of the egalitarian form of respectability in the antebellum era, were frequently at odds with other black reformers such as Frederick Douglass who felt African Americans were best served when they showcased the most decorous and accomplished of the race. I read Simons's political writings and McCune Smith's ennobling sketches of the lives of everyday black persons, *Heads of the Colored People, Done with a Whitewash Brush* (1852–1854), to theorize respectability's democratic capacity and why it is democracy's highest personal virtue.

Simons, McCune Smith, and similarly inclined proponents of respectability believe all persons deserve respect simply because they are persons. They did not base that claim on appeals to human dignity or on a conviction that persons possess some sort of inviolable intrinsic value. In this regard, they shared Immanuel Kant's perspective on dignity and respect, which, as Oliver Sensen writes in his groundbreaking explication of Kantian moral philosophy, holds that "[i]t is not because others have a value that one should respect them, but it is because one should respect them that they have an importance and a dignity."⁵⁰ I have no evidence that early black writers read Kant, nor am I interested in establishing them as unwitting proto-neo-Kantians. But my reading of Kant alongside their work heeds their refusal to cede the terrain of political theory to (white) thinkers who are more self-consciously philosophers. Charles Mills writes, "The moral and political agenda of those persons not originally seen as full persons will be significantly different from the agenda of those whose personhood has traditionally been uncontested, and we need concepts, narratives, and theories that register this crucial difference."⁵¹ This book responds to this call in its study of (formerly) enslaved persons' and their antebellum descendants' judgments of democracy and its features. If our world was shaped by a "normative architecture based on racist Kant-like principles," as Mills writes, the writers and cultural producers I explore in *Pragmatics of Democracy* offered narratives that help topple that architecture and craft blueprints for the rebuilding of American democracy in more robust and equitable formations.⁵²

Black feminist thought has taught us that care is at the core of this effort. How individuals give and receive care shapes homes, communities, and political bodies. Early black thinkers dwelled on the question of the meaning of care and the interconnectedness of persons in (racial) groups, or what now we call relationality, especially in the decade leading up to the American Civil War when separatist black nationalism emerged as a dominant discourse in black political thought. The most ruminative, sociologically complex fictive rendering of care politics, relationality, and democracy in African American letters before Emancipation is Frank J. Webb's *The Garies and Their Friends* (1857). Webb's novel of manners follows the lives of black Philadelphians across the class spectrum whose struggles for self-determination and communal improvement are beset by quotidian racist affronts and a massive race riot. Chapter 5, "Care," reads *The Garies and Their Friends* as a profound meditation on the ways care in and around the home countervails the effects of white supremacist practices and logics in America. The novel posits regimens of domesticity that foster personal, familial, and neighborly care as the primary front in the realization of democratic flourishing, especially in a multiracial polity.

An emphasis on the actions of and effects on human bodies anchors my explication of care in *The Garies and Their Friends*, as it does every chapter of this book. In this regard, I hope to build on the new materialism in political theory that starts from the premise that the human body "is inevitably a vehicle for the exercise of [political] agency" but exists, according to Sharon Krause, in a "material world" that "establishes the conditions of possibility for the exercise of [such] agency." *Pragmatics of Democracy* theorizes the emergence of democratic habitus out of this "corporeal context."[53] Its readings of African American literature before Emancipation yield new elaborations of materialist accounts of democratic socialization by way of largely untapped intellectual resources in political philosophy; likewise, it aims to expand critical hermeneutics and frames in early African American literary studies.

1 · Ecstasy

One of the most remarkable phenomena in the history of black life in British North America is the century-and-a-half-long resistance to Christianity among enslaved Africans. The primacy of the church to the development of African American politics, culture, and community seems to belie the incredible failures that defined proselytization campaigns in the era. Slaveholder opposition to black Christianization is certainly part of the story: there were ubiquitous fears that giving enslaved persons the gospel would disrupt work habits, and worse, that conversions and baptisms would necessitate manumissions. Some colonial legislatures assuaged the latter concern with laws declaring that receiving the holy sacraments "doth not exempt [slaves] from bondage"; for the former, ministers developed a minor homiletic literature which argued that black Christianization not only engendered more "serviceable, obedient, and obliging . . . servants," but also fulfilled an apostolic duty to save "the souls of our Negroes."[1] As slaveholders relented and welcomed proselytizers onto their plantations and into their homes, however reservedly, enslaved persons found little conceptual or practical material in Christianity that made it germane to their conditions. African theologies thus retained for them religious and political salience, even as devotional and doctrinal specifics faded in New World settings.

Consider the struggles of the Society for the Propagation of the Gospel in Foreign Parts (SPG), the missionary organization the Church of England founded in 1701 with the express purpose of converting all persons in the British Americas to Anglicanism. Ecclesiastical authorities did not foresee just how hard the SPG's work with the enslaved would be. They fretted over "difficulties" such as language barriers and "Pagan Rites and Idolatries" that made Africans "prejudiced against other religions, and more particularly against the Christian."[2] But correspondences suggest the SPG never fully appreciated that enslaved persons understood how Anglicanism furnished institutional, if not spiritual, reinforcements to chattel slavery. When the Reverend Francis Le Jau oversaw SPG efforts in parts of South Carolina, for example, he required a sworn oath from black candidates pledging they would not cite their baptism to press for freedom.[3] Such measures rendered Christianity hostile to the worldly interests of the enslaved, only compounding the peculiarity of Anglican noetic-textual traditions that alienated persons reared in West and West Central African religions.

Among the small numbers of black Anglican converts, some did discern a liberatory potentiality in Christianity that conflicted with the assurances proselytizers gave slaveholders and lawmakers. An enslaved man Le Jau called "the best scholar of all the negroes" in one of his parishes emerged from a reading of the gospel with a prophecy that alarmed local authorities. Because of "the Sins in these latter days" he saw around him, the man "told his Master abruptly that there wou'd be a dismal time and the Moon wou'd be turn'd to Blood, and there wou'd be dearth of darkness."[4] The prophecy caused an uproar in the community, and Le Jau had to reassure several constituencies that his teachings did not encourage rebellion or any other form of defiance. The historians Sylvia R. Frey and Betty Wood call the man's prophecy and hermeneutics the "earliest extant record of the millennial theme in African American Protestant Christianity."[5] For millennialist and other forms of African American Protestantism to take hold, large numbers of enslaved persons had to convert and make the religion their own. What occasioned these conversions were wholesale transformations in the meanings and praxis of colonial American Christianity that began in the 1730s.

These radical changes in theology and worship modalities conditioned the affective and intellectual revolutions that came to be known as the First Great Awakening (1733–1745). Enslaved and free black persons emerged from the Awakening with the belief that the prevailing metrics for measuring persons' value flouted God's word because all persons are equal as God's children.[6] Thus they embraced the anti-hierarchism at the core of evangelical theology, crafting a slave morality they then translated into any number of secular campaigns for abolition and black civil rights.

This chapter explores how ecstasy was paramount to enslaved and free black persons' elaborations of evangelicalism's democratic significance. Religionists drew on African traditions of full-bodied religious worship such as spirit possession to make Christianity appealing to black populations throughout British North America. The evangelical call to be seized by God through the Holy Spirit evoked repertoires of African religionism and refashioned Christianity as something very different from the pro-slavery theology proselytizers such as Le Jau and the SPG propounded; that any person could be possessed by the Holy Spirit and achieve such direct intimacy with God was proof of the equality of personhood. These beliefs disposed black evangelical writers such as Phyllis Wheatley, Richard Allen, and Jupiter Hammon to inaugurate and participate in Anglo-American literary cultures as forms of democratic dissent and personal fulfillment. They recognized how central literary discourse was to American political culture and regarded themselves as worthy contributors with the same authority as their white counterparts.

EVANGELICAL ORATURE AND DEMOCRATIC PERSONALITY

The New Light clergyman and evangelist Samuel Davies spearheaded the first lasting and successful crusade to teach enslaved persons in the colonial American South, if not all British North America, to read and write.[7] The earliest resident Presbyterian minister in the Virginia Piedmont, Davies began making inroads in literacy among the enslaved in 1751 after procuring support from the London-based Society for Promoting Religious Knowledge among the Poor, an evangelical tract society lay dissenters founded in 1750 to distribute gratis Bibles, Testaments, spelling primers, and Isaac Watts's hymnals, among other texts. In a series of solicitation letters to society benefactors, Davies hails the "poor . . . NEGROE SLAVES" of Hanover as "the most proper objects of the SOCIETY's Charity" because of the singular ardency with which they sought to rectify their "Want of [Christian] Instruction" and thus pursue the "Means of Grace."[8] He could not satisfy enslaved parishioners' demand for books. They spent what little leisure time they had learning to read and worshipping with these texts, doing so on their own or in small societies, often holding night-long meetings in Davies's home. He writes: "Sundry of them have lodged all night in my kitchen; and, sometimes, when I have awaked at two or three a-clock in the morning, a torrent of sacred harmony poured into my chamber, and carried my mind away to Heaven. In this seraphic exercise, some of them spent almost the whole night. I wish, Sir, you and their other Benefactors could hear one of these sacred concerts: I am persuaded it would please and surprise you more than an Oratorio, and a St. Cæcilia's Day."⁹ Davies embraced music in his evangelism, making him a pioneer among American dissenting proselytizers, but enslaved parishioners' worship milieu instantiated a broader phenomenon of (African) American religious life: black evangelicals grounded their devotional and intellectual habits in their belief in the interanimation of the embodied and the textual.¹⁰

Put differently, the advent of black literacy and eventually literature in British North America was in many ways a religio-cultural event that emerged from slaves' and their descendants' refusal to dissociate or hierarchize the oral and the literary, but to hold these communicative technologies in symbiotic relation. Performance theorists understand this relation as one of orature, a conception that "goes beyond a schematized opposition of literacy and orality as transcendent categories; rather, it acknowledges that these modes of communication have produced one another interactively over time and that their historic operations may be usefully examined under the rubric of performance."¹¹ Orature became the dominant communicative paradigm of mid-eighteenth-century evangelical cultural productions because it empowered New Light ministers and proselytizers to cultivate demotic, often extemporaneous performance forms that promised direct, readily achievable access to the divine. This repertoire of ecstatic embodied practices—dancing, shrieking, frenzied gesticulations, and rapt transfixion, among other behaviors that collectively came to be known as *shouting*—consolidated into a distinctive worship style that not only countered the noetic rhetoric and textuality that ecclesiastical authorities upheld as doctrinal necessities in order to reinforce sociopolitical hegemony, but also implored persons to experience God personally and without intercession, which is a sacred imperative of evangelicalism. The somatic prioritization and theological tenets constitutive of that style engendered a field of interracial contact and acculturation theretofore nonexistent in British North America, and furnished the phenomenological and symbolic means for those who had ignored or rejected Christianity to view the religion as a positive resource for their spiritual and secular betterment. Indeed, the remarkably latitudinal matrix of evangelical orature compelled even the most outcast persons of the colonial population to reimagine Christianity, ecclesial and civil polities, and their standing within each.[12]

For the enslaved, shouting achieved the greatest significance within cultures of evangelical orature. W. E. B. Du Bois identified shouting, or "frenzy" as he termed it, as one of the three "essential[s]" of slave religion and "the one more devoutly believed in than" the other two—the preacher and the music.[13] Shouting became the experiential foundation of slave evangelicalism because it affirmed an interrelation between God and person that gave the lie to the divine abandonment the brutalities and privations of New World chattel slavery ostensibly signified. It did so by way of the intimacies of individual bodies: a person shouts when the Holy Spirit of God seizes her or his body. Enslaved persons construed shouting as confirmation of their eventual deliverance from all forms of human suffering, when the soul would reside with God after death. Yet shouting also produced this-worldly effects, the most fundamental of which was the vivification of a democratic appreciation of the self. Such an understanding posits that the dignity of each individual boasts no less, but never more, value than that of another because all persons have equal access to God. For enslaved (and free black) evangelicals, this felt sense of the sanctity of the person substantiated the abstracted individualism around which contemporaneous economic and political liberalisms cohered. In effect, shouting prepared black persons, affectively and intellectually, for their encounters with and (re)formations of the institutions, practices, and subjectivities constitutive of modernity.

Shouting's eschatological and temporal meanings prompted enslaved persons to inaugurate a series of projects that would bear witness to, archive, and promulgate the democratic notions they acquired when filled with the Holy Spirit. Knowledge of (divine) individuation that orients much of evangelical praxis demands such publicity, yet the peculiarities of black life within the dispensation of New World chattel slavery often moved enslaved persons and their descendants to cultivate expressive formations that were distinct from, even if not always oppositional to, those of white evangelicals. The most conspicuous feature of this activity was the institutional provenance of African American religion (e.g., independent congregations, churches, and denominations), but the cultural materials they developed were just as consequential to the testimony-based innovations and interventions they carried out in their respective locations and polities. Of this cultural production, the emergence of literacy and literary subjectivities is uniquely striking because of the dearth of such pursuits among black populations of British North America hitherto. Hence any understanding of the beginning of black American writing in all of its aesthetic, formal, or political complexities must return to the revivals, churches, and other worship spaces that instantiated eighteenth-century evangelicalism: it was from shouting in these spaces that enslaved persons and their descendants recognized by and for themselves that they possessed the power and authority to take up writing for the same reasons their white counterparts did.

But what was it about shouting, and about cultures of evangelical orature more broadly, that disposed enslaved persons to identify the compositional and material technologies of written discourse as viable mechanisms with which to claim their (political) interests across spheres of colonial and early national American life? To pursue this line of inquiry is to demur to analyses that prioritize these persons' exposure to religious texts during the First Great Awakening; such narratives are too facile insofar as they hinge on an *a priori* assumption that slaves' exposure to texts (as repositories of sacred wisdom and writ; as curiosities that "talk") would necessarily have spurred them to turn to the writing of their own texts and to claim an interventionary force for that writing. Rather, the aim must be to identify the cultural conditions and intellectual contexts out of which such a view of black authorship began to obtain among enslaved persons. This chapter argues that juncture occurred in the wake of the rise of evangelical shouting, mobilizing the historiography of early African American Protestantism to clarify how the existential-conceptual notions fostered by black shouters established the theoretical groundwork for the "transitive beginning" of African American literary work.[14] These ideas emerged from significant theological discontinuities between shouting and its most direct antecedent: practices of spirit possession in traditional African religions. In fine, shouting revolutionized an enslaved person's understanding of God's involvement in her or his life and thereby reoriented her or his sense of self vis-à-vis the world. The resultant posture might best be called democratic insofar as democratic names a positionality that not only hails equal dignity among persons but also strives for "self-expression, resistance on behalf of others, and receptivity or responsiveness (being 'hospitable') to others."[15] However incipient or inhibited, the democratic affects and ideas that black shouters acquired revealed to them the viability and necessity of black authorial presence. That ecstatic religious experience was the originary source of that presence goes a long way toward explaining why cultures and strategies of performance were among the dominant topoi, organizing principles, and chief rhetorical tactics of the first generations of African American writers.

My construal of the political orientation of early black American writing is not to suggest that all written discourse is inherently democratic; in this case, it is to say enslaved evangelicals began to identify and deploy Anglo-American literary culture as a worthwhile enterprise by means of which to craft new forms of dissent and aesthetic fulfillment. Such writing represents features of what Nancy Ruttenburg calls "democratic personality"—that is, "a distinctive mode of political (and later, literary) subjectivity," forged in colonial settings like those of the First Great Awakening by "a process of individuation unconnected to the concept of citizenship" that compelled persons from positions of "social invisibility to speak with power and authority in a newly constituted—and uncannily transient—public sphere."[16] Like other marginalized populations across colonial settings, the enslaved grasped the tremendous liberating power inherent to evangelical procedures of individuation, but their realization was cast less in the literal and figurative proliferation of a "popular voice" to which any person might contribute and more in the phenomenology of personal ecstatic embodiment.[17] In other words, shouting was the principal medium through which enslaved persons cultivated democratic personality and, as such, marks the point when the "American" in African American achieved its first real and lasting substance, cognitive and somatic.

ECSTATIC "FIRE": FROM SPIRIT POSSESSION TO SHOUTING

Shouting's corporeality and theology enacted a permanent epistemic rupture with African ways of ordering the world for African-descended persons in British North America that, among other consequences, animated them to turn to written discourse.[18] Scholars concur that African traditions of danced or performed religions served as primary conduits of black conversion to Protestantism in the mid-eighteenth century in that they resonated with the evangelical emphasis on fervent physicality as an essential devotional paradigm. Indeed, the full-bodied nature of evangelical worship, especially in revivals, performed the important task of legitimating elements of a religious heritage enslaved persons carried with them across the Atlantic. In the seventeenth and early eighteenth centuries, they found virtually no articulation of this heritage in the Christian proselytisms they encountered, especially in the dominant Church of England, which deemed African forms of bodily and emotionalist worship brutish heathenism. Beginning in the 1730s, so-called New Light reformations within Anglicanism and dissenting denominations poised enslaved and free black persons to recognize Protestantism as a resource for spiritual fulfillment and thus existential amelioration; new rhetorical styles, new modes of address, and deeply interactive settings were among the most significant of these communicative formations. These practices strove to conduct persons to the point of ecstatic bodily expression of communion with God through the Holy Spirit—that is, acts of shouting as the climax of worship—which enslaved persons deemed, however unconsciously, a ritual effort that aligned with such aspects of traditional African worship as spirit possession. Yet core theological differences between shouting and spirit possession are what propelled black evangelicals toward a fundamentally *American* habitus, setting in motion the democratic habits of mind, heart, and action that I understand as the motive force of African American writing.

These differences concern divine interest and participation in the world. Enslaved persons and their ancestors from West and West Central Africa were polytheistic peoples who believed in some form of a supreme God, but one that was "too great to condescend so much as to trouble himself or think *of* Mankind," as the Fidasians (Guinea) explained to the seventeenth-century Dutch merchant and travel writer Willem Bosman.[19] Instead, they reserved the great bulk of their blessings, prayers, and sacrifices for lesser deities bound to nature and thus to the common workings of the earthly realm. Interacting with their local gods was constitutive of the everyday lives of these and other West and West Central African peoples, who, consequently, often regarded the supreme God as less crucial than lower members of their pantheons. Spirit possession was the most charged of such interactions. Much like the gods it venerated, the particularities of spirit possession varied from community to community, but performers across the region did share a basic framework for the practice: devotees gave over their bodies in such a way that a specific deity's entrance into or of the body caused the devotees to shed their personal identities, even as they maintained enough somatic control for the deity's presence to be identifiable through the devotees' comportment. Each deity possessed its own precise compositions and choreographies, which devotees had to master in arduous training programs and spectators had to learn to recognize as such. Hence traditional African spirit possession was organized by the logic of theatricality, which Diana Taylor defines as a performance practice "structured in a predictable, formulaic, and hence repeatable fashion." Theatricality "flaunts its artifice [and] its constructedness," and "strives for efficaciousness, not authenticity. It connotes a conscious, controlled, and, thus, always political dimension that performance need not imply."[20] Such performances necessitate a set of carefully preserved texts and social arrangements with which to maintain separation between the initiated and the uninitiated, between the expert and the ignorant, and between performers and spectators.

The demographic and material conditions of chattel slavery in British North America precluded the survival of the texts (choreographies, musical scores, and utterances) and social arrangements (cult houses and instructional regimes) dedicated to the pantheons of West and West Central Africa. But as the "death of the gods" (as Albert J. Raboteau calls the process) ensued, enslaved Africans did preserve the commitment to the fullness of the body as material for spiritual veneration and thus a worthy resource with which to make sense of the world, its limits, and one's ability to conceive that world anew.[21] Moved by doctrine and pragmatism, evangelical proselytisms appealed to this conviction, offering African and African-descended persons for the first time a brand of Christian thought and praxis that accorded with their ancestral customs of ecstatic religious performance. In short order they developed a fairly stable revivalist spatial framework across colonial locations, from congregations and private homes to backwoods "hush harbors" and open-air assemblies on plantations, within which enslaved and free black persons might grapple with evangelicalism's "plain Truth for plain people" and thereby come to experience God firsthand.[22] The various realizations of this milieu came to be what Joseph Roach theorizes as "vortices of behavior," whose purpose "is to canalize specified needs, desires, and habits in order to reproduce them." They constitute "a kind of spatially induced carnival, a center of cultural self-invention through the restoration of behavior. . . . Although such a zone or district seems to offer a place for transgression, for things that couldn't happen otherwise or elsewhere, in fact what it provides is far more official: a place in which everyday practices and attitudes may be legitimated, 'brought out into the open,' reinforced, celebrated, or intensified."[23] While revivalist evangelical vortices occasioned performances that resonated with corporeal features and affective registers of traditional African religions, they simultaneously engendered new theological-existential formations by way of those very performing bodies: the supreme God is concerned with the affairs of mankind and all persons can commune with God through the Holy Spirit. That God descends regularly to alleviate or even rectify temporal matters, sometimes in the humblest of animate forms, was particularly enthralling for populations that bore the brunt of the physical and psychological agonies of life in the New World.[24]

The ideological and morphological differences between spirit possession and evangelical shouting mark a decisive epistemic rupture from enslaved persons' African religious pasts, notwithstanding their relative somatic isomorphism. With shouting all persons, not just select trained devotees, have the capacity to be seized by the divine—and the divine that seizes persons is the supreme God through the Holy Spirit. Once the Holy Spirit takes hold of the body, the shouter cannot manage the moves and sounds the body produces because its presence is too formidable to fit any choreography or script; more to the point, the Holy Spirit does not assume prescribed shapes and sounds through the body the way an African god does on its devotees' bodies. Thus shouting names an idiosyncratic, spontaneous, and unrehearsed form of religious ecstasy that rejects theatricality. With shouting comes a sort of "Confusion" and uncontrollable "Screamings and Shrieking," as well as "exhorting," "singing," "laughing," "congratulating one another by shaking hands," and "sometimes kissing" that Charles Chauncy and other eighteenth-century anti-revivalists abhorred.[25] Yet for the enslaved, shouting focalized and arrayed the person (body and soul) as sacred matter abounding with dignity in the face of daily brutalities. Their shouting experiences enacted processes of divine individuation, rousing an aggregation of democratic affects and ideas that would percolate and erupt well beyond religious contexts.

Enslaved persons shouted whenever they felt the presence of God through their bodies, for its spiritual and secular entailments were too weighty to confine the practice to more official occasions such as revivals, church services, or congregational meetings. Shouting attained a rejuvenating force that buoyed the enslaved through the quotidian travails of bondage, becoming the most distinctive and lasting "condensational event" that evangelicalism's revivalist vortices of behavior produced. As Roach explains: "The principal characteristic of such events is that they gain a powerful enough hold on collective memory that they will survive the transformation or relocation of the spaces in which they first flourished."[26] Firsthand observations and the historiography of slave religion abound with evidence of enslaved persons shouting beyond revivalist settings, and accounts of twentieth- and twenty-first-century black evangelicalism make clear that, as a condensational event, shouting's purchase on African American imaginaries remained incredibly firm well after Emancipation. In "Down at the Cross: Letter from a Region in My Mind" in *The Fire Next Time* (1963), for example, James Baldwin's eloquent portrait of the Pentecostal congregation he served as a teenage minister reveals morphologic uniformity between enslaved persons shouting and African Americans shouting centuries later.[27] Particularly notable in Baldwin's description is that his diction and imagery are reminiscent of, and at times identical to, that used by enslaved persons when they described shouting. Condensational events give rise to fairly rigid and delimited linguistic and visual lexicons that mark concern with (the preservation of) the originary significance of the event itself.

The most striking term in the lexicon that attends shouting is *fire*—a term that not only denotes evangelical ecstasy but also intimates the surge of democratic personality such ecstasies produced. In the Judeo-Christian tradition, such significations of fire derive from the book of Jeremiah in the Hebrew Bible (Jeremiah 20:9). Jeremiah was the first of the Hebrew prophets to expound the idea that every individual is born with the capacity to experience God firsthand. The most well-known aspect of his influence on (African) American culture is the rhetorical form of the jeremiad, the lamentation of societies whose wickedness and moral shortcomings have brought about their own ruination. But enslaved persons sensed in Jeremiah's prophetic witness a more immediate avowal that concerned the interrelation of their spiritual and temporal lives: one's positionality in the world has no bearing before God. Centuries before the apostle Peter declared "God is no respecter of persons," which became a favored refrain among African American orators and writers of the late eighteenth and the nineteenth century, Jeremiah prophesied that under an imminent covenant with God, individuals "no longer will teach their neighbor, or say to one another, 'Know the Lord,' because they will all know [God], from the least of them to the greatest" (Acts 10:34; Jeremiah 31:34). Evangelical fire convinced enslaved persons that this covenant was in force, as their groans, grunts, screams, thrashes, trances, and other shouting behaviors substantiated jeremiadic claims that they, "the least" of the American polity, knew God personally and without any form of intercession.

Probably the earliest black-authored literary meditation on shouting and its relation to black subjectivity, Richard Allen's dialogic poem "Spiritual Song" (1800), opens with a comment on evangelical fire. An apologist for religious zeal encounters his interlocutor, Brother Pilgrim, returning from church and asks,

> Is your heart a-glowing, are your comforts a-flowing
> And feel you an evidence, now bright and clear;
> Feel you a desire that burns like fire,
> And longs for the hour that Christ shall appear.[28]

A discomposed Brother Pilgrim cannot even fathom the possibility, because the "groaning and shouting" he just witnessed makes him "fear such religion is only a dream."[29] His displeasure notwithstanding, Brother Pilgrim describes a scene of shouting that ranks among the most vivid literary portrayals of evangelical fervor in the period.

> The preachers were stamping, the people were jumping,
> And screaming so loud that I neither could hear
> Either praying or preaching, such horrible screeching,
> 'Twas truly offensive to all that were there[.]
> ....
> No place for reflection, I'm fill'd with distraction
> I wonder that people could bear for to stay
> The men they were bawling, the women were squaling,
> I know not for my part how any could pray;
> Such horrid confusion, if this be religion,
> Sure 'tis something new that never was seen,

For the sacred pages that speak of all ages,
Does no where declare that such as ever has been.
. . . .
The scripture is wrested, for Paul hath protested,
That order should be kept in the houses of God,
Amidst such clatter who knows what they're after,
Or who can attend to what is declared;
To see them behaving like drunkards a-raving
And lying and rolling prostrate on the ground,
I really felt awful and sometimes was fearful,
That I'd be the next that would come tumbling down.[30]

Fire serves at once a descriptive and a figural function: it mediates the gap between cause (e.g., "bawling," "squaling," "confusion") and effect (e.g., "heart a-glowing," "comforts a-flowing," "desire"), signifying the tenability of a causal relation between ecstatic worship and positive spiritual fecundity. Accordingly, fire emerges as the keyword in the debate regarding the social and theological proprieties of religious zeal that "Spiritual Song" stages.

Despite the poem's methodical dialogism, shouting's seemliness was a pressing matter for an emergent clergyman like Allen, who was in the process of consolidating the doctrinal, institutional, and liturgical features of his fledgling black Methodism. He aspired to ecclesiastical self-government, so protocols of worship and the suitability of shouting therein were significant considerations in his pursuit of ecclesial and communal sanction. (In 1816, the Pennsylvania Supreme Court granted several allied black Methodist congregations' plea for independence from the white-controlled Methodist society. They incorporated themselves as the African Methodist Episcopal Church, and consecrated Allen as its first bishop.) The revivalist fervor Brother Pilgrim describes threatened to undercut the legitimacy Allen sought for black evangelicalism, especially since that behavior evoked African barbarism in the dominant racial imagination. "Spiritual Song" thus contributed to (and archives) a critical discourse regarding shouting that enslaved and free black persons had to negotiate in their efforts to build autonomous, theologically robust socioreligious communities.

The poem's format and circulation history underscore the import Allen accorded to shouting: he printed it as a broadside that he sold to the public out of his Philadelphia home.³¹ The few critics who have studied "Spiritual Song" all read it as Allen's position on shouting in black worship; to that end, most have followed Dorothy Porter, who published the poem in her groundbreaking 1971 collection *Early Negro Writing, 1760–1837*, and claimed Brother Pilgrim's remonstrations as Allen's own.³² But the poem's dialogic asymmetries suggest otherwise: while both characters ground their arguments in the Bible and early church history, the apologist speaks for seven of the eleven octaves and his command of scripture far outstrips Brother Pilgrim's. If anything, Brother Pilgrim's complaints establish a set of logical predicates for the apologist to refute and thereby erect an opposing conceptual framework with which to expound an eschatology that prioritizes full-bodily worship.

In the apologist's hermeneutic, scenes of congregational pandemonium are affirmations of divine presence and consecration. He adduces Old Testament figures like David who "came running / And dancing" before the Ark of the Covenant, and members of the "Jewish nation" who "wept and some prais'd, and such a noise there was rais'd" after they "rebuilt the temple at Ezra's command." He describes how

> Ezekiel, the teacher,
> Was taught for to stamp and to smite with his hand,
> To shew the transgression of that wicked nation,
> That they might repent and obey the command.³³

He also reminds Brother Pilgrim of the scene of performance at the first Pentecost in the New Testament:

> When Peter was preaching, and boldly was teaching,
> The way of salvation in Jesus' name,
> The spirit descended and some were offended,
> And said of the men they were fill'd with new wine.
> I never yet doubted but some of them shouted,
> While others lay prostrate by power struck down,
> Some weeping, some praying, while others were saying,
> They are as drunk as fools, or in falsehood abound.³⁴

Homologizing Pentecost with contemporary black shouting, the apologist recalls the apostolic prophecy that ecstatic worship among slaves in particular signifies the imminent fulfillment of God's promise of deliverance and salvation. That is, the mention of Peter preaching is an allusion to his proclamation in the midst of Pentecost: "And it shall come to pass in the last days, saith God, I will pour out of my Spirit upon all flesh: and your sons and your daughters shall prophesy, and your young men shall see visions, and your old men shall dream dreams[;] And on my servants and on my handmaidens I will pour out in those days of my Spirit; and they shall prophesy" (Acts 2:17-18). Thus an enslaved person (i.e., a servant or handmaiden) swept up in evangelical fire should understand her or his shouting as an instantiation of a tradition of Pentecostalist revelations that traces back to the very first. The intertextual, hermeneutical apparatus of "Spiritual Song" works to affirm the notion that ecstatic worship does not corrupt the spirit, but rather constitutes a ravishment of the spirit that substantiates a first principle of evangelicalism, the doctrine of universal priesthood: all persons, regardless of their station, have direct access to God.

The story of Pentecost also functions as a cautionary tale for Brother Pilgrim and the persons the figure represents. In this formulation, contemporary critics, those who censure shouting and other acts of evangelical fervor as "falsehood" making persons "drunk as fools," become latter-day versions of the detractors who rebuked the apostles and their disciples at the time of Pentecost; these critics are out of the fold of salvation, "Spiritual Song" suggests. By degrees the poem's admonitory tone becomes more explicit, finally blazoning its homiletic crux in the apologist's final stanza:

> Our time is a flying, our moments a dying,
> We are led to improve them and quickly appear,
> For the bless'd hour when Jesus in power,
> In glory shall come is now drawing near.[35]

At this point the apologist is no longer interested in maieutic exchange, so he reconfigures their relationship and ministers to Brother Pilgrim. The poem underscores this new hierarchy by returning to the fire trope: whereas the apologist opens "Spiritual Song" by asking Brother Pilgrim if he "burns like fire" in anticipation of Christ's arrival, his concluding words enjoin Brother Pilgrim to follow his lead "and now pray together, / That your precious soul may be fill'd with the flame."[36] Brother Pilgrim follows the directive, and the poem ends with him, perhaps for the first time, assured of his salvation: for his "heart is a glowing."[37]

Brother Pilgrim's epiphany is the upshot of the poem's dialogic structure. The dialogue was a favored literary technique among contemporaneous evangelical and social reform writers because they recognized a pedagogic force within the form that could be used to guide ambivalent or skeptical readers toward some sort of theological or political clarity. Allen was steeped in the aesthetic and political currents of the early national US literary public sphere. Coauthored with Absalom Jones, his *Narrative of the Proceedings of the Black People, during the Late Awful Calamity in Philadelphia, in the Year 1793: And a Refutation of Some Censures, Thrown upon Them in Some Late Publications* (1794) is a pioneering pamphlet of (African) American politico-literary history. That Allen, who while enslaved underwent an emotionally powerful conversion experience and as a minister preached to induce revivalist worship among his own congregants, should use the rationalist mechanisms of dialogism to appraise the thoroughly sensory act of shouting might seem ironic, if not paradoxical; but Allen's choice exemplifies his full embrace of prevailing literary aesthetics, modes, and technologies, which reflects his more general pursuit of the democratic ideals of the American Enlightenment.

JUPITER HAMMON AND BLACK LITERARY INDIVIDUATION

This orientation was by far the dominant ideological charge of black writers through at least the 1820s. However geographically or sociologically diffuse, the aggregate of their work evinces a corporate literary subjectivity dedicated to the inclusionary aims and means of early black nationalism. (Emigrationism and other modes of race-based separatism would not anchor black nationalist action and thought until the 1850s.) Following Paul Gilroy, I understand that corpus as a project animated by "the politics of fulfilment," which functions by way of "the notion that a future society will be able to realize the social and political promise that present society has left unaccomplished." It "demands that bourgeois civil society live up to the promises of its own rhetoric. . . . The politics of fulfilment is mostly content to play occidental rationality at its own game. It necessitates a hermeneutic orientation that can assimilate the semiotic, verbal, and textual."[38] Phyllis Wheatley's poetry,

Olaudah Equiano's *The Interesting Narrative* (1789), and Allen and Jones's *Narrative of the Proceedings of the Black People*, among so many other lesser-known and lesser-studied black-authored writings from the period, bear critique of the praxis of American Enlightenment that emerges from within and by means of the Enlightenment's spheres of cultural production; that is, these texts "resist" to the extent that, in this instance, resistance names activity that strives to remove discursive and material hindrances that impede full democratic inclusivity. Even literary productions that do not center on slavery or race-based exclusion, such as Allen's "Spiritual Song" or Wheatley's neoclassical aestheticism, entail a (racialized) political valence because they instantiate and often elaborate on dominant creeds and prevailing aesthetic-representational norms.

Recognizing early African American writing as a consequence and conduit of the politics of fulfillment goes a long way in addressing the underlying query that organizes Gene Andrew Jarrett's important theorization of a "political genealogy of early African American literature." Since "the racial identity of authorship was not always a reliable predictor of the political nature of early African American literature[,] nor were the literary intentions and productions always reliable indicators of it," Jarrett writes, "the taxonomic insecurity of these political definitions prompts us to ask why contemporary readers regarded early African American literature as political, so to speak, in the first place."[39] Through an extended reading of David Walker's *Appeal to the Colored Citizens of the World* (1829) and its critical engagement with Thomas Jefferson's *Notes on the State of Virginia* (1785), Jarrett concludes that because Americans across racial lines "had ideologically overlapped in privileging intellectual culture [i.e., the inextricability of literature and politics] within conceptions of political representation and self-governance," African American literary productions like Wheatley's poetry could not help but become fodder for political contestation because they served as "flashpoint[s] for a broader intellectual debate over genius, race, and representation."[40] While this argument certainly resonates with my reading of early African American writing as a corpus pitched toward the fulfillment of the democratic ideals of the American Enlightenment, Jarrett's rigorous analyses obscure what I believe is the more primal reason why critics and readers in the era politicized black-authored literary discourse regardless of its subject matter: for the enslaved, the formerly enslaved, or their descendants, the very act of taking up writing signaled an assumption of power, a slave morality, in an "intellectual culture" that used violence, the law, and domestic mores to keep them from doing just that. The politicization of early African American writing was part and parcel of a broader clash over these writers' breach of the prescriptive limits that defined American cultural productions.

Such claims to power had to derive from elsewhere, away from the networks and syndicates of early national intellectual culture. As I have argued, that elsewhere was the revivalist evangelical spaces wherein by acts of shouting black persons acquired feelings of personal authority and standing—that is, democratic personality—in the face of quotidian abjection and marginalization. Those feelings were the aftereffects of shouting's ecstatic visions of deliverance from all forms of personal suffering and eternal salvation, "utopian" yearnings that articulate Gilroy's notion of a "politics of transfiguration." As he argues, the politics of transfiguration "emphasizes the emergence of qualitatively new desires, social relations, and modes of association within the racial community of interpretation and resistance and between the group and its erstwhile oppressors. . . . The politics of transfiguration strives in pursuit of the sublime, struggling to repeat the unrepeatable, to present the unpresentable. Its . . . hermeneutic focus pushes towards the mimetic, dramatic, and performative."[41] To my mind, shouting was the most consequential expression of the politics of transfiguration among black populations in eighteenth- and early nineteenth-century America, not least because it spurred them to create and contribute to several secular enterprises (e.g., literary discourse) dedicated to the realization of the broader society's most excellent aims and pronouncements. In other words, the transfiguration of enslaved persons through shouting propelled them to hail themselves as central actors in the fulfillment of American democracy through writing.

In this regard, the genesis of African American literary production constitutes an instance of a harmonious, even determinative relationship between the repertoire (i.e., shouting) and the archive (i.e., written discourse). Centering on that relationship not only reveals the underlying conceptual and contextual attributes that fostered the advent of black authorial presence in British North America and the early United States; orienting one's critical purview in this way also helps to account for several of the formal-rhetorical dimensions that configure early black literary and textual productions. Elizabeth Maddock Dillon has modeled this approach. Hers is an effort to theorize new, counter-Habermasian models of public sphere formation and the circulation of culture therein by centering on the functionality of the formal conditions of performance (embodied action, presence, and lived space) in the constitution of incipient black literary codes, networks, and assemblages in the last quarter of the eighteenth century. She argues that attending to "scenes of performance that inform print production . . . significantly augments and shifts our understanding of the public sphere such that [early black] texts . . . reveal central dynamics of race, embodiment, and performance in relation to the social and political belonging that characterizes the public sphere."[42] This critical orientation stresses the ways in which early African American writers used performance culture, as semiotic and subject, to counteract the racialized frameworks of the cultural and civic order that stratified early American polities. Such writing invests deeply in the experiential and the interested, as it works toward the achievement of an alternative "*sensus communis* [i.e., an assemblage] at the limits of an Enlightenment reason that holds a contradictory racial politics at its core."[43]

In their determination to forge bonds of communal affect, expressivity, and reciprocity constitutive of such performative assemblages, early black texts intimate a broader ethic of collectivism: an aesthetic, rhetorical, and social predisposition that opposes the precepts and pursuit of liberal individualism. According to the historian Craig Steven Wilder, collectivism pervaded West and West Central African societies and, as a result, shaped the coalitions, institutions, and networks enslaved persons and their free descendants created to withstand early American racism and racialism. Wilder's crucial socio-intellectual history explains the political character and demographic heterogeneity of black associationalism in the period, but the stark ideological and intellectual divergences across the black-authored texts that circulated within spaces of black association render race-based collectivism an inadequate hermeneutic with which to conceptualize or explain the beginnings of African American written discourse. Indeed, even when performance occasioned a *sensus communis*, the only politico-ethical claims black writers felt the need to uphold within that assemblage were those that accorded with their individual aims and sensibilities. Accordingly, early African American writing archives structural and affective features of the shift from past African dispositions (e.g., collectivism) toward future American inclinations that performed slave evangelicalism set in motion.

No corpus instantiates this development with greater clarity than that of the enslaved writer Jupiter Hammon. Even though Hammon was the first black poet to be published in what became the US, and his sermons and political orations invigorated audiences in New York and Connecticut, there are no major monographs and only a handful of article-length treatments concerning his life and work.[44] This scarcity registers an over-investment in the "oppositional" or "radical" in black literature from the era of slavery (and beyond) that continues to impoverish our understanding of the contingencies, depth, and intricacies of African American thought and culture.[45] The mainstream of African American literary criticism disregards Hammon's writing as a subject of rigorous, sustained analysis because his Calvinist traditionalism is anathema to the ideological currents that structure the field. The thrust of his work evinces little concern with "the end of slavery in a temporal, civil sense," as Cedrick May writes. "Such matters fell into the realm of secular politics, which did not interest Hammon except where they contradicted his sense of religiosity."[46] This principle organizes his most well-known text, "An Address to the Negroes in the State of New-York," which Hammon wrote for the African Society in New York in 1786 and then published for general circulation in 1787. The "Address" enjoins enslaved persons to remain obedient to their masters and to maintain the highest of standards of personal rectitude, even if their masters and free white persons do not. Hammon writes: "Some of you to excuse yourselves, may plead the example of others, and say that you hear a great many white-people, who know more, than such poor ignorant negroes, as you are, and some who are rich and great gentlemen, swear, and talk profanely, and some of you may say this of your masters, and say no more than is true. But all this is not a sufficient excuse for you."[47] Hammon argued that a higher moral law obliged enslaved persons to maintain righteousness, and as their reward at God's "judgment seat" their "slavery will be at an end, and though ever so mean, low, and despised in this world, we sit with God in his kingdom as Kings and Priests, and rejoice forever, and ever."[48] Obedience and patience within one's station as positive (spiritual) goods run through his creative and political writings, nullifying whatever antislavery inklings one might tease out of the "Address."[49] Despite these proslavery concessions, Hammon's speech galvanized the African Society and, in pamphlet form, engendered the publication of a number of other text-based assemblages in New York and Philadelphia, if not elsewhere.

Hammon's prioritization of individual piety and probity was at odds with the collectivism that vitalized associations such as the African Society, but he was assured and determined in his capacity to promulgate his convictions among even the most unsympathetic of audiences.[50] The *Address* begins with Hammon's admission that he had longed to help mitigate "the poor, despised and miserable state" of black people, and to contribute to the quashing of their "ignorance and stupidity, and the great wickedness of the most of" them. But the subject too often "pained [him] to the heart," moving him "to turn [his] thoughts from the subject."[51] Overcoming these affective barriers as well as the inclination to reticence he felt due to his "own ignorance" and "unfitness to teach others," Hammon bolsters his rhetorical ethos by adducing the wisdom of his old age, the success of his earlier writings, and his identity as a "negro," among other things. He writes, "I think you will be more likely to listen to what is said, when you know it comes from a negro, one your own nation and colour, and therefore can have no interest in deceiving you, or in saying any thing to you, but what he really thinks is your interest and duty to comply with."[52] This amalgam of self-effacement and self-aggrandizement marks Hammon's familiarity with the conventions of late eighteenth-century oratory, but it is the broader rhetorical genealogical context within which he positions the *Address* that frames early African American writing as a culmination of evangelical imaginaries and passions: Hammon aligns himself with the apostle Paul, a writer empowered and duty-bound to speak out against the obstacles, self-imposed or otherwise, that impede his "nation" from fulfilling its most excellent potential.

This posture dominates Hammon's literary and oratorical work. His poem "The Kind Master and Dutiful Servant" (n.d.) is even more forthright in its insistence on the necessity of Hammon's prophetic-apostolic intervention, and it too relies on techniques of performance, albeit textualized, to reinforce the legitimacy of his voice and authority. The poem imagines a dialogue between a master and his servant (most certainly an enslaved person), both of whom are concerned with morality and obedience, a scenario that recurs in Hammon's writings. Unlike the *Address*, "The Kind Master and Dutiful Servant" does not exhort enslaved persons to resist the temptation to conform to the example of their depraved masters or free white counterparts because the titular kind master is an exemplar of moral rectitude and virtue. He implores his servant to follow his lead because it will bring them both closer to God: it is his obligation as master to provide pathways of Christian servility and tuition, just as it is the servant's obligation to set out upon those paths. The first half of the thirty-stanza poem stages their conversation by way of alternating quatrains of dialogue in which both participants voice traditional Calvinist doctrine. Set in rigid common meter, their banal dialogue makes for a fairly conventional eighteenth-century religious poem. With its predictable content in tidy form, "The Kind Master and Dutiful Servant" placed contemporaneous readers and auditors on familiar poetic terrain.

Yet Hammon unsettles expectations midway through the dialogue. Between stanzas fifteen and sixteen, he writes: "A Line on the present war."[53] Over the course of the next eight stanzas, master and servant discuss the ongoing American War of Independence, construing the death and destruction it brought as God's handiwork:

> *Master.*
> This is the work of God's own hand,
> We see by precepts given;
> To relieve distress and save the land,
> Must be the pow'r of heav'n.
> *Servant.*
> Now glory be unto our God,
> Let ev'ry nation sing;
> Strive to obey his holy word,
> That Christ may take them in.[54]

These and the other thirteen stanzas that make up the second half of "The Kind Master and Dutiful Servant" maintain the Calvinism that begins the poem, but ground it in a specific time, place, and event. That is, whatever "line" (i.e., gloss) on the war Hammon promises is shot through with his religiosity, and any sort of allegiance (i.e., Patriot or Loyalist) or political commentary is conspicuously absent.[55] The only way to end the armed conflicts of the war with Great Britain, or indeed any temporal discord, is total submission to the word of God, the poem argues.

Hammon further emphasizes his religious prescriptions in another distinguishing, unexpected move: from stanza twenty-four to twenty-five, "The Kind Master and Dutiful Servant" transforms from a dialogue to a soliloquy–political sermon:

> *Servant.*
> Thus the dialogue shall end,
>   Strive to obey the word;
> When ev'ry nation acts like friends,
>   Shall be the sons of God.
> Believe me now my Christian friends,
>   Believe your friend call'd Hammon
> You cannot to your God attend,
>   And serve the God of Mammon.
> If God is pleased by his own hand
>   To relieve distresses here;
> And grant a peace throughout the land
>   'Twill be a happy year.
> 'Tis God alone can give us peace;
>   It's not the pow'r of man:
> When virtuous pow'r shall increase,
>   'Twill beautify the land.[56]

For the final third of the poem, Hammon assumes the role of the servant and speaks directly to his readers and auditors. His identification of the American War of Independence as divine compensation for the combatants' religious shortcomings and moral turpitude reflects the jeremiadic sensibility that animates the poem. Critics have not positioned "The Kind Master and the Dutiful Servant" or any other Hammon texts within genealogies of the African American jeremiad because his Calvinist accommodationism runs counter to the religious and political norms we prefer to ascribe to this literary-rhetorical tradition. Yet Hammon claimed the same authority and aptitudes other black (literary) Jeremiahs in the era did, and it is that gesture and its catalyzing agent—namely, ecstatic evangelical performance—that established the conditions for the rise and flourishing of African American written discourse and, eventually, literary cultures. The performance devices that configure "The Kind Master and Dutiful Servant" (e.g., soliloquy, direct address, masking and unmasking, and epilogue) and the decision to publish the poem alongside Hammon's sermon "An Evening's Improvement" throw this process into stark relief.

My account of the provenance of African American writing as a consequence of evangelical performance culture and its procedures of democratic individuation (i.e., shouting) dovetails with Alexis de Tocqueville's more general theorization of modern democracy as a by-product of Christian thought and practice, especially its more radical Protestant strains. In his introduction to the first volume of *Democracy in America* (1835), Tocqueville sketches the ways in which the leveling capacity at the core of Christianity (i.e., "Christianity, which has made all equal before God, will not flinch to see all citizens equal before the law") empowers lowborn persons to take on economic and political elites and thereby disrupt prescriptive social hierarchies and their underlying frameworks.[57] While economic (e.g., laws of entailment and inheritance) and political (e.g., common consent, civic accountability, and administration) concerns dominate his schema, Tocqueville remained keen on how essential the cultural front is to processes of democratization. "From the moment when the exercise of intelligence had become a source of strength and wealth . . . [p]oetry, eloquence, memory, the beauty of wit, the fires of imagination, all these gifts which heaven shares out by chance turned to the advantage of democracy," he writes. "Literature was an arsenal open to all, where the weak and the poor could always find arms."[58] While holding Tocqueville's distinctive providentialism at bay, I argue that the origins of African American writing affirm his thesis regarding the slave morality of Christianity as an authorizing episteme of democratic cultural praxis, especially for the "weak and the poor." It took the felt ecstasies of shouting for the enslaved to recognize that episteme as legitimate and viable in light of their enslavement; they did not merely absorb its democratic potentiality by osmosis or rationalist deduction. Thus, as a democratic effect, enslaved and free black evangelicals' turn to literature did not bring about anything close to politico-ideological uniformity in the writing itself. Rather, their writings posit idiosyncratic, very often divergent means of aesthetic and political fulfillment for the slavery and post-slavery milieus they endured. The differences in form and normative political claims that characterize early African American writing, ranging from Jupiter Hammon's conservative poetry to David Walker's militant *Appeal to the Colored Citizens of the World* (1829), simply reflect the phenomenology of ecstatic evangelicalism itself: no person caught up with the Holy Spirit will shout like any other.

2 · Impersonality

The steady deterioration of African Americans' rights and freedoms in the 1850s caused a ground swell of black nationalist politics. The Fugitive Slave Act of 1850, the opening of Western territories to chattel slavery with the Kansas-Nebraska Act of 1854, and the notorious Dred Scott decision in 1857 proved to activists that American political infrastructures were all aligned against them. Strategies grounded in appealing to the nation's collective conscience to effect social change on behalf of black people had failed. And reformers once dedicated to nonviolent liberalism began to see physical resistance as necessary and viable. Frederick Douglass was the most prominent among those reformers. He posited a morality of anti-slavery violence in the mid-1850s as the culmination of his embrace of political violence.

Beyond its pragmatism, Douglass's tactical shifts instantiate his evolution as a thinker more and more concerned with ethics, normative politics, and the metaphysical. He developed new ways to maintain faith in democracy despite its many corruptions and failures. American Transcendentalism was one of his most valuable resources. It furnished a system of political-philosophical conceits with which to refigure, reorient, and thus revitalize abolitionism and civil rights activism in the face of several crushing defeats. At the core of that system is an understanding of the propinquity of God to man that paralleled early black evangelicalism: the divinity of human lowliness. Douglass teased out the political implications of a shared divinity across persons—that is, *impersonality*—to reclaim the viability of democracy for black life in America.

Douglass's fullest elaborations of impersonality emerged in his refutations of racial biologism, particularly the pro-slavery science of the American School of Ethnology. His metaphysics rests on an idea of the impersonal that spurns racial ontologies and their political ascriptions. Through an extended reading of his "Claims of the Negro, Ethnologically Considered" (1854), I describe how he repudiated antebellum ethnology to contend that all we can know about persons, black or otherwise, is that they are persons of equal divinity and thus worthy of the same rights as all other persons. If not for (racial) prejudice, he argued, that truth was beautiful and obvious to behold. "Claims" is Douglass's most systematic expression of slave morality.

THE DEMOCRATIC CAPACITY OF IMPERSONALITY

In a June 1854 editorial for *Frederick Douglass' Paper* (*FDP*), Frederick Douglass told his readers that physical "resistance," which included the murder of "kidnappers" (i.e., slave catchers) employed to recapture fugitives in free states and territories, was "wise as well as just."[1] To murder such "monsters who deliberately violate" the "rights and liberties of the [human] race" was an act of compensation, a fitting "penalty" for those who transgress the laws that "the All-Wise has established." He wrote: "As human life is not superior to the laws for the preservation of the physical universe, so, too, it is not superior to the eternal law of justice, which is essential to the preservation of the rights, and the security, and happiness of the [human] race."[2] Fewer than three months before Douglass published these sentiments in *FDP*, Ralph Waldo Emerson made the same claims in his lecture "The Fugitive Slave Law," which he delivered at the Tabernacle in New York City. Emerson said, "slavery is disheartening; but Nature is not so helpless but it can rid itself at last of every wrong. But the spasms of Nature are centuries and ages, and will tax the faith of short-lived men. Slowly, slowly the Avenger comes, but comes surely. . . . 'For evil word shall evil word be said, / For murder-stroke a murder-stroke be paid. / Who smites must smart.'"[3] He justified killing enslavers as a natural, ineluctable requital administered to those who violate the will of Nature whose "voice . . . pronounces Freedom."[4]

Emerson affirmed the inevitability of such world-corrective action well before 1854, describing it in the essay "Compensation" (1841) as a "levelling circumstance that puts down the overbearing, the strong, the rich, the fortunate substantially on the same ground with all others."[5] But if in the 1840s Emerson understood acts of compensation to be primarily the work of Nature, in the 1850s he more regularly recognized and encouraged the leveling function that positive human action performs, especially in regard to the eradication of chattel slavery: "Whilst the inconsistency of slavery with the principles on which the world is built guarantees its downfall, I own that the patience it requires is almost too sublime for mortals, and seems to demand of us more than mere hoping."[6] Here and in other reform speeches throughout the decade, Emerson intimates a transcendentalist politics that "urges solidarity—indeed mobilization" on behalf of the downtrodden, notwithstanding his idiosyncratic demurrals from "public questions," which he called "odious and hurtful, and it seems like meddling or leaving your work."[7] So even if Emerson "never failed to regret the time he spent publicly opposing slavery" because "immersion in [political] activity may . . . be a huge distraction from the life of the mind" that he craved, as George Kateb argues, Emersonian Transcendentalism provided activists a new philosophical basis from which to launch their campaigns. Douglass's controversial embrace of killing slavecatchers and, later, armed insurrection among the enslaved as acts of compensation in service to the "All-Wise," for example, instantiated the metaphysical logics and rhetoric with which some abolitionists in the 1850s legitimated their most radical schemes.

Douglass's very notion (and epithet) of the "All-Wise" as a force that necessitates a counterpoising relation between the "moral and social world" and the "physical world" is strikingly akin to what Emerson termed the "Over-Soul," the impersonal that animates and inhabits nature and thus all humankind.[8] Emerson writes: "In all conversation between two persons, tacit reference is made, as to a third party, to a common nature. That third party or common nature is not social; it is impersonal; is God."[9] This affirmation of an all-encompassing common nature is at the core of what political theorists call Emersonian democratic individuality—a theory that demands we recognize how the impersonal that produces the infinitude of the world works through all persons without bias and produces the very same dignity and infinitude in each and every person.[10] I understand it as an expression of slave morality. Douglass discerned an egalitarian drive in Emerson's insistent searching and striving beyond "the merely *visible* part of things," and as he read and heard more Emerson from the late 1840s onward, he came to believe that the transcendentalist logic of essential and immutable human sameness might exert a democratic (e.g., anti-slavery) pressure in the nation's collective consciousness that the realms of economics, law, and formal politics could not muster.[11] He was one of several of Emerson's antebellum black readers and listeners who believed Emersonian abstractions bore heavily on the political in that they delivered a powerful repudiation of biological models of racial essentialism antebellum publics used to justify chattel slavery and race-based inequities.[12] When Douglass endeavored to confound the pro-slavery biological researches of the authoritative American School of Ethnology—his "The Claims of the Negro, Ethnologically Considered," an address he first delivered as part of the 1854 commencement exercises at Western Reserve College in Hudson, Ohio (what is now Case Western Reserve University in Cleveland), then made available to a wider reading public in pamphlet form—he relied most assuredly on a metaphysics that is strikingly Emersonian in both substance and tone.[13] Only one month after he endorsed murdering slavecatchers as compensation to the All-Wise, Douglass grounded his fullest dismissals of the ethnological arguments of the American School on a transcendentalist notion of the impersonal that invalidates race and, therefore, race-based policies and perceptions.

With "Claims," Douglass offered a performance-text that draws its most acute interventions from the democratic capacity of impersonality. My claim might seem paradoxical in light of his in-depth engagement with the American School's ethnological-materialist contentions throughout the address. Yet I argue that whatever positivist or scientistic arguments Douglass puts forward in "Claims" ultimately serve to reinforce the transcendentalist claims of impersonality around which he organized the speech. In so doing, I recognize "Claims" less as a performance-text that marks Douglass's "shift" toward "empiricism" and privileging the materialist than as a performance-text that lingers rather uneasily with the empirical and the material only in order to arrive at the metaphysical, where Douglass, in 1854, seemed to be most comfortable politically.[14] The metaphysical, and impersonality in particular, allowed Douglass to imagine the self in ways that forestall—or, better, dissolve—categories of identity polities use to discriminate. One finds such notions of impersonality in Emerson and Thoreau, but in Douglass the dissolution of those categories becomes doubly burdensome and significant because he could not take for granted that his audiences would always accept the full personhood of the black and enslaved. Thus what emerges most forcefully in "Claims" is a quasi-materialist disquisition that upholds "the negro is a MAN" as means to make the overriding idealist claim that "all mankind have the same wants, arising out of a common nature."[15]

In this way, Douglass's impersonal differs from Emerson's insofar as there is never a "missing sense of the person," which Sharon Cameron calls the "great shame" of Emerson's impersonal. This absence accounts for what she describes as Emerson's "barbarous idealism," an idealism that "sanctions the drama of injustice by denying its existence or by *justifying* its existence."[16] The impersonal in Douglass, by contrast, remains fixed on the person (the affective, the corporal, the psychical) because he wants to keep to the fore that its presence within all persons constitutes an inviolable democratic mandate: a common and equal right to positive freedom and negative liberty. Thus if "the pressure put on the personal to dissipate into what is impersonal is the guiding force of how American Transcendentalism thinks about subjectivity," as Branka Arsić suggests, then Douglass's critical position within the intellectual history of American Transcendentalism rests in large part on his preoccupation with, and elaboration of, the first principles of impersonality: namely, all persons are capable of—and should have the latitude to pursue—the ecstasy of self-abandonment, a ravishment of the sort that Emerson famously imagined in the "transparent eye-ball" passage from *Nature*.[17]

When Douglass composed "Claims" in 1854, he had good reason to fix his audiences upon these principles, considering the increasingly prevalent cultural, ethnological, and theological discourses that questioned and, in some cases, outright denied "the negro's manhood."[18] But his affirmation of an impersonal that all persons can access because that impersonal inhabits all persons was in significant ways a rehearsal of mainstream transcendentalist dogma. Decades before, Emerson had already conceived of impersonality as an all-encompassing force, an "Over-Soul," described most cogently in an 1841 essay of that title: "In youth we are mad for persons. Childhood and youth see all the world in them. But the larger experience of man discovers the identical nature appearing through them all. Persons thus acquaint themselves with the impersonal." Thus all persons share an "identical nature"—what he describes elsewhere as a "common heart" and "the great, universal mind"—not only with the natural world but also with each other.[19]

Within the intellectual-historical context of antebellum America, when professional ethnologists and cultural producers alike promulgated theories of inherent black inferiority and racial difference to great effect, Emersonian impersonality had profound political implications. Emerson himself explicated those implications in the address that propelled him from anti-slavery to abolitionism, "Emancipation in the British West Indies" (1844): "The civility of no race can be perfect whilst another race is degraded. It is a doctrine alike of the oldest, and of the newest philosophy, that, man is one, and that you cannot injure any member, without a sympathetic injury to all the members. America is not civil, whilst Africa is barbarous."[20] Since Emerson understood all persons to stem from, and share in, the impersonal—this is what makes us "one"—the abolition of slavery is not only an act of social justice, but also an act of profound self-care: "If you put a chain around the neck of a slave, the other end fastens itself around your own," he said.[21]

For Emerson's detractors, however, such perpetual returns to the individual, not to mention his characteristic abstractions that lack an emphatically oppositional charge, ultimately undercut his transcendentalism's potential for progressive dissent. John Carlos Rowe is perhaps most categorical in making the case when he concludes: "Emersonian Transcendentalism and political activism in mid-nineteenth-century America were inherently incompatible."[22] Coeval with Transcendentalism, this judgment has begun to fall out of favor in some critical circles, as new interpretations of Emerson's work have made clear that his aversion to associational agitation and formal politics did not preclude an interest in (re-shaping) the political.[23] Critics working in this vein rely most on his anti-slavery speeches of the mid-1840s and his literary and oratorical protest against the Fugitive Slave Act of 1850; but, as I argue above, Emersonian Transcendentalism was fully oppositional from the very first because its most foundational philosophical idea—impersonality—proscribes slavery, capitalist exploitation, and other systems of oppression that inhibit self-culture. That is, even if Emerson never engaged political questions directly, his ostensibly apolitical essays such as "The Over-Soul" (1841), "Compensation" (1841), and other early works from the so-called "small canon" already evinced a mind bent on the most revolutionary of social reforms.[24]

Sharon Cameron identified the impersonal as the "centrally recurring idea . . . in Emerson's essays." In so doing, she not only gave the lie to readings that malign Emerson as the philosopher *par excellence* of "the egotistical, the subjective, and the solipsistic"; she also directed Emerson's readers downward, to the democratic, to the very "weed by the wall" Emerson claimed to be in "Circles."[25] She writes: "I understand Emerson's impersonality to be *related* to, but not identical with, [Richard] Poirier's genius, [Harold] Bloom's energy, [Barbara] Packer's powers, as his corrective to the deformation of personal identity. These terms rely on a Neoplatonic, upward, sublimatory movement away from material particularity, whereas Emerson's impersonal moves in the opposite direction. For in impersonality Emerson is elaborating a paradox that truth to the self involves the discovery of its radical commonness."[26] In calling this reading of Emerson's impersonal a gesture toward the "democratic," I mean to underscore the ways in which his transcendentalism issues from an ethics of shared embeddedness or sociality that demands we create the conditions necessary for all persons to live out lives of full autonomy—that is, self-reliance. Such worldmaking must be, Emerson suggests, because all persons are elementally the selfsame: "The heart and soul of all men being one, this bitterness of *His* and *Mine* ceases. His is mine. I am my brother and my brother is me. If I feel over-shadowed and outdone by great neighbors, I can yet love; I can still receive; and he that loveth maketh his own the grandeur he loves," Emerson writes in "Compensation."[27]

In such scenes of impersonality, "where the interest of Emerson's essays lies," the condition of subjectivity remains open to question: does the impersonal fully negate the person or does it work ravishingly *with and through* the person that it "contrives" in the first place?[28] In either case, accessing the impersonal most abundantly requires equal rights and protections for all persons, for one cannot fully honor his own divinity if he infringes on that of another since they are constitutive of the same divinity, the Over-Soul. In other words, Emerson's theological affirmations are utterly political, because personal restraint and social contingency constitute the preconditions of self-reliance—and what is self-reliance for Emerson other than the most divine of human efforts? "Through egalitarian moral respect," Jack Turner argues in slightly different terms, "the [truly] self-reliant register their commitment to human equality and signal their transcendence of the base desire to establish one's dignity through others' degradation. Conditioning one's dignity on the subjection of others is not strength but weakness, an exposure of the spiritually slavish need to dominate, and an admission of a lack of self-trust."[29] Emersonian Transcendentalism turns out to be more than suitable for social reforms such as abolitionism because its most rudimentary principles necessitate an ethical orientation that rejects the sorts of self-serving egotisms (e.g., racial supremacy) on which institutions of collective domination (e.g., chattel slavery) thrive.

Impersonality and self-reliance thus yield a robust democratic ethos because, in my view, they are born of slave morality above all else. Even if the most striking and well-known scenes in the canon of American Transcendentalism exalt solitude, the way of life Emerson imagined requires a sociality of radical equality because such a life pursues impersonality above all. Or, as Branka Arsić puts it, "if the impersonal is the social in its highest form, it is the social itself that leads there."[30] In Emerson's transcendentalism, then, abides his most rigorous defense of liberty and common equality. To be sure, his strained activism and prescriptions for social change that smack of a self-defeating conservatism (e.g., compensated emancipation) marred his standing as a galvanizing reformer, but these actions do not vitiate the radicalism of Emerson's impersonal as a critique of the corruptions of democratic life. And yet it holds that in order to mobilize any real political authority, Emersonian impersonality needs a voice other than Emerson's, one far less vexed and aloof from the messiness of practical reform. Frederick Douglass's voice, if not his very *person*, emerged to enact that authority in 1854, when he set out to counter the weighty pro-slavery arguments of the American School of Ethnology. At the core of Douglass's most painstaking refutation of ethnological racism lies a notion of the impersonal that not only parallels Emerson's but also enhances it.

BODY POLITICS: FREDERICK DOUGLASS AND THE AMERICAN SCHOOL OF ETHNOLOGY

After Emerson converted to abolitionism, he and Douglass found themselves working the same lecture circuits and, at times, speaking on the same bill.[31] Each esteemed the other as a model of self-reliance, and the two deepened their respective understandings of individualism as at its most excellent when it rejects self-interestedness but works in service toward a world of moral and political equality. For Emerson, Douglass was the "Anti-Slave" and embodied the "might & the right" of a struggle that would lift "the civilization of the world."³² For Douglass, Emerson philosophized the boons of self-trust in a way that was not only intellectually moving but also affectively resonant with his own life journey from enslaved chattel to leading social reformer. With increasing frequency, critics have elucidated the considerable reach of these lines of influence and thereby debunked the idea that the intellectual relationship between Emerson and Douglass was mainly one of "conscious refusal."³³ Jack Turner goes as far as to claim Douglass as a principal elaborator of Emersonian individualism because of the "intensity with which [Douglass] attended to freedom's [material] prerequisites. Douglass, unlike Emerson, could never take for granted that he would have both the negative liberty and positive economic wherewithal to lead a free life." And still, Turner concludes that Douglass's "self-reliance was more Franklinian [i.e., Benjamin Franklin] than Emersonian [because] it focused less on freedom's ethics and more on freedom's practicalities."³⁴ What seems to hinder critics from identifying Douglass's intellectual debts to American Transcendentalism is a refusal to appreciate Emerson's claim in "Circles" (1841) that the "practical" is one of the "degrees of idealism."³⁵ In response to the mounting defeats of rationalist abolitionism in the 1850s Douglass did just that, as he increasingly tackled the question of what to do (i.e., the practical) from the vantage of transcendentalist idealism. His 1854 "The Claims of the Negro, Ethnologically Considered" is an exemplar of this methodological approach.

First given for the literary societies of Western Reserve College, "Claims" marks both a national and a personal first: it was the first time an African American spoke at the commencement of an American college or university, and it was Douglass's first prepared scholarly address.³⁶ The address rests on a conception of equal humanity among all persons that rejects the American School of Ethnology's proposition that African-descended persons were essentially dissimilar from their white counterparts at the level of their physical and mental makeup. For ethnologists, the most convincing proof of inherent human difference across race was the craniology of Samuel G. Morton, the founder of the American School, and his work led many to adopt the theory of polygenesis: multiple creations of man or numerous sets of Adams and Eves scattered across the globe that the Bible does not account for. Some polygenists would go so far as to claim that the persons descended from these "different pairs of the human race, of different complexions and physical conformations," constituted different *species* of the genus *Homo* (i.e., Man).[37] Validated by the researches of the American School, theories of constitutional dissimilarity readily sanctioned dissimilar and thus unequal relations in the polity. As Douglass put it, "the whole argument in defense of slavery, becomes utterly worthless the moment the African is proved to be equally a man with the Anglo-Saxon."[38]

In setting out to prove that the humanity of the African is inherently the same as that of the Anglo-Saxon, Douglass announces that his discourse on "the claims of the negro, general and special," shall proceed "in a manner . . . not scientific."[39] With this admission Douglass reveals not only his limitations as a scientific thinker but, more tellingly, the limitations of the work of the American School as *science*. Fundamentally, ethnologists understood the anatomical as the vehicle by means of which to arrive at the ontological—that is, the nature of one's character, intellectual powers, and capacity for virtue. For this reason, Jared Hickman has identified the arguments of the American School as a "pretention to 'science,'" since those who adhered to those arguments understood them as revelations of "divine truths." Hickman writes: "The debate that swirled around the American School might be thought of as the last hurrah of the natural theology that the imminent Darwinian revolution would squelch."[40] Thus the aim of Douglass's contest with the American School was not simply to refute its cranial and corporeal specificities but, more importantly, to invalidate the *metaphysical* conclusions those specificities reputedly signified. "In Douglass' reading of the American School of Ethnology, the black body c. 1855 has not been emptied of transcendental meanings," Hickman argues, "rather it is supercharged with them."[41]

The question of the transcendental significance of the black body—its divinity—thus calibrates the analytical thrust of "Claims" because Douglass understands deeply that that significance has real-world consequences. In this way, he recalls Emerson's insistence on a positive link between idealism and the practical. The sentence that immediately follows Emerson's affirmation of the practical as a degree of idealism reads: "We learn that God is; that he is in me; and that all things are shadows of him."[42] Emerson's ability to presume common human divinity here allows him to continue to outline his theory of the relation between the forever abiding impersonal and the flux of historio-cultural succession he calls "circles," which culminates in an acknowledgment of our "insatiable desire to forget ourselves ... to draw a new circle.... The way of life is wonderful. It is by abandonment."[43] While such rhetoric might give the impression that the highest priority of Transcendentalism is "radical disengagement" from political and social spheres, one must remember that the prerequisite of Emersonian abandonment is a faith in all persons as infused with the impersonal, that they are its "shadows."[44] For his part, Douglass seemed to have believed he did not have the intellectual latitude to assume *a priori* common human divinity because in "Claims" he takes seriously propositions that question common humanity across racial difference. For before Douglass could argue that the impersonal necessitates common equal rights, and thus draw on the radically democratic potentiality at the core of Transcendentalism, he had to deal with the "first general claim" that "respects the manhood of the negro."[45]

The belief that the Negro is fully human Douglass calls an "elementary claim, simple enough, but not without question. It is fiercely opposed."[46] He cites what he believes is the opinion of "a respectable public journal," the *Richmond Examiner*, which deemed the Negro "destitute" of "will and intellect" and thus possessed of no right to "his liberty and the pursuit of his own happiness ... BECAUSE HE IS NOT A MAN!"[47] "There are three ways to answer this denial," Douglass suggests—by "ridicule," "denunciation," or "argument"—and while he "hardly [knew] under which of these modes my answer today will fall," his response becomes both the keynote and, as I will argue, the most settled epistemic terrain of the entire address:

> Man is distinguished from all other animals, by the possession of certain definite faculties and powers, as well as by physical organization and proportions. He is the only two-handed animal on the earth—the only one that laughs, and nearly the only one that weeps. Men instinctively distinguish between men and brutes. Common sense itself is scarcely needed to detect the absence of manhood in a monkey, or to recognize its presence in a negro. His speech, his reason, his power to acquire and to retain knowledge, his heaven-erected face, his habitudes, his hopes, his fears, his aspirations, his prophecies, plant between him and the brute creation, a distinction as eternal as it is palpable. Away, therefore, with all the scientific moonshine that would connect men with monkeys; that would have the world believe that humanity, instead of

resting on its own characteristic pedestal—gloriously independent—is a sort of sliding scale, making one extreme brother to the ourang-outang, and the other to angels, and all the rest intermediates! Tried by all the usual, and all the unusual tests, whether mental, moral, physical, or psychological, the negro is a MAN—considering him as possessing knowledge, or needing knowledge, his elevation or his degradation, his virtues, or his vices—whichever road you take, you reach the same conclusion, the negro is a MAN. His good and his bad, his innocence and his guilt, his joys and his sorrows, proclaim his manhood in speech that all mankind practically and readily understand.[48]

That Douglass would entertain the notion that the Negro is not fully human with such seriousness is surprising, though his considered counterattack might suggest he did not want to reject arguments that disputed the Negro's full humanity out of hand and thereby cede ultimate rhetorical authority to his rivals by exhibiting a lack of intellectual curiosity. In short, Douglass first had to affirm the full personhood of the Negro if the political claims he was to make on her behalf were to have any merit.

The operative phrase thus becomes "the negro is a Man," and Douglass proclaims it four times over the course of the address. "Claims" suggests that the very act of questioning (black) personhood constitutes blasphemy because it is to grant credence to an evolutionary paradigm (one that "would connect men with monkeys" on a "sort of sliding scale," as he describes it) that negates divine human creation. Hence Jared Hickman's astute observation that Douglass "dares the American School ... to make the Negro subhuman, and therefore, less than a child of God endowed with inalienable rights," since doing so one "will have to get in bed with the evolutionists." The American School would not have identified as evolutionist because of the "association of evolutionism with social radicalism and the revolutionary upheavals of the previous decades"; besides, two of the most-discussed theories of the ethnological debate were those of natural theology: monogenesis and polygenesis.[49] By explaining racial descent and difference as a consequence of either of these theories, Douglass intimates, even the most hostile and pro-slavery of ethnologists admitted to the divine personhood of all persons, however obliquely, because theological narratives of human genesis, mono- *or* poly-, recognize persons as God's "children."[50]

"Claims," therefore, enacted Douglass's shrewd understanding of what antebellum ethnology actually is: less a science, and more a sort of positivist investigational regime in pursuit of theological and transcendental truths. Ethnology, as he defines it, "is connected with eternal as well as with terrestrial interests. It covers the earth and reaches heaven."[51] With his first claim—that is, "the negro is a MAN" and thus endowed with the very same divinity as her white counterparts— Douglass believed he successfully exemplified the logic of the physical (the "terrestrial," "the palpable") disclosing the metaphysical (the "eternal"), and it is this method of investigation that he uses for the rest of "Claims." But he encounters a problem when he relies on this logic to uphold monogenesis, his second claim, because "viewed apart from the authority of the Bible, neither the unity, nor the diversity of the human family can be demonstrated."[52] To be sure, on the side of monogenesis he adduces an "instinctive consciousness of the common brotherhood of man" as well as a political calculus that estimates if one grants "that the human race are of multitudinous origin, naturally different in their moral, physical, and intellectual capacities, [he] . . . at once make[s] a plausible demand for classes, grades and conditions, for different methods of culture, different moral, political, and religious institutions, and a chance is left for slavery, as a necessary institution." But affect and prognosis do not constitute physical evidence that all races "descended from a common ancestry" or single stock.[53] Thus in his most comprehensive treatment of ethnology, Douglass has no choice but to leave the question of racial descent hanging conspicuously in the balance because of the insufficiency of his analytical method.

Incredibly, in a move that clashes with his earlier prognosis, Douglass declares that the factuality of monogenesis should have no bearing on the substance of human relations. He asks: "What, if we grant that the case, on our part [monogenesis], is not made out? Does it follow, that to enslave and imbrute him [i.e., the Negro] is either *just* or *wise*? I think not."[54] By allowing theories of a multitudinous human origin any degree of plausibility, Douglass breaks from abolitionists, black ethnologists, and anti-slavery ministers who found in polygenesis justifications of chattel slavery and race-based exclusionary practices. But Douglass can tolerate polygenesis because human descent from distinct pairs of ancestors does not in any way negate the fact that the persons who descend from those lines are indeed *persons*—and it is their standing as persons, their "manhood" and divinity, that warrants their right to full self-determination and political autonomy.

This is the substance of Douglass's impersonal, and "Claims" culminates in an elucidation of transcendental impersonality and its inviolable social and political meanings. He writes:

> Human rights stand upon a common basis; and by all the reason that they are supported, maintained and defended, for one variety of the human family, they are supported, maintained and defended for all the human family; because all mankind have the same wants, arising out of a common nature. A diverse origin does not disprove a common nature, nor does it disprove a united destiny. The essential characteristics of humanity are everywhere the same. In the language of the eloquent [John Philpot] CURRAN, "No matter what complexion, whether an Indian or an African sun has burnt upon him," his title deed to freedom, his claim to life and to liberty, to knowledge and to civilization, to society and to Christianity, are just and perfect.[55]

That the climax of Douglass's much-anticipated two-hour lecture on ethnology propounds a metaphysic of impersonality as the foundation for his existential and political claims on behalf of the Negro suggests an investment in idealism that he could not make in materialism, scientific or otherwise.[56] For one, Douglass believed ethnological methods and the data they uncovered could not truly answer the field's two most politically meaningful research questions: monogenesis vs. polygenesis; and the relationship of sub-Saharan Africans to ancient Egyptians. (As with monogenesis, Douglass finds one cannot conclude definitively that Africans are "but one people"; they "*probably*" are, he says.[57]) Moreover, Douglass anticipates a day when advances in ethnological research might uncover incontrovertible proof of polygenesis and that the civilizations of Northern Africa and sub-Saharan Africa are unrelated; thus, he cannot risk conceding matters of government and sociality to scientism. Instead, Douglass proposes in "Claims" that impersonality should always remain philosophically and politically viable because its transcendental conceptions of personhood elude the contingencies of empiricism, and for Douglass universal human freedom and the liberty to pursue self-culture should never be contingent.

Douglass's discontent with the scientific also stemmed from what he discerned as a refusal of objectivity among ethnologists, whom he branded as "men who reason from *prejudice* rather than from facts."[58] Their prejudices were not only personal but also pandering to what he called a "characteristic American assumption" against black persons: "It is the province of prejudice to blind; and scientific writers, not less than others, write to please, as well as to instruct, and even unconsciously to themselves, (sometimes,) sacrifice what is true to what is popular."[59] For Douglass, this prejudice was most evident in the lack of cranial and facial parity between whites and blacks in the American School's craniometrics. The most egregious and well-known example of race-based cranial discrepancy occurs in a chart in George R. Gliddon and Josiah C. Nott's *Types of Mankind* (1854), a book Douglass denounced as "the most compendious and barefaced" of "all the attempts ever made to disprove the unity of the human family, and to brand the Negro with natural inferiority."[60] In that chart, the head of the Apollo Belvedere represents the "white" cranium, while the "Negro" crania and heads correspond directly to the primate crania and heads that are also pictured.[61] Douglass told his audience that such renderings were rife in the scientific literature, because if a "phrenologist, or naturalist undertakes to represent in portraits the differences between the two races—the Negro and the European—he will invariably present the *highest* type of the European, and the *lowest* type of the Negro." To counteract such "ethnological unfairness towards the Negro," he demanded racial equivalence: "If the very best type of the European is always presented, I insist that *justice*, in all such works, demands that the very best type of Negro should also be taken." Douglass recommended several black men whose "heads," "all better formed, and indicat[ing] the presence of intellect more than any pictures [he had] seen in [ethnological] works," the craniologist should use were he to do "justice" to his subject.[62] And although he did not list himself, those who heard or read the address usually put forward Douglass above all others as one whose "head" evinced that black persons were as intellectually gifted as their white counterparts. Or, as the editor of a local Ohio newspaper, the *Summit Beacon*, put it in his review of Douglass's performance of "Claims," "the address was written, and in point of scholarship and literary merit, it will rank,—should it be published,—with the most successful efforts of the ripest scholars."[63]

In proposing several accomplished African Americans whose crania signified the capacity of black erudition, Douglass did not mean to suggest that black persons deserved freedom and full civil inclusion because members of their race attained cultural and intellectual distinction. Rather, he hoped to clarify that one could find the full range of human corporeality, life, and achievement among African and African-descended persons. To that effect, Douglass "admitted that there are negroes answering the description given by the American ethnologists and others" because "there is every description of head among them, ranging from the highest Indoo Caucasian downward."[64] He attributed somatic differences within and across races to what he called "the effect of circumstances," and pitched his environmentalism in direct contestation to the essential racial truths the American School argued the black body signified: "The form of the *negro* . . . has often been the subject of remark. His flat feet, long arms, high cheek bones and retreating forehead, are especially dwelt upon, to his disparagement, and just as if there are no white people with precisely the same peculiarities. I think it will ever be found, that the *well* or *ill* condition of any part of mankind, will leave its mark on the physical as well as on the intellectual part of man."[65] In this view, the body is raw material where the natural and social worlds impress their "marks"; thus the deplorable corporeal and mental constitutions the American School recognized as particular to black persons could take shape among any group of persons who endured similar conditions. Douglass argued that one only needed to look to "the common people of Ireland" for proof: "Never did human faces tell a sadder tale. . . . [T]hese people lacked only a black skin and woolly hair, to complete their likeness to the plantation negro. The open, uneducated mouth—the long, gaunt arm—the badly formed foot and ankle—the shuffling gait—the retreating forehead and vacant expression—and, their petty quarrels and fights—all reminded me of the plantation, and my own cruelly abused people."[66] Hence Douglass recognizes no correlation between racial identity and human immanence because anatomical and intellectual disparities among racial groups are consequences of environmental and sociocultural differences, not of God or Nature.

Throughout "Claims," Douglass's meditations on cultural, linguistic, physiological, and sociohistorical differences return to this principle of transcendentalist impersonality: essential human sameness. In effect,

Douglass had found a way to turn ethnology itself against the American School, charging the field's greatest authorities with intellectual dishonesty because in his estimation the only objective metaphysical claims an ethnological investigation could yield invalidated race as a transcendental ideal. Put another way, in "Claims" ethnology simply becomes another "mode of reasoning" that negates inherent racial difference in favor of the impersonal, a notion that organizes much of his political thought and social criticism in the decade. As he put it in an 1850 editorial for *The North Star* called "Prejudice against Color": "Wherein does the white man differ from the black? Why, one is white and the other is black. Well, what of that? Does the sun shine more brilliantly upon the one than it does upon the other? Is nature more lavish with her gifts toward the one than toward the other? Do earth, sea and air yield their united treasures to the one more readily than to the other? In a word, 'have we not all one Father?' Why then do you revolt at that equality which God and nature instituted?"[67] While the notion of impersonality that organizes this succession of rhetorical questions (with its not-so-subtle echoes of transcendentalist diction) remained axiomatic for Douglass, the ethnological research he carried out for "Claims" became the materialist, even if not quite scientific, scaffolding upon which to hoist such assertions of essential human sameness across race.

Moreover, Douglass's impersonal distinguished him from several of his most incisive black contemporaries who also fought to topple chattel slavery and achieve full political autonomy and rights for African Americans but appealed to black chauvinism and "complexional institutions" and "distinctions."[68] Such appeals flout impersonality and, for Douglass, reify the very categories and conceptions of human difference polities rely on to legitimate race-based proscriptions of freedom and citizenship. In a significant way, Douglass's habitual, almost reflexive recourse to the "oneness of the human family" relegated black chauvinists like the abolitionist and amateur ethnologist Martin R. Delany to the same moral plane as the American School and their adherents: both groups understood race as an inexorable biological force that shapes individual endeavor and social relations.[69] Douglass, by contrast, perceived race as a superable sociohistorical force, and he maintained a form of race consciousness that was grounded in, and strove toward, an idea of impersonality that nullifies races. "My cause first, midst, last, and always, whether in office or out of office," Douglass reflected in 1892, "was and is that of the black man; not because he is black, but because he is a man, and a man subjected in this country to peculiar wrongs and hardships."[70] Thus if Douglass found "little space for black transcendence in the antebellum era," as Maurice S. Lee argues, it does not necessarily follow that he "privileged the material fact of race over transparent selfhood."[71] Rather, Douglass's aim was to help foster that very space where all persons, black or otherwise, might work to achieve transcendence without having to overcome undue and unjust barriers that dishonor human dignity and divinity. The achievement of "transparent selfhood," which I understand as the achievement of impersonality, remained the highest privilege Douglass sought for himself and for all persons. He battled persistently with the "fact of race" because he viewed racial affect—from pride to prejudice—as a hindrance and offense to the impersonal.[72]

The analytical priority Douglass maintained on the encumbrances of race marks his standing as a distinctive theorist of transcendentalist impersonality. He could never settle in the purely reflective or philosophical as Emerson often did—and he never wanted to—knowing that these moods and modes too easily occluded, and moved past, the anxieties, brutalities, and proscriptions that beset bodies such as his. Instead, Douglass spoke directly and politically on behalf of "the lonely and despised ones, with whom [he] was cradled, and with whom [he had] suffered" because their dignity and divinity as persons had too quickly and too often been snubbed; in fact, their very personhood had often come under question.[73] While Douglass found such doubts absurd, he decided to engage them, however sardonically, because of their far-reaching consequences. In "Claims," he leans on the field of ethnology to demonstrate that all we know for sure about the Negro, his nature, and his natural history is that he is a person and, as such, possesses the same dignity and divinity as all other persons. Douglass's ethnological consideration of the "claims of the negro" ends up most firmly on transcendentalist ground, affirming the shared political promise of impersonality: "Human rights stand upon a common basis[:] . . . all mankind have the same wants, arising out of a common nature," he concludes, "God has no children whose rights may be safely trampled upon."[74]

The overriding appeal of "Claims" lies in its call on its readers and listeners to recognize and honor the divinity in all persons—black, slave, or otherwise. In fact, the address very often positions the face (and head) of the person before its audiences to facilitate such an encounter—the person being both its ethnological subjects and the performing Douglass himself. In this way "Claims" might be Douglass's most enduring contribution to what Sharon Cameron calls a "reinvented American heroic[,] reinvented in the sense that its emphasis on face-to-face confrontation with the divine is originally Homeric as well as Old Testament." The American heroic bears an indissoluble relationship to Emersonian impersonality, she suggests, since the "*content* of Emerson's impersonal implies a heroic *context*: an encounter with the real, however indecipherable its name." Cameron finds that Emerson ultimately lacks the "authority to speak of the soul's manifestations of divinity" because his "statements are *insufficiently* personal," but she identifies Dickinson, Whitman, Melville, and Thoreau as writers who understood that the heroic "implies a *person's* contact with the real."⁷⁵ To this list I would add Douglass, for he not only foregrounded the import of the person in the heroic encounter, but more importantly, elucidated that all persons are worthy of taking part in that encounter because all persons are equally divine. In "Claims," Douglass stakes his abolitionism and political demands on behalf of the Negro on nothing more—but nothing less—than her divinity and our willingness to encounter it.

Looking back at "Claims" for the revised edition of his final autobiography, *The Life and Times of Frederick Douglass* (1892), Douglass called the address "a very defective production."⁷⁶ In both his public writing and his private correspondence he remembered his text and performance of it as something of a low point in his oratorical career. Certainly the rarefied setting and novelty of the event—Douglass had no formal schooling and had been enslaved longer than he had been free at that point in his life, yet there he was delivering a college commencement address—produced whatever anxieties marred the address or his memory of it. But I take his qualms to be indicative of the political magnitude of "Claims": it was what Jason Frank calls a "constitutive moment," an event in which "the underauthorized—imposters, radicals, self-created entities—seize the mantle of authorization" to "speak in the people's name, even though those claims explicitly break from the authorized procedures or norms for representing popular voice."⁷⁷ Frank reads Douglass's famed "The Meaning of July Fourth for the Negro," delivered in Rochester, New York on July 5, 1852, as a constituent moment *par excellence*, when Douglass lacked "authorization to speak for the people" yet "claimed to speak on their behalf . . . from an indeterminate or paradoxical position, insofar as he spoke at once as a slave—representing in his words 'a people long dumb, not allowed to speak for themselves'—and as part of a political collectivity still without social determination." Such moments become "felicitous" when the people emerge as such, however affective or spectral, and enact new conditions for political authority, representation, and voice.[78] With "Claims" Douglass also called forth the people as a political body (the *demos*), but what distinguishes it from the "July Fourth" speech is that he does so by way of an ontological query of the human (i.e., What is the nature of the Negro? What are his needs?) rather than by way of political-philosophical cunning with the Constitution and the American founding as he did in Rochester. Here democratic subjectification for Douglass and the persons for whom he speaks, especially black persons, emerged from the affirmation of common personhood and its recognition amid the dominance of antiblack racial scientific discourses that shaped all aspects of American life.

From the vantage of the ascendancy of Darwinism and American Pragmatism in the late nineteenth century, "Claims" lacks the empirical heft to be called a philosophy of science. But the source and force of the intervention "Claims" enacted resides elsewhere: in a transcendentalist logic that not only refutes the "materialist" racism of the American School of Ethnology, but also upholds impersonal life as radically democratic and self-actualizing. Douglass thus broadens the political significance of American Transcendentalism, beckoning us to confront the ways racial difference shrouds our perception of the other's dignity and divinity. At the same time, his idiosyncratic absorption and deployment of transcendentalist idealism in his activism, social criticism, and political thought in the 1850s marks Douglass's turn to the metaphysical as both an explanatory frame for, and emancipatory power from, the problem of chattel slavery.

In a review of an anti-slavery lecture Emerson gave in 1855, Douglass wrote: "The hugest enormity that ever confronted heaven laid outspread before [Emerson,] and that enormity was SLAVERY; and yet, in the lecture, you will find very little which, to the common eye, bears any sort of relation to the question he came among us to discuss; and yet in that lecture, he *did* discuss slavery, very directly and very profoundly, and showed, with his own *unique* richness of ideas, the real foundation of slavery." Because chattel slavery was an "enormity" that transcended the physical world, Douglass suggests that toppling the institution would require embracing what he called "the spiritual mysteries of mankind."[79] Equal human dignity and divinity was the spiritual mystery he sought to reveal in "Claims," trusting that the recognition and adoration of such radical commonality was not only heroic but also the foundation for the most vigorous forms of free, democratic life.

3 · Violence

Harriet E. Wilson's *Our Nig; or, Sketches from the Life of a Free Black* (1859) is the great outlier of African American literature before Emancipation. A fictionalized autobiography, the novel chronicles Wilson's childhood as an abandoned black girl in New Hampshire but flouts the first-person narrative form that dominated contemporaneous black life writing. It also lacks the sentimentalism that readers in the era craved from women's fiction and domestic novels. Wilson said she wrote the book to make money. "Deserted by kindred, disabled by failing health," she explains, "I am forced to some experiment which shall aid me in maintaining myself and my child without extinguishing this feeble life."[1] These financial motivations make her decision to eschew prevailing literary conventions all the more puzzling.

This enigma has baffled readers since Henry Louis Gates Jr. rediscovered *Our Nig* in the early 1980s. Most critics have attempted to solve it by deciphering whom the book is for, but that pursuit has proven just as difficult. Wilson "sincerely appealed to [her] colored brethren universally for patronage," but the strangeness of the novel's form combined with black financial precarity in the late 1850s ensured a tiny market of black buyers—an amalgam of factors she surely knew. As for white readers of women's fiction, especially those that made Harriet Beecher Stowe's *Uncle Tom's Cabin* (1852) a smashing success, the unsparing rebuke of Northerners' priggish antiblack cant that *Our Nig* stages was unpalatable. White middle-class women emerge as sinister brutes, and Wilson's "antislavery friends" as uncaring hypocrites.[2] The search for audience has gotten us no closer to making sense of the formal anomalies that distinguish *Our Nig* in the antebellum literary canon.

The key to unraveling the novel's narrative architecture, I believe, lies in the primary event it details: the torture of its protagonist, Frado. Frado, Wilson's fictionalized self, is victim to a catalogue of abuse at the hands of her foster family, the Bellmonts—especially the matriarch, Mrs. Belmont, and her daughter Mary. The abuse begins when she is six, very shortly after they take her in, with "words that burn," "frequent blows on [the] head," and beatings with "a raw-hide."[3] And the abuse lasts, and worsens, for the next twelve years. Wilson did not "divulge every transaction" of Frado's horrifying upbringing, almost certainly leaving out instances of sexual assault and exploitation.[4] But the torture she does describe—everything from starvation and psychological harm to beatings, maiming, and knockout thwacks—molds the novel's *sui generis* form. I understand that form as a textualization of what Jennifer Nash calls "the great insight of black feminist theory": that "injury is never *really* shared; [that] identity-work always requires elisions."[5] The novel's peculiar shape instantiates the fundamental peculiarity of injury itself.

Wilson did not have the talent (or even interest) to develop representational modalities that might approach the fullness of what Frado endures. But she was savvy enough to know that popular literary conventions were inadequate for her project. Her interventions emerge from how she rejected, altered, and reoriented those conventions. The most significant of her tacks is an inversion of the liberation-through-violence model that hails the violent overthrow of white oppressors as the primary means toward black freedom and thus toward the cultivation of one's "true" black self. Once a person overcomes violence with violence, this model holds, he becomes both "heroic and political."[6] Liberation-through-violence has organized nationalist and radical strands of black politics from David Walker's *Appeal to the Colored Citizens of the World* (1829) to ongoing reverberations of the Black Power concept. But *Our Nig* turns that model on its head. Frado is defeated time and again, and she is anything but heroic. Yet it is from her lowly vanquished position that she emerges with new political life: the capacity for speech.

This chapter reads Wilson's inversion of the liberation-through-violence model as an allegorical exemplum of slave morality. Wilson's espousal of slave morality in *Our Nig* is her response to the ways America deemed certain persons deserving of indiscriminate violence simply because of who and what they are. She suggests these are persons who lack the power and force to change their condition, persons who are always already defeated. *Our Nig* is a tale of how some of them have come to seize a liberatory potentiality within their own vanquishments: from the depths of the hell into which they are beaten, they discover their voice and speak. Speech is an unparalleled political power and slave morality esteems it as such. How else might one undermine master morality except through argumentation, eloquence, and persuasion? Slave morality, which might be democracy itself, has no other instrumentality but speech.

"THE LADDER OF INFAMY": PARODY AND AMERICAN SOCIAL VALUE

Our Nig begins on what would have been very familiar literary terrain for mid-century readers. A Lothario has seduced Frado's mother, Mag Smith, out of her virginity; Mag's friends and neighbors have refused to offer succor or companionship; and she has decided to "seek an asylum among strangers." Mag's first words in the novel are "God be thanked," which she says because the "unwelcomed" weeks-old baby has died. "No one can taunt *her* with my ruin."[7] Mag ultimately moves into a deserted hovel on the outskirts of town, where she has little to no contact with others. Only a few pages in, Wilson has thrust readers into the mire of the seduction novel, the hugely popular genre of antebellum fiction that was also a common narrative template in anti-slavery writing.

The opening thus operates as a sort of double fiction: the generic trappings of the seduction novel couch Wilson's fanciful account of Mag's life leading up to Frado's birth. Wilson had no qualms about concocting actions, conversations, thoughts, and movements concerning Mag's predicament because her aim, above all, is to clarify the discursive and ideological forces that animate the novel and its politics. The evaluation of the novel's status as "fiction" versus "autobiography" has occupied critics for decades now. But that critical endeavor has too easily obscured the far more salient point that, as Priscilla Wald puts it, *Our Nig* is a "*narrative about* what writing for a particular market does to this African American woman in pre-Civil War New England and, more generally, *about* cultural identity."[8]

Wilson believed an identity-based axiology was the conceptual spine of how American culture takes shape. She described it as "the ladder of infamy," a rhetorical figure that signifies a valuation of persons and their consequent status in the polity.[9] The ladder of infamy evokes the Great Chain of Being in its hierarchization of life, though one does not remain fixed in place on the former as one does on the latter. Mag is born a white woman with the privileges that identity entails in antebellum America, but she loses her position and slides down the ladder of infamy once she "surrendered" her "priceless gem" to a man who claimed her virginity as a "trophy" to display alongside "those of other victims."[10] Within the narrative logic of the conventional seduction novel, she has reached rock bottom.

But *Our Nig* suggests Mag has further to fall. Its first chapter is titled "Mag Smith, My Mother," which means Mag has procreated with a black man to birth Frado. "You can philosophize, gentle reader, upon the impropriety of such unions, and preach dozens of sermons on the evils of amalgamation," Wilson writes, but "poor Mag. She has surrendered another bond which held her to her fellows. She has descended another step down the ladder of infamy."[11] For white persons, sexual relationships and reproduction with African-descended persons were violations of the American racial contract, acts of personal depravity tantamount to national betrayal. Never mind that Mag had already been cast into a state of penury and despondency; never mind that the "publicity of her fall" made her a regular target of "some foul tongue" and "averted looks and cold greetings" everywhere she turned; never mind that the black man with whom she had two children "furnished her with a more comfortable dwelling, diet, and apparel" until the day he died. Nothing is worse than a "union with a black": it was what "expelled [Mag] from companionship with white people; this last step . . . was the climax of repulsion."[12]

Wilson describes the man in Mag's union, Jim, as a "kind-hearted African."[13] Biographers have almost certainly identified the real-life Jim in historical records. He was a cooper named Joshua Green of Milford, New Hampshire, and he is listed on Wilson's marriage and death certificates as her father. (Green died in 1829 or 1830.) Jim courts Mag while delivering wood to her hovel, a detail that might also be true given Green's occupation. In the novel, his approach is clear-eyed expedience devoid of all romance: "You's down low enough. I don't see but I've got to care of ye. 'Sposin' we marry! . . . You's had a trial of white folks, any how. They run off and left ye, and now none of 'em come near ye to see if you's dead or alive. . . . Take me Mag, I can give you a better home than this, and not let you suffer."[14] With her life in the balance and vagrancy her only other option, Mag accepts his proposal. The novel offers no indication as to whether she ever loved Jim romantically, but she remained committed to him until the very end, when "she nursed him faithfully and true to marriage vows till [his] death released her."[15]

Yet Jim loved Mag deeply. Why? Wilson explains his reasoning in a stunning scene of reverie and soliloquy:

> [Jim] belted his barrels, with many a scheme revolving in his mind, none of which quite satisfied him, or seemed, on the whole expedient. He thought of the pleasing contrast between her fair face and his own dark skin; the smooth, straight hair, which he had once, in expression of pity, kindly stroked on her now wrinkled but once fair brow. There was a tempest gathering in his heart, and at last, to ease his pent-up passion, he exclaimed aloud, "By golly! . . . She'd be as much of a prize to me as she'd fall short of coming up to the mark with white folks. I don't care for past things. I've down things 'fore now I's 'shamed of. She's good enough for me, any how."[16]

Jim's train of thought runs through the affective logics of sentimentality and scientific racism, leaving him an avatar of what we now call internalized antiblack racism. But everything is so theatrical, so inflated, so rhapsodic, that to regard anything here as "internal" in any real sense is to miss the rhetorical ironies at play in the scene and throughout the novel. *Why* Jim loved Mag does not matter, at least not in *Our Nig*, but Wilson uses the occasion of his "love" to pinpoint pillars of American social value that she wants to expose and thereupon launch her critique.

The narratology of the scene thus calls for a hermeneutic attuned to irony. Jim is alone, no one hears his thoughts or words, and Wilson was not even born when it took place: the scene is pure invention. His ratiocination, twisted in the most hackneyed racialism, culminates in euphoric catharsis. Wilson ironizes the moment of intellectual clarity and affective sanction that anchors American literatures of sentimentality: Jim becomes the sentimental hero *par excellence*. Sentimentality's representational norms refuse to judge black persons' feelings—if they are judged to have feelings at all—as philosophically illuminative or politically meaningful. Precisely because it was utterly ridiculous under normative affective logics, Jim's assumption of the role of sentimental hero exposes the lie of humanitarian inclusion via emotional similitude across race and every other category of social stratification.

Wilson was especially censorious of the sentimentalism that vitalized bourgeois white women's public culture. The political core of their culture was a "compassionate liberalism," as Lauren Berlant terms it, that "wants to dissolve all that structure through good intentionality, while busily exoticizing and diminishing the inconvenient and the noncompliant."[17] Wilson rejected such liberalism as a cruel, self-serving pietism; she deemed it the humbug of "professed abolitionists, who didn't want slaves at the South, nor niggers in their own houses, North. Faugh! to lodge one; to eat with one; to admit one through the front door; to sit next to one; awful!"[18] Her effort to expose the debasements of the sentimentalist publics bourgeois white women governed was more than a "demand [of] its reorganization"; it was a call for that public's demise.[19]

That work required coming to terms with the imbrication of race, sex, and desire, a feature of American antebellum sociality bourgeois women reformers sublimated into regimes of personal abstemiousness and social puritanism. Wilson decried the sexualized and racialized aesthetics that for them anchored white supremacist epistemes and, quiet as it was kept, benefited these reformers who publicly demurred to carnality. In the American intellectual tradition, Thomas Jefferson's theory of white persons' "superior beauty" in *Notes on the State of Virginia* (1785) was the first major philosophical statement on the intersections of beauty, race, and sexuality. Jefferson asks: "Are not the fine mixtures of red and white, the expressions of every passion by greater or less suffusions of colour in the one, preferable to that eternal monotony" of blackness? "Add to these, flowing hair, a more elegant symmetry of form," he continues, and black persons' "own judgment in favour of the whites, declared by their preference of them, as uniformly as is the preference of the Oranootan for the black women over those of his own species."[20] Jim apes Jeffersonian racial aesthetics and, in the way he chooses Mag, becomes the ape ("Oranootan") of Jefferson's metaphor. Yet he does refute Jefferson's schema insofar as his emotions, "the tempest gathering in his heart" and his "pent-up passion," burst out plainly for all to see despite the "eternal monotony" of his "immovable veil of black" skin. Jim thus becomes every type of man: the sentimentalist and the brute; the aesthete and the ape. Wilson layers these ironies of character, form, and genre with such theatricality that the best, perhaps *only*, way to read Jim is as a figure of parody.

Parody can be "aestheticist" in the sense that it trains its energies on what it imitates, mocks, or travesties. It can also be "political" if it consciously targets someone or something *beyond* the parodied object or text. In *Our Nig*, it is political. Wilson parodies sentimentalism and the seduction novel through the figure of Jim to target white bourgeois women and their reformist politics. Jim loves Mag because she is a white woman; he never mentions anything about her as an individual that appeals to him. Her white womanhood makes her a "prize" and a "treasure."[21] The irony here is that the other white women in the novel to this point, Mag's "former companions," have been cruel, unforgiving, and oppressive. Then, once Mag decides to leave Frado with the Bellmonts after Jim's death, Mrs. Bellmont is introduced as a "right she-devil" with a reputation for sadism and barbarity—a reputation she lives up to throughout the rest of the novel.[22] The parodies that shape Mag and Jim's "love" story reveal what Wilson takes to be the malicious core of bourgeois white women's compassionate liberalism.

Julia Stern has written about the ways these rebukes in *Our Nig* revolve around the kitchen. The kitchen was the most treasured space of white liberal women, "domestic sentimentalists," who esteemed it in their activism and literature as the locus of racial transcendence and America's "moral regeneration."[23] In the novel, it is the site of much of the violence, insult, and humiliation that Frado endures. The kitchen offers no escape from the cold, brutal vagaries of the racist public sphere; the ostensible comforts of home-cooked food, table talk, women's charity, and fellow feeling are, in actuality, grisly intimacies that furnish different kinds of brutalities for black persons, especially black women and girls. As Stern writes, "in Wilson's fictional universe the kitchen becomes an inverted figure, a lively type of Hell."[24] The kitchen does not dissolve or destroy the ladder of infamy and its social valuations; rather, it reifies them and maintains the structure of the outside world, albeit in "womanly" form. Wilson admonishes her "colored brethren universally" that there are no spaces where they can be safe from the hellscapes of America: the sooner they embrace this reality, she suggests, the sooner they might develop a political vision that will bring about equal standing and personhood for African Americans in the polity.

COLOR AND HAIR

Wilson spurned the nostrums of mid-century American liberalism. In her judgment, bourgeois feminists, anti-slavery crusaders, temperance advocates, and poverty reformers offered little but empty promises. She called on African Americans to see those promises as fool's gold that would plunge them into different types of hell. With *Our Nig* she exposes how the social fantasies of antebellum liberalism not only confine black persons to the bottom of the social order, but require them there at the bottom for their own coherence and legibility.

Color was one mark of their ascription. In *Our Nig*, color is a major thematic that shapes everything from plot and character formation to sociology and political meaning. The most remarkable example of color's structuring force concerns Mrs. Bellmont's insistence that Frado never shield herself from the sun so that her skin will darken. "At home, no matter how powerful the heat when sent to rake hay or guard the grazing herd, [Frado] was never permitted to shield her skin from the sun," Wilson writes. "Mrs. Bellmont was determined the sun should have full power to darken the shade which nature had first bestowed upon her as best befitting."[25] Frado's skin color unsettles the color line—she is referred to as "yellow" and "handsome and bright, and not very black, either"[26]—and Mrs. Bellmont's effort to shore it up is both punishment (to her mind) and an affirmation of white racial accord.

Yet her attempts to "blacken" Frado reveal the relative precarity of color as determinant of one's status. As Orlando Patterson writes: "Color, despite its initially dramatic impact, is in fact a rather weak basis of ranked differences in interracial societies." He finds that it was "differences in hair type that become critical as a mark of servility in the Americas.... Differences between whites and blacks were sharper in this quality than in color and persisted for much longer with miscegenation. Hair type quickly became the real symbolic badge of slavery."[27] How hair shaped one's standing in antebellum America captivated Wilson. While she was writing *Our Nig* she was manufacturing and selling her own line of hair products to make ends meet. Her interests in hair converged on its functionality as an object of self-definition and a site of cultural judgment, two issues her black female customers negotiated with especial sensitivity.[28]

Wilson narrates these concerns in *Our Nig* with hair as a divider, separating the beautiful from the not beautiful, the master class from the slave class. These are not Wilson's social judgments but her parodic acknowledgment of America's.[29] In Jim's reverie about Mag, for example, he recalls her "smooth, straight hair, which he had once, in expression of pity, kindly stroked on her now wrinkled but once fair brow."[30] Even though Mag had fallen to the low rungs of her white community, she could still boast the hair of the master class. For Jim, a simple stroke of her hair is a kind of recompense for his pity. That stroke becomes a driver of his passion, fueling the scene's parody and Wilson's cultural commentary. Mag might be an outcast of polite white society and Jim might have the wherewithal to improve her material conditions and restore her health, yet "white hair" maintains its significance as the mark of which of the two belongs to the superior class of persons.

The ascriptive power of hair, its texture and growth pattern, that Wilson parodies in Jim's reverie becomes violent in Frado's story. Frado has "long, curly black hair" that others admire.[31] To Mrs. Bellmont that is an outrage, so she shaves off Frado's "glossy ringlets."[32] Jack, one of Mrs. Bellmont's sons, says his mother cut off the curls because she thought Frado was "getting too handsome." It is "the same old story," he concludes, "knocks and bumps."[33] Jack deems the haircut a violent act, marking Wilson's recognition that, as Jasmine Nichole Cobb writes, "violence is the chief imprint on [black] hair's imbrication in struggles for Black liberation."[34]

One way to read Frado's hair is that it is insufficiently "black." Her "glossy ringlets" are an ambiguous racial signifier, too "white" in their signification. They pose a threat to the social order and to Mrs. Bellmont's authority that "black hair" does not. "In the Americas," Patterson explains, "blacks' hair was not shorn because ... leaving the hair as it was served as a powerful badge of status. Shaving it would have muted the distinction."[35] Frado's hair must be cut off, then, because it troubles the social distinctions hair is supposed to demarcate. Mrs. Bellmont deems Frado's hair, just as she does Frado's skin color, too close to hers and her family members'. (The novel often compares Frado's features and comportment to Mary Bellmont's.) Shaving her hair and "blackening" her skin clears up the slipperiness of race as a category of social ascription.

Moreover, the characterological drives that shape Mrs. Bellmont compel her to cut off Frado's hair simply because it is fetching. Throughout the novel, she strives to strip every bit of joy from Frado's life; all Frado is to give is basic service, never delight to others or herself. Thavolia Glymph's description of the role white women's violence played in the administration of the plantation household in the American South pertains to its functionality in the Bellmonts' New Hampshire home. Glymph writes: "Violence permeated the plantation household, where the control and management of slaves required white women's active participation and authorized the exercise of brute or sadistic force."[36] The extended subtitle of *Our Nig* says that the novel's purpose is to show "that slavery's shadows fall even" in the free North.[37] "Wholly imbued with *southern* principles," Mrs. Bellmont is the most significant figuration for that project.[38] Her pleasure comes from whipping, beating, kicking, punching, and torturing Frado; she "indulge[s] her vixen nature" through such violence. "No matter what occurred to ruffle her, or from source provocation came, real or fancied," Wilson writes, "a few blows on Nig seemed to relieve [Mrs. Bellmont] of a portion of ill-will."[39] Cutting Frado's hair was among her many sadistic pleasures, which I argue are deeply libidinal and belong to the set of life experiences Wilson said she would not disclose. In its revelations of "slavery's shadows" as just as intimate and personal as they are operational and structural, Mrs. Bellmont's character is more than a malevolent trope in the (melo)drama of the story; it is a mirror within which northern white women might recognize themselves and their own villainies.

The violence of hair and color in *Our Nig* thus clarifies any uncertainties about what place African-descended persons occupy in the American polity: not only are they at the bottom rungs, but that position renders them subject to violence and all manner of violation with little to no recourse. The "maiming and destruction of black life," one of American chattel slavery's "central tendencies," obtained beyond the slave societies of the South and West.[40] *Our Nig* narrativizes that reality of black life in the free North, too, where, as Frederick Douglass put it, black people were "not slaves to individuals, not personal slaves," but "the slaves of the community."[41] Wilson believed black people must not delude themselves into thinking they were anything other than the slaves of the community. A politics rooted in something other than this clear-eyed judgment—a politics of sentimentalist reformism or compassionate liberalism, for example—would do nothing but entrench their oppression and exacerbate their delusions.

LIBERATION-THROUGH-VIOLENCE: A ROMANCE

Frederick Douglass agreed with Wilson's assessment of black life in late 1850s America. The evolution of his political thought over the decade and a half leading up to the Civil War was marked by increasing disillusionment with liberal reform and a more enthusiastic embrace of violence as the solution for chattel slavery and black oppression. Violence racked black life in slavery and freedom, so violence must be its remedy, he concluded. With this judgment Douglass severed any lingering connection to Garrisonian pacifism, joining the ranks of thinkers such as David Walker, John Brown, Henry Highland Garnet, and Charles Lenox Remond who deemed violence essential to black liberation.

Douglass's editorials and speeches in the 1850s constitute a groundwork for a morality of violence as both social pragmatism and political virtue. His short story "The Heroic Slave" (1852) imagines violence as a regenerative force that obviates the animus and bewilderments that racial difference breeds, thereby restoring society to a path of perfectibility. When Douglass co-founded the Radical Political Abolition Party in 1855, he sponsored a platform that championed violence as a solution to the limitations and shortcomings of the US Constitution. "If [the Constitution] says the nation has no power of self-protection, no power to shelter its subjects from enslavers, then give us REVOLUTION," the Radical Abolitionists declared.[42] "Enslavers" here meant not only those who participated directly in chattel slavery's operations and financial transactions, but also those who craved and cast its "shadows" in the North and elsewhere.

This period marks Douglass's studied merging of violence and politics, but violence had already figured prominently in his well-known narrations of his life story and the examples they staged. His epic battle with the notorious overseer and slave breaker Edward Covey is the climax of his first autobiography, *Narrative of the Life of Frederick Douglass, An American Slave* (1845). Douglass, whose owner rented him to Covey for a year so that he might "be broken" and work as a field hand for the first time in his life, framed the battle with what has become the most famous chiasmus in American letters: "You have seen how a man was made a slave; you shall see how a slave was made a man."⁴³ Their two-hour fight ends in a draw, and Covey never had Douglass whipped or beaten as punishment. Through physical struggle Douglass's "long-crushed spirit rose, cowardice departed, bold defiance took its place; and I now resolved that, however long I might remain a slave in form, the day had passed forever when I could be a slave in fact. I did not hesitate to let it be known of me, that the white man who expected to succeed in whipping, must also succeed in killing me."⁴⁴ His decision not to submit but to meet violence with violence reanimates his desire for freedom and, as such, furnishes the advent of his "manhood."⁴⁵

The liberation-through-violence model that unfolds across Douglass's autobiographies, especially the *Narrative*, has become a mythos in modern black political thought.⁴⁶ That mythos has spawned narratives of (black) freedom that are deeply masculinist in their features and aims. Feminist critics have explained the functional problematics of how these narratives "collapse freedom and manhood" such that freedom means "ending constraints on the capacities of the black body most associated with masculinity and ending threats to the male body."⁴⁷ What is missing or obscured in the masculinist purview are "specific threats to those who possess feminine embodiment, the capacities of the body and the material labors that have come to define the feminine," as Shatema Threadcraft writes. Hence a politics attuned to "liberation from sexual and reproductive violence that paves the way for unconstrained choice in sexual partners and unrestrained relationships with children" cannot emerge.⁴⁸ Those who are feminine and otherwise-not-manly-enough are mostly incidental to the political vision that conventional readings of Douglass's battle with Covey in the *Narrative* produce.

Claudia Tate has argued that the "masculine discourse" in Douglass's writings is the upshot of how quickly he moves past the sexual assault and other bodily violations of women. His recognition of the "pervasiveness of the sexual oppression of female slaves" at the beginning of the *Narrative*, she says, is but a cursory gesture toward the text's more forceful affirmation of "abstract humanistic abolitionist arguments that drew heavily on the republican discourses of American Revolution."⁴⁹ Like so many other feminist critics, Tate turns to Harriet Jacobs's *Incidents in the Life of a Slave Girl* (1861) to formulate conceptions of freedom that are conspicuously absent from antebellum black men's writings, conceptions that home in on "the intimate sphere" and its centrality in the "black freedom project."⁵⁰ *Incidents* has become a sort of theoretical *urtext* in black (American) feminisms that seek to redress forms of dispossession and domination that beset black familial and sexual lives, especially those of women. That project finds in Jacobs the beginnings of a radical and necessary repudiation of the public-private binary that has obtained in liberal thought since the eighteenth century: black women's "private" lives were nothing if not "public" matter.

One of the most remarkable features of these critiques as they take up Douglass's political thought is that they almost always rely on his *Narrative* and very rarely consider the rest of his autobiographical oeuvre, such as *My Bondage and My Freedom* (1855). This second autobiography is a thoroughgoing revision of the *Narrative* at over four times its length. The polymath and co-founder of the Radical Political Abolitionist Party James McCune Smith deemed the book Douglass's grand declaration of independence from William Lloyd Garrison and his brand of activism and social movement politics. The earlier *Narrative* is the product of a mind and temperament too beholden to Garrisonianism, McCune Smith argued. McCune Smith was part of a cohort of black critics and thinkers who believed Garrisonian "principles," especially racial paternalism and the refusal to engage in formal state politics, marred the first decade and a half of Douglass's public career. "These gentlemen [the Garrisonians]," McCune Smith writes in his introduction to *My Bondage and My Freedom*, "failed to fathom, and bring to the light of day, the highest qualities of his mind; the force of their own education stood in their own way: they did not delve into the mind of a colored man for capacities which the pride of race led them to believe to be restricted to their own Saxon blood."⁵¹

That readers should gauge the Garrisonian influence on the *Narrative* and its (gendered) conceptions of freedom is not to excuse Douglass of his blind spots. Rather, it is to be mindful of the philosophical delimitations that constrained his thinking and from which he famously broke free. McCune Smith understood Douglass's relationship with the Garrisonians as a kind of intellectual thralldom. He even correlated their split to the battle with Covey: "The same strong self-hood [that] led him to measure strength with Mr. Covey" drove Douglass to "wrench himself from the Garrisonians."⁵² For McCune Smith, the *Narrative* and other early works are so rife with Garrisonianism that they constitute a deeply misleading, if not nugatory archive of Douglass's mature thought.

How the two autobiographies treat violence illustrates McCune Smith's judgment. In the *Narrative*, violence is never a proactive instrumentality but always the last resort, always an unavoidable act of self-defense and self-preservation. Garrison, one of antebellum America's leading pacifists, taught his disciples to view violence this way, but it was wholly alien to Douglass's life experiences, free and enslaved. It is one of the "abstract humanist" principles that Tate and other critics see as the conceptual armature of the *Narrative*. But wouldn't it be most accurate to regard it as an instantiation of Garrison's political priorities rather than Douglass's?

Garrison writes in his Preface to the *Narrative* that the book's "most thrilling" scene is of Douglass "as he stood soliloquizing respecting his fate, and the chances of his one day being a freeman, on the banks of the Chesapeake Bay." In that moment, Garrison continues, readers encounter "a whole Alexandrian library of thought, feeling, and sentiment—all that can, all that need be urged, in the form of expostulation, entreaty, rebuke, against that crime of crimes,—making man the property of his fellow-man!"[53] He deemed Douglass's famed apostrophe to the ships on the Chesapeake Bay the climax of the *Narrative* because he believed the scene's sublimity and affective splendor would move unconverted readers to see the evils of chattel slavery: it was moral suasion in textual form. For Garrison and other staunch advocates, the rhetorical praxis of moral suasion is impervious to the barbarities that attend human greed and the corruptions that shape politics; they saw it as nothing less than the means toward a shared transcendence and the total sanctification of humankind itself.

But in *My Bondage and My Freedom*, violence emerges as a necessary instrumentality with which to bring about the end of human suffering and purify one's soul. The entire Covey episode in this book is rife with sanguinary imagery such as "warm blood," "blood marks," "clotted with dust and blood," and "bleeding, and almost bloodless."[54] Douglass's language evokes martyrdom and prefigures his "resurrection" into "manhood," but the prominence it gives to the *materiality* of embodiment, of felt anguish and corporeal breakdown, marks his rejection of the "abstract humanistic abolitionist arguments" that Tate says structure the *Narrative* and that I argue is Garrisonianism through and through. The scene indexes the robust political vision African American thinkers in the 1850s, from McCune Smith and Garnet to Martin

Delany and Mary Ann Shadd Cary, cultivated that was built on black self-determination above all and rejected all forms of racial custodianship and paternalism associated with Garrison and white liberal reform.

The Covey episode in *My Bondage and My Freedom* also broadens the significance of sex and gender in Douglass's liberation-through-violence model. In the *Narrative*, he tells us Covey owned one enslaved person, a twenty-year-old woman named Caroline whom Covey used as "*a breeder*."[55] After this brief mention she disappears from the *Narrative*. Here is a signal instance of what Threadcraft describes as the practice of "male-authored [slave] narratives [to] reference," but which does "not contain a sustained focus on, the gender-specific threats to the female body, the slave system's constraints on the aspects of the body and the material labors most associated with femininity."[56] In *My Bondage and My Freedom*, Douglass offers a thoughtful reflection on the practice of slave breeding, analogizing the plight of persons like Caroline to that of cattle. But to Threadcraft's point, there is still very little "sustained" attention paid to the specifics of female and feminine subjection.[57]

Yet Caroline goes on to play an important role in the battle scene in *My Bondage and My Freedom*. In the middle of the fight, Douglass catches Covey off guard with "a kick which sent him staggering away in pain," causing him to "lose his usual strength and coolness. [Covey] was frightened, and stood puffing and blowing, seemingly unable to command words or blows."[58] Dumbfounded and unsteady, Covey called out to Caroline and enslaved persons nearby for help. Douglass says that she "threatened my present advantage" because "she was a powerful woman, and could have mastered me very easily, exhausted as I now was." But she refused to help Covey, making herself a target for bloody retribution. As Douglass explains:

> As soon as she came into the yard, Covey attempted to rally her to his aid. Strangely—and, I may add, fortunately—Caroline was in no humor to take a hand in any such sport. We were all in open rebellion, that morning. Caroline answered the command of her master to "take hold of me," precisely as Bill had answered, but in her, it was at greater peril so to answer; she was the slave of Covey, and he could do what he pleased with her. It was not so with Bill, and Bill knew it. Samuel Harris, to whom Bill belonged, did not allow his slaves to be beaten, unless they were guilty of some crime which the law would punish. But,

poor Caroline, like myself, was at the mercy of the merciless Covey; nor did she escape the dire effects of her refusal. He gave her several sharp blows.

In this "open rebellion," Caroline is a central actor. Her bravery in the face of possibly fatal retribution from the region's most notorious slave breaker, her owner, is heroic: she makes Douglass's entry into "manhood" possible.

In the Covey episode and elsewhere in *My Bondage and My Freedom*, Douglass hails women as indispensable figures in the liberation-through-violence model, however "masculinist" the model might read. He argues that the very public, cross-gender venture of "open rebellion" will rectify the violations and indignities that women and other feminine-embodied persons endure in the intimate private sphere. Caroline's sexual freedom, reproductive rights, and self-governing motherhood are just as much at stake as, and never deemed less important than, Douglass's literacy, political autonomy, and "manhood." *My Bondage and My Freedom* favors triumph by means of revolutionary violence because it begins the work of rehabilitating the dispossessed while meting out retributive justice to their oppressors.

In the history of black thought, Frantz Fanon's essay "On Violence" in *The Wretched of the Earth* (1961) has become the cornerstone treatment of black revolutionary violence. Like Douglass, Fanon emphasizes violence's regenerative potentiality for oppressed persons and populations. "The underprivileged and starving peasant is the exploited who very soon discovers that only violence pays," he writes. "At the individual level, violence is a cleansing force" that "emboldens" and "restores the self-confidence" of the oppressed.[59] That violence fosters the act of self-(re)creation has become a commonplace claim in Black Studies, especially with the absorption of G. W. F. Hegel's allegory of lordship and bondage, the so-called "master-slave dialectic," in *Phenomenology of Spirit* (1807), in the 1990s. (Fanon engaged the allegory as early the late 1940s, but it took decades before it obtained in the field as an analytic.) Hegel posits the violent clash between the lord and his bondsman—a "life-and-death struggle"—as *the* means toward self-consciousness which, in turn, allows the person to create himself anew. This notion of identity formation has appealed to theorists of modern racialization because its emphasis on (the real possibility of) death speaks to the ways (the real possibility of) death was the ground zero of colonialism and New World chattel slavery. For example, Achille Mbembe argues that, at the point of death, the vanquished "gives way to the other, submits to the other, and recognizes the other without reciprocity. The victorious consciousness then accedes to the status of the master.... Meanwhile, the defeated consciousness is reduced to the condition of the *slave*."[60] Mbembe does not racialize his schema; so, the black subject *could* emerge as "the master" and the white subject as "the slave." What is most important, though, is that victor becomes master regardless of who he or she is.

The possibility of masterhood after enslavement has enchanted these and other philosophers of black revolutionary violence, not to mention its poets and storytellers. They have adopted the romance as their preferred generic form.[61] That antiblack violence prevails in archives of modern black life even though those archives contain relatively few victorious episodes for non-white subjects has not dampened romance's appeal for "reinventions" of these archives in culture and historiography.[62] Romance projects a future that vindicates (black) pasts rife with harm, insult, and violation: it does not necessarily claim that suffering was justified but holds that it won't be for naught.

But history, not to mention the present, compels us to consider what we make of the defeated (black) subject. Can his or her loss produce more than knowledge of self, which in this case is the self-as-the-enslaved? That is, can vanquishment dispose the defeated toward something other than (regarding himself as) what Hegel called a "negative in the permanent order of things?"[63] Douglass and his legatees do not help address these questions because their model of liberation-through-violence culminates in triumph and masterhood. What is required is a text in which the subject/protagonist suffers defeat and never achieves any sort of masterhood. In antebellum African American letters there is no better text for these queries than Harriet Wilson's *Our Nig*.

SPEECH AND THE PERFORMATIVITY OF SLAVE MORALITY

In *Our Nig*, Frado is defeated time and again. She never overpowers the Bellmonts or even fights them to a draw as Douglass does Covey. The constant abuse and toil wreck Frado's body to such a degree that she is so "reduced as to be unable to stand for any great length of time," having to sit to complete her tasks until she hears "the well-known step of her mistress [when] she would rise till she returned to her room, and then sink down for further rest."[64] Despite her youth, she is often "seriously ill" with "no relish for food."[65] Frado has no prospects for masterhood, no opportunity to act as Douglass or Caroline did in their "open rebellion" against Covey. Whenever she asserts herself even in the slightest, Mrs. Bellmont beats her back into humiliating submission. Even Frado's grief for a dying member of the Bellmont family results in her being "whipped with the raw-hide" and given an "injunction never to be seen snivelling again." She is left with "no solicitude about the future."[66]

After years of such treatment, Frado develops what we now call suicidal ideation. In a chapter titled "Spiritual Condition of Nig," someone overhears Frado clamoring for her own death. Believing she is alone with her dog, she asks: "Why was I made? Why can't I die? Oh, what have I to live for? No one cares for me only to get my work. And I feel sick; who cares for that? Work as long as I can stand, and then fall down and lay there till I can get up. No mother, father, brother, or sister to care for me, and then it is, You lazy nigger, lazy nigger—all because I am black! Oh, if I could die!"[67] Frado has come to recognize herself as (the) "black," and for the first time hails herself as such. Her "spiritual condition" is less about religious belief than about the facticity of (her) blackness, which, as Fanon writes, marks those located in the "zone of non-being." Fanon describes the zone of non-being as "an extraordinarily sterile and arid region, an incline stripped bare of every essential from which a genuine new departure can emerge."[68] This anti- or para-ontology of blackness is one freighted with total deprivation, lacking all the stuff that makes one human under the normative logics of modernity. Wilson sets that deprivation within the hellscape of the domestic sphere. Frado's is a world where she has "no mother, father, brother, or sister to care" for her. She comes to see death as her only form of escape.

"In most cases," Fanon writes, "the black man cannot take advantage of this descent into [the] veritable hell" of the zone of non-being.[69] He identifies two primary psychological barriers that prevent black persons from doing so: delusion and fear. Delusional black persons, he says, believe they are fully assimilable to the dominant imperial, colonial, and enslaving culture, that they are capable of "whitening" themselves into being the metaphysical "human" of modernity. But among those who recognize this delusion and know they do not have the capacities to assimilate as such, most are too afraid to do anything about it. Fanon argues black persons cannot do anything substantive about exiting the zone of non-being until they overcome these psychologies. Once they do, they can get to the work of remaking the world. For Fanon, that work begins with revolutionary violence. The oppression of black peoples across the globe "will only yield," he writes, "when confronted with greater violence."[70] Black revolutionary violence is not about grievance or revenge. Rather, it is about the development of a consciousness grounded in the needs and desires of the revolutionaries which they learn through "violent praxis": it will be nothing short of the beginning of liberation.[71]

Wilson found such ideas infeasible and jejune. (Calls for black revolutionary violence were ubiquitous among American radical abolitionists in the 1850s.) American history and her life in New England, ostensibly the country's most racially progressive region and a hotbed of anti-slavery activism, had shown her that the attainment of black masterhood through violence was impossible. Wilson believed advocates of black revolutionary violence were the delusional ones, even dangerous in how they misled African Americans into believing they could overcome chattel slavery and white supremacy through physical struggle. The "physical" resistance that did work, Wilson suggests in *Our Nig*, is death. Death has been a long-standing form of black resistance that runs from sites of capture in West and West Central Africa and the Middle Passage to Margaret Garner's infanticide in the mid-1850s and beyond.

Wilson posits another option besides death: speech. Nearing the end of her time with the Bellmonts, Frado is sent to retrieve wood. She does not return fast enough for Mrs. Bellmont's liking, and the woman meets her at the pile, grabs a stick, and moves to beat her with it. Frado's response creates her character and the world anew.

> "Stop!" shouted Frado, "strike me, and I'll never work a mite for you more"; and throwing what she had gathered, stood like one who feels the stirrings of free and independent thoughts.
>
> By this unexpected demonstration, her mistress, in amazement, dropped her weapon, desisting from her purpose of chastisement. Frado walked towards the house, her mistress following with the wood

she herself was sent after. She did not know, before, that she had a power to ward off assaults. Her triumph in seeing [Mrs. Bellmont] enter the door with *her* burden, repaid of her former suffering.

[...]

This affair never met with an "after clap," like many others.[72]

Over the next year Mrs. Bellmont refrained from the "former tempests" but for a "few weeks." Frado considers turning to others for help but decides against it because she is black "and no one would love her." Then, Wilson writes, "[Frado] remembered her victory at the wood-pile. She decided to remain [at the Bellmonts'] to do as well as she could; to assert her rights when they were trampled on.... She learned how to conquer."[73] Speech is Frado's power and with it she can "conquer." Of course, Frado does not literally conquer Mrs. Bellmont and invert the novel's master-servant relationship; after all, Mrs. Bellmont ends up carrying the wood she requested for herself, not for Frado. Speech is the great leveler, as neither figure emerges with masterhood.

Wilson ironizes the liberation-through-violence model in that the "conquering" party, Frado, never fights back and is always vanquished in her battles. The liberation of Frado's speech functions as an anticlimax of sorts, with none of the retributive justice or revolutionary romance we have come to crave from black liberation narratives. But the novel had been working toward that moment because it foregrounds Wilson's judgment of how African Americans should respond to the many forms of violence they endured: they can overcome violence not with violence, *pace* Douglass, but with speech. Her argument is not that one need only declare "Stop!" as Frado does to put an end to his oppression; rather, she posits a normative claim about speech *qua* speech as the most prudent medium for self-fashioning and worldmaking for black persons.

The conceptual significance of Frado's speech act accretes over the course of *Our Nig* with the recurrence of a figure: Frado's stuffed mouth. Mrs. Bellmont often stuffs her mouth with a towel or a block of wood while "beating her inhumanely."[74] Her hope is to "silence, or privatize, [the] abuse" because she does "not want to make public the open secret of her abuse by having Frado call attention to [the] violence."[75] But the figure recurs so frequently that it operates beyond plot and character and becomes a trope that amplifies Hannah Arendt's idea that violence precludes speech and thus politics. The stuffed mouth signifies suppressed personality, thought, and self-expression. When Frado shouts "Stop!" then, she offers a political response to the anti-politics of violence. (A remarkable aspect of the scene is that they are at the woodpile, yet no wood ends up stuffed in Frado's mouth.) With her speech act comes intellectual autonomy ("the stirring of free and independent thoughts") and rights talk ("assert her rights when they were trampled on") for the first time. It enacts a new beginning and becomes its own sort of founding, however figurative.

The worldmaking capacities of the speech act, or what we call performativity, are central to Arendt's political philosophy. Not only does she understand speech as that which makes man "a political being" but she theorizes speech as both architect and activity of the political realm. She writes, "the political realm rises directly out of acting together, the 'sharing of words and deeds.' Thus action not only has the most intimate relationship to the public part of the world common to us all, but is the one activity which constitutes it."[76] Arendt argues that action, the "words and deeds" we perform in public, is the means by which we reveal ourselves to ourselves and to others. In theatricalizing personal distinction and social contestation, action manifests and is the material of "the space of appearance," which is Arendt's definition of the political sphere.

The scene at the woodpile, intimate and domestic, does not have the hallmarks of the Arendtian space of appearance (the *polis*), but Frado's speech act makes it so. Self-revelatory and agonistic, Frado's performativity countervails Mrs. Bellmont's violence to create a realm, however transitory, of and for different voices. "Politics exists because of the fact of plurality, the existence of many people," John McGowan writes. Violence and other forms of domination "want to destroy the political— and will aim to destroy the political in its rage against the primal fact that others, not just myself, live in this world and have the right to do so."[77] Wilson did not believe that violence readily submits or loses out to performative political action. Violence is always the greater physical force of the two; it "can always destroy [political] power" and achieve the "most effective command, resulting in the most instant and perfect obedience."[78] Mrs. Bellmont epitomizes this sort of masterhood but, as *Our Nig* makes clear, her character represents systems of domination and intimate violation that brutalize black persons as such, particularly chattel slavery and its "shadows." Wilson sees violence as the greatest source for a robust African American political vision, calling on her "colored brethren" to reject the idea that they should attempt to match the violence that sustains these systems as the means to overcome them. I read Frado's "Stop!" as a response to Wilson's contemporaries who espoused black revolutionary violence in America. Instead, she offers political life—that is, speech—as the engine of true liberation and human flourishing.

Wilson's and Arendt's parallel views on violence and political performativity work toward radically different ends. Arendt developed her theory of action in *The Human Condition* (1958), her famously antidemocratic text. There she elaborated her bifurcation of the "social realm" and "the political realm." The social realm is a "relatively new phenomenon whose origin coincided with the modern age," she argues, that "transformed all modern communities into societies of laborers and jobholders; in other words, became at once centered around the one activity necessary to sustain life."[79] Labor and other forms of vital activity are too base for the realm she conceptualizes as the political: in the political sphere persons distinguish themselves in the presence of others, they *perform*, and reveal themselves "explicitly."[80] The political realm is the domain of the strong and power must remain there, with and among them, for the good of the polity. "Power corrupts indeed when the weak band together in order to ruin the strong, but not before," she writes.[81]

Democracy, of course, aims to distribute power equitably in the polity, and it is especially invested in redressing fortuities of birth and history to which individual members fall subject.[82] The most potent way democracy strives to accomplish this objective is to open the political sphere to all and their interests and concerns, to collapse what Arendt calls "the social" with "the political" and "extend the broad egalitarianism of ordinary lives into public life."[83] This commitment is the dominant political charge of African American literature before Emancipation. These works render the social as enveloped by the problematics of race and the procedures of the political indispensable to their remedy.[84] *Our Nig*, for one, narrativizes the ascension of the weak to the level of the strong by means of speech-through-action: the performativity of slave morality.

Frado's story illustrates the promise of slave morality and its rhetorical functionality as a democratic instrumentality.[85] It aims to persuade Wilson's fellow African Americans that speech acts, oral and textual, given in the presence of others is their best course of action in the struggle against antiblack oppression. She argues that violence, revolutionary or otherwise, is a losing game for black persons, a judgment that runs counter to that which structures a now global black political vision extending from David Walker's *Appeal to the Colored Citizens of the World* (1829) to Frantz Fanon and contemporary black nationalisms. Although unremitted violence prompted Wilson's performative self-creation and political assertion through her fictionalized self, Frado, her story upholds slave morality, however agonizingly protracted in its fulfillment, as African Americans' most effective political morality.

4 · Respectability

Is there a more scorned concept in African American studies than respectability? Conjuring all manner of retrograde black cultural politics, respectability has come to describe behaviors that are far different from those Evelyn Brooks Higginbotham theorized under the rubric of "the politics of respectability" in her study of black Baptist women negotiating *fin-de-siècle* Jim Crow America. These are behaviors that in some way signify assimilationist capitulation to hegemonic norms, especially when redolent of bourgeois moralizing. Popular elaborations of respectability as a behavioral hermeneutic of minority cultures have redoubled its ever-increasing definitional slipperiness. Of course, any specialized argot will lose much of its technical specificity and conceptual texture as soon as it enters popular discourse, but the transposition of the politics of respectability from African American women's historiography to the public sphere has been nothing short of the mangling of an idea. The great majority of the African American women Higginbotham studied were self-styled "daily toilers," menials, domestic servants, and field workers whose intellectual and social labors did not emerge from a desire to fulfill others' expectations of black womanhood or to mollify white racial anxieties.[1] Theirs was a form of respectability that derived from their own aims and interests as poor and working-class persons beset by Jim Crow segregation, lynch laws, and the stigmatization of black (female) sexuality and reproduction: it called on others to recognize that society's lowliest are as good as and thus equal to all others in the polity. Yet prevailing notions of respectability invert the crux and political terms of these women's stories such that respectability now names (black) performances of middle-class mores that seek to curry favor with majoritarian institutions and other social hegemons. Thus, respectability has become an epithet of sorts, a condemnation of minoritarian subjects guilty of a cowardly, self-effacing acquiescence to dominant social mores and demands.

The irony of these inversions of meaning is that they obscure everyday black persons' creativity and intelligence, which respectability's critics decry conventional historiographies for undervaluing. The poor and working-class women in the late nineteenth century who built organizations to mitigate communal privations formed library societies and crafted liberation theologies grounded in black feminist hermeneutics claimed respectability to mark such deeds as acts of self-imposition free of the degradation of another's personhood. For them, respectability named problem-solving activity and self-directed assertions of equality. This idea was not new, but a long-standing philosophical commitment in nineteenth-century black political culture. Indeed, even though we now commonly associate the late 1890s with the rise of respectability politics, African Americans began to develop a bottom-up form of respectability over a century earlier with the advent of free black communities and institutions. (More familiar top-down concessions to bourgeois hegemony I will call "uplift.") Its most robust theorizations come from the crucible of post-Emancipation New York City, most vividly in the work of the labor activist Peter Paul Simons and the abolitionist-intellectual James McCune Smith as they clashed with other black reformers who insisted African Americans were best served when they showcased the most decorous and accomplished of the race. The abolition of chattel slavery in the state in the late 1820s resulted in a set of demographic and economic conditions in the city unlike those anywhere else; out of that milieu respectability emerged as a viable, widespread political project whose assumptions and predications called out for critical, literary, and philosophical explication.[2]

This chapter reads free and enslaved black persons' everyday practices, Simons's public disputes with African American leaders dedicated to the politics of moral elevation, and James McCune Smith's ennobling sketches of the lives of everyday black persons, *Heads of the Colored People, Done with a Whitewash Brush* (1852–1854) to theorize respectability's democratic capacities. In clarifying the egalitarian ends toward which poor and working-class black persons embodied respectability, I will also take up the role of honor in modern democracy, which has resurfaced as an important concern in normative political philosophy.[3] Black writers knew deeply that the cultivation of honor depends on interpersonal power relations fully at odds with the democratic tenets of equal human value, self-ownership, and civil parity. And what practice in American life, grounded in such asymmetries of power, was more readily available for the achievement of honor than slave ownership? African American literary discourse before Emancipation is replete with narratives that explicate the inextricability of honor and chattel slavery, but few thinkers were as adamant as Simons and McCune Smith in their insistence on respectability as the most prudent alternative with which to attain equal standing in the American polity. A striking philosophical feature of their writing is its attentiveness to the fact that undeserved shame, the negative obverse of honor, is among the greatest hindrances to respectability. The quotidian assaults and slights African Americans endured because of their race and the labor they performed made overcoming undeserved shame especially burdensome; any effort to do so left them even more vulnerable to cruel reprisals. Nevertheless, the subjects of Simons's activism and McCune Smith's writings forged ahead and claimed respectability by way of spectacular and unprecedented ventures. Most of the time, though, they did so with actions as simple as taking a walk.

TOWARD A THEORY OF RESPECTABILITY: CREATIVE INTELLIGENCE AND THE ASSUMPTION OF PUBLIC SPACE

Sometime in early 1852, the African American flâneur William J. Wilson found himself awhirl at Broadway and Fulton Street, not far from City Hall in Manhattan. After cutting through the hustle and bustle of commerce and congestion, Wilson finally gained a more "congenial current" and began his stroll up Broadway to observe some of the city's goings-on. Writing under the pseudonym "Ethiop" as the Brooklyn correspondent for *Frederick Douglass' Paper* (FDP), he reports one "would readily perceive that the whites exhibited the two features, wealth and poverty; while the blacks exhibited an intermediate one." White walkers showed evidence of their race's "propensity for grasping and appropriating," for it was "indelibly stamped in every face, as the mark of Cain." Ethiop's readers would have delighted in the ironies of his projection of the demerits of physiognomic examination, and the pro-slavery implications of Cain's plight, onto whiteness. But with black walkers "the scene is changed!!! We have now a medium."[4] Medium here means African Americans' position in the spectacle's social order: they embody the "intermediate" position between "wealth and poverty." In Ethiop's analysis these are not economic categories; he knew black New Yorkers were overall much poorer than the collective of white persons. Rather, "wealth and poverty" connote manners of cultural judgment, style, and vitality. Unlike the gluttonously insouciant wealthy or the cowardly enervate impoverished, the black persons who made up the scene's "intermediate" stratum embody "all the requisites of a mighty people[:] ... bones and muscle and intellect; and above all, life and vivacity; great power of endurance." Ethiop ends his epistolary column with a call for its black readers to assume these powers so that they might "not only get, and have money like the whites, but thrive also."[5] For (black) persons to thrive, he suggests, they must pursue socially estimable acts of self-enrichment that do not depend on oppression, financial accumulation, or ostentatious display. Iterable and quotidian, such pursuits are the substance of respectability.

Ethiop grounds his notion of respectability and the broader political sociology it organizes in readings of black street culture. By the mid-1850s, the streets of New York City had become political fodder for the whole range of concerns in contemporary ethics and urbanity, spurring a minor literature of journalistic and proto-ethnographic accounts of city life such as Charles Dickens's *American Notes* (1842) and George Foster's *New York by Gas-Light and Other Urban Sketches* (1850). For black persons, the appeal of thoroughfares like Broadway was that they engendered points of contact and exchange that dominant racial codes precluded elsewhere. They claimed these vibrant, spectacular forums to (re)mold culture and social practices in accordance with their own sensibilities. Ethiop was among the most perspicacious evaluators of the novelty, dynamism, and eccentricities of black street culture. Nothing was more vital to his analysis than black walkers' demand for respect, the most basic aspect of which is respect's most basic denotation: to look at (from the Latin *specere*) again (re-). The "easy negligence, careless abandonment, and refined freedom" they bodied forth enjoined onlookers to *look at us, again*.[6] Their venture required (1) the assumption of public space (e.g., the street), and (2) the performance of creative intelligence (e.g., gait, pace, style, élan). These are two actions by which one claims respectability.

The assumption of public space is a central feature of one of the most abiding mythoi of American democracy. It is a story that renders the act of everyday persons laying claim to the streets to protest draconian or inequitable distributions of (state) power an apotheosis of democratic expression and intervention. Events such as the Boston Massacre, the Boston Tea Party, Civil Rights–era marches, and present-day demonstrations for equitable treatment from policing forces stand out as grand instantiations of this judgment. But more quotidian actions sustain its seeming veracity. Consider the history of racial manners on American walkways. Well into the twentieth century, a black person's refusal to yield the sidewalk to white persons signified a profound breach of the civic order.[7] His or her bold act of defiance could have been met with invective or violence, responses that dominant social codes warranted. More than a violation of the protocols of racial deference, such encounters enact an abiding struggle over the racialization of American public spaces. That struggle began with the onset of emancipation decrees and the proliferation of manumissions in the late eighteenth and early nineteenth centuries; it remains one of the more long-standing fronts in the battle for equal rights and protections in the US.

The question of who has access to what public spaces, when, and why almost always plays out in localized and interpersonal encounters. It is mainly for this reason that black persons' dramatic assumptions of public spaces have received uncommon scrutiny and acquired heightened political significance. In the summer of 1821, for example, black persons became the featured attraction of Sunday strolling on Broadway in Manhattan. A sort of weekly ritual that emerged in response to the so-called Blue Laws that mandated the theatre, circus, and other entertainment venues be closed on the Sabbath, these promenades allowed New Yorkers to exhibit personal flair, build camaraderie, discover new wares, and experiment with sartorial trends *du jour*. Once a critical mass of black strollers burst on the scene, blithely sauntering and belying racial expectations, accounts of their contributions and interventions began to appear in city newspapers and journals. They were enslaved, formerly enslaved, and freeborn black persons administering a sort of stress test on the boundaries of civic life amid New York's tortuous transformation into a free state. Their Sunday strolls theatricalized the cultural audacity, intellectual ingenuity, and fierce backlash that characterized the effort to flee the "long shadow of slavery" that haunted the city's politics and social economies through Reconstruction and beyond.[8]

In a report for his *National Advocate*, editor Mordecai Noah describes a procession of these "black dandys and dandizettes" en route to a black-owned pleasure garden. He writes:

> Among the number of ice cream gardens in this city, there were none in which the sable race could find admission and refreshment. Their modicum of pleasure was taken on Sunday evening, when the black dandys and dandizettes, after attending meeting, occupied the side walks in Broadway and slowly lounged toward their different home.... Accordingly, a garden has been opened somewhere back of the hospital called African Grove.... The little boxes in this garden were filled with black beauties "making night hideous"; and it was not an uninteresting sight to observe the entree of a happy pair. The gentleman, with his wool nicely combed, and his face shining through a coat of sweet oil, borrowed from the castors; cravat tight to suffocation, having the double faculty of widening the mouth and giving it a remarkable protuberance to the eyes; blue coat fashionably cut; red ribbon and bunch of pinchback seals; wide pantaloons; shining boots, gloves, and a tippy rattan. The lady with her pink kid slippers, her fine Leghorn, cambric dress, with open work, corsets well fitted; reticule, hanging on her arm. Thus accoutered and caparisoned, these black fashionables saunter up and down the garden, in all the pride of liberty and unconsciousness of want.[9]

Wrapped in Noah's derisive and condescending report is an extraordinary tale of persons demanding respect—to be looked at, again. Like their assumption of public space, that demand rested on the basic fact of their personhood, that as persons they can make such demands legitimately without special pleading or apology. Noah ends his account by remarking that "they fear no Missouri plot; care for no political rights; happy in being permitted to dress fashionable, walk the streets, visit African Grove, and talk scandal."[10] He misconstrues the absence of politics talk as apoliticism: what he missed or refused to acknowledge was that the black dandys' and dandizettes' political interventions were located squarely in the phenomenalism of their embodiment. In fact, a symptomatic reading of Noah's meticulous documentation of their clothing and comportment suggests that he sensed the politics of their respectability in this scene were carried out through the body, not the spoken word.

These and other black Sunday strollers who claimed respectability did so without recourse to theological (see chapter 1) or transcendentalist (see chapter 2) assertions of human dignity. That persons are endowed with some sort of inviolable intrinsic value and thus possess certain natural rights or social privileges never shaped their (civic) judgments; they had little interest in such legitimation. Rather, the careful nonchalance with which black dandys and dandizettes seized attention reflected an ethical judgment that a person deserves respect simply because he or she is a person among others. I understand their notion of respect as very similar to the one that organizes Immanuel Kant's moral philosophy. Kant argues that humans must be treated with respect because of their humanity, those ratiocinative features that allow them to pursue rational ends and, as such, distinguish them from all other animate beings. Oliver Sensen explains in his groundbreaking explication of how respect figures in Kantian ethics that "it is not because others have a value that one should respect them, but it is because one should respect them that they have an importance and a dignity."[11] In this formulation, dignity denotes a valuation of relational entities: humans have dignity because they are "raised above" other animals and things. This comparative juxtaposition is their source of "elevation or sublimity" in the world.[12] Black dandys and dandizettes did not aim to position themselves above white persons; rather, they sought to clarify that their humanity was equal to all others'. African Americans' Sunday strolls captured Noah's eye precisely because they commanded his respect and thereby compelled him to grapple with their dignity, however obliquely. Their performances of respectability openly flout prescriptive racisms and the political mores they underwrite, which is why black persons were often put down with calumny, insult, or violence.

In a reading of African American political thought from the era of chattel slavery through the twentieth century, Nick Bromell explains how black thinkers have explicated how dignity requires sociality. He argues that "our dignity is something we cannot ever be the sole creators or possessors of; we need relations with others in which they recognize it; by its nature, dignity is something socially produced and affirmed (or denied).")[13] Black dandys and dandizettes compelled onlookers to confront the possibility of African-descended persons' dignity; if detractors like Noah denied it, black persons, at least, affirmed it among and for themselves. Bromell argues that to "sense one's [own] dignity" will not "necessarily lead to or take the form of resistance. Dignity . . . refers to the always-present possibility that a person might recover, remember, or reclaim her sense of intrinsic self-worth through intersubjective exchanges in which that very thing is being slighted or denied."[14] Such exchanges characterize black Sunday strolls in 1820s Manhattan: those performances produced and enacted (black) dignity as a relational effect of persons respecting each other as such.

The notion that dignity results from the respect persons deserve *qua* persons is a central input of Kant's formula of humanity (FH): that is, one must never treat persons as a mere means to an end. The FH does not preclude our use of others to acquire or reach ends but requires that we only do so with their reason-based consent. African Americans did not need Kant's erudition to arrive at a similar idea. Chattel slavery, drudgery, and sexual assault, among other forms of racialized subjection, proved to them its virtue and necessity; indeed, the history of black life in colonial North America through Emancipation (and beyond) is in many ways a history of systematic violations of the FH. Humanity's capacity for "fidelity to promising" and "benevolence from principle (not from instinct)" is Kant's sole justification for his FH. He regards "skill and diligence in work" as well as "wit, lively imagination, and humor" as lesser human faculties because they "have a market price" and "fancy price," respectively.[15] Kant's axiology notwithstanding, early American society esteemed industriousness and creativity not only as marketable social goods but also as markers of personal virtue and public utility. Dominant social thought deemed African-descended persons especially deficient in these areas and therefore unsuited for the privileges and responsibilities democracies confer on free and equal citizens. These were the terms of engagement by which black persons had to intervene in American politics and its civic rituals. They knew their bodies and minds, let alone their moral capacities, were generally held in disrepute.

Thomas Jefferson's Query XIV in *Notes on the State of Virginia* (1785) is the foremost statement on black constitutional deficiencies in Anglo-American thought before Emancipation. Query XIV's vilification of African-descended persons' corporeality, intellect, reasoning powers, and capacity for culture-making galvanized the field of antebellum black political thought, beginning with David Walker's magisterial *Appeal to the Colored Citizens of the World* (1829). One of the most significant (though underappreciated) aspects of the query is that Jefferson's stated objective is to detail Virginia's "administration of justice and description of the laws."[16] His race-based cultural criticism (which included literature) and racial typology might seem like tangents but are vital frameworks for his explication of Virginia's demography, law, and administrative state. Race becomes central to the query because Jefferson believed an all-white Virginia was vital to its democratic future. His colonization scheme was a blueprint for the African Colonization Society's efforts later in the nineteenth century: emancipate and train enslaved black persons in "tillage, arts or sciences"; remove them from Virginia to somewhere in Africa; and resettle into the state "an equal number of white inhabitants" from Europe as a replacement labor force.[17] Jefferson imagines a thrifty interlocutor's rejoinder, "Why not retain and incorporate the blacks in the state, and thus save the expence of supplying, by importation of white settlers, the vacancies they will leave?"[18] He finds this plan impractical because black persons' physiological and mental defects leave them unfit for freedom and democracy. He concludes that only by examination via "Anatomical knife, to Optical glasses, to analysis by fire, or by solvents" can philosophy and science ever fully account for black corporeal lack.[19]

Jefferson ascribes the creative and ratiocinative shortcomings he finds endemic in African-descended persons to constitutional flaws of the black body. His dismissal of contextual factors such as condition, environment, or experience to account for black persons' deficiencies in "reason" and "imagination" vis-à-vis other races anticipated craniology, phrenology, eugenics, and other racist biologisms.[20] He adduces slavery during classical antiquity to substantiate his racialism: "Yet notwithstanding ... [the] discouraging circumstances among the Romans, their slaves were often their rarest artists. They excelled too in science, insomuch as to be usually employed as tutors to their master's children. Epictetus, Terence, and Phaedrus, were slaves. But they were of the race of whites. It is not their condition then, but nature, which has produced the distinction."[21] Here and throughout Query XIV, Jefferson claims modern chattel slavery as practiced across North America, and especially in Virginia, offered enslaved black persons advantages which were unheard of under older forms of slavery, but nature rendered them unable to capitalize on them. He posits their culture, or lack thereof, as proof of the deficiencies that inhere in persons of African descent, which exposure to and participation in Anglo-American culture could not remedy.

> Many millions of [black persons] have been brought to, and born in America. Most of them indeed have been confined to tillage, to their own homes, and their own society: yet many have been so situated, that they might have availed themselves of the conversation of their masters; many have been brought up to the handicraft arts, and from that circumstance have always been associated with the whites. Some have been liberally educated, and all have lived in countries where the arts and sciences are cultivated to a considerable degree, and have had before their eyes samples of the best works from abroad.... But never yet could I find that a black had uttered a thought above the level of plain narration; never see even an elementary trait of painting or sculpture.[22]

That Jefferson was truly interested in identifying black artists who met his standards is dubious. Indeed, his infamous summary dismissal of Phyllis Wheatley's poetry, that it is "below the dignity of criticism," reflects a mind so committed to antiblack notions of race and personhood that it cannot even be bothered to go through the motions to confirm its biases.[23] Yet Jefferson's negative judgment of Wheatley's work, and of black artistic possibility more broadly, is an important marker of many early Americans' belief that a people's (e.g., race's) culture should be determinative of the modes of governmentality they deserve and require. As such, the cultural realm—which includes not only art objects but also the manners, aesthetic taste, and moral sense those objects instantiate—became the dominant arena within which black persons waged political struggle before Emancipation.

Richard Iton has described black political actors' "hyperactivity on the cultural front" as "a response to some sort of marginalization from the processes of decision-making or exercising control over one's own circumstances.... American blacks are not 'different' in this respect because they have chosen to be but because of the exclusionary and often violent practices that have historically defined black citizenship and public sphere participation as problematic and because of the recognition that the cultural realm is always in play and already politically significant terrain."[24] If political activism via culture is definitional of the history of black American politics, enslaved and free black persons initiated that history with no choice in the matter: culture and politics were virtually the same enterprise in early America. Black cultural objects, even and perhaps especially the most formally aestheticist such as Wheatley's neoclassical poetics, were necessarily politicized because they were fodder for conceptualizing and legitimizing forms of government and sociality best suited for black populations. These objects, including the most intra-racially oriented, have always been scrutinized for political meaning and social prescription.

For thinkers like Jefferson who deemed themselves progenitors of the incipient field of political *science*, culture was "data." By the turn of the nineteenth century, their racialized epistemologies dovetailed with an emerging philosophy of culture—namely, modernity—that regarded cultural formations as the materialization of rational cognition and human development. Not "a reservoir of inexhaustible novelty," which James Snead argues is in any case "unthinkable," modern cultural achievement was marked by innovative transformations of existing materials toward something like a perfection of affect and form.[25] The novelty of Romanticism's interventions, for example, was in their revelation of aspects of the world that custom, ignorance, and fidelity to received knowledge obscured. Walt Whitman, the greatest of the American Romantics, practiced a poetics that was nothing other than the unveiling of ourselves in all our majesty and messiness. Among the shrewdest lessons of Whitman's poetry is its insistence that if the artist wants to sing the world's "untold latencies," he must adopt forms and modalities that derive from the subject matter itself.[26] Genius emerges from what one does with what is given, from producing something novel from something existent. Parmenides' dictum *ex nihilo nihil fit*—that is, "nothing comes from nothing"—is a first principle of the philosophical foundations of modern American cultural theory, from eighteenth-century neoclassicism and Transcendentalism to Pragmatism. A promise of the newly formed United States, the founders claimed, is that it extended to all persons the latitude necessary to innovate and thus contribute meaningfully to its culture; despite his economic or social stature, all that mattered was a person's willingness to exert himself or herself. For example, the black dandies and dandizettes who strolled along New York City streets offered new sartorial and visual economies that belied the Jeffersonian claim that their race was bereft of creativity and thus of the wherewithal to be free in the modern world. Their threat was the undeniably political dimension of their street performances, which I call political because of the ways in which they subverted dominant claims of the impossibility of black genius. The cunning means with which they demanded respect made onlookers confront the fallacies of American racialism and its attendant politics.

The creative intelligence black strollers theatricalized in their promenades and struts reflected their desire for redistributions of power in the city and beyond. To assume public space as they did was an unmistakable exercise of liberty. Liberty requires such practices, such forms of human action that actualize liberty's conceptual rudiments and horizons. From the time of the founding, everyday black persons have seized on the normative force of democracy: all one needs is his mind and his body to disrupt and reconfigure the polity. While political realists and pessimists might dismiss this judgment as a distressing and naïve credulity, the harsh and often violent backlash that regularly attends black inclusionary politics on streets and in other public spaces suggests otherwise. Despite strictures upon their thought, movement, and assembly, black persons have used their bodies to project themselves as exemplary bearers of national possibility. They have bodied forth a decidedly bottom-up democratic ethos—what I understand as respectability—that does not require its practitioners to accumulate, hold, or expend might of any sort.

THE PROBLEM OF HONOR AND ZIP COON IDEOLOGY

Respectability is a product slave morality: it spurns might as a hindrance to the realization of democracy's most righteous ends. Friedrich Nietzsche argues that the disdain for might, whether it be "age and ancestry" or physical brawn, enfeebles individuals and society because it rejects the logic of domination and its "badge" is "compassion or in doing things for others or in *désintéressement*."[27] Nietzsche regarded the exaltation of selflessness as a blight that Christianity wrought upon the world, as one of the great shames of modern society because it precludes true human greatness and repute. Without capital, that is, persons and cultures cannot achieve greatness because greatness requires singularity, a distinctive and marked separation from the commonality. For Nietzsche, only a return to the moralities that organized the ancient world could revive persons' ability to realize their full potentialities and thereby spur a new epoch of real human flourishing. "Difficult to appreciate today [and] difficult to unearth and uncover," classical models are explicit in their "severity in the fundamental principle that we have duties only to our peers; that we have the right to behave towards beings of lower rank, towards everything alien, as we deem fit or 'as the heart dictates.'"[28] Such underlying power imbalances render human subjugation necessary, indeed salutary. Even with alternative courses of action, there are times when aristocrats, noblemen, warriors, and the mighty feel they *must* mete out harsh treatment when dealing with the weak because the maintenance of their goodness and the goodness of the society itself depends on it. The powerful, whom Nietzsche calls "the good," have an obligation to dominate those below, whom he calls "the bad," and even those in their peer group when times call for it; to do so is to uphold their personal integrity. If they distinguish themselves in the process, they might achieve honor.

That only the powerful can achieve honor instantiates its fundamentally antidemocratic makeup. Based in a morality of the masters and rulers, this conception of honor comes from classical antiquity. It defines honor as a motivational force that propels acts of bravery and sacrifice in the face of danger. The recognition of such acts as worthy of honor must come from the broader community; one cannot legitimately honor oneself. Cicero, who wrote the most thorough philosophical treatment of classical honor, accentuates its externalities as well as the limits of eligibility. In Book Two of *On Duties* he writes:

> But not all people require affection equally; whether one needs to be esteemed by man, or it is enough to be esteemed by a few, must be tailored to the life built by each. . . . So perhaps not all people require as much honor and glory and goodwill from their fellow citizens. . . . Therefore, people commonly admire everything that they believe is great and surpasses their own opinion, but particularly if they perceived in individuals certain good qualities that are not opined. And so they look up to and extol these men with the greatest of praises, believing they perceive in them certain excellent and singular virtues.[29]

Although Cicero's emphasis on those who "require" honor intimates a sort of psychological need, it also suggests persons covet honor because their social station demands it. His notion of a "life built by each" is anchored in who one is and what one does in society. There is no expectation of honor for those who were not the mighty and "the good" because honor was outside their grasp. As such, honor helped cement a hierarchy that positioned "the good" as always better and of higher value than their inferiors.

Cicero understood how corruption and monstrosity could taint an act that society deems honorable. He insists justice must guide persons if they are to attain honor. But Cicero's conception of justice is largely absent from the prevailing narratives by which the classical world recognized honor. For example, the glorification of the warrior figure that surfaces from these narratives, none better known than Achilles's story in the *Iliad*, too easily minimizes the demerits of bloodthirst and vainglory. While it took until the middle of the eighteenth century for Ciceronian justice to come to frame honor's functionality in political thought, Christianity and chivalry in the Middle Ages worked to disarticulate vice from honor centuries before. "Chivalric honor," as the political theorist Antong Liu calls it, merged "the provocative power in the love of victory and the restraining power in Christian humility in creative [i.e., seemingly less contradictive] ways."[30] This intervention proved crucial for late Enlightenment thinkers such as Montesquieu, Rousseau, and Adam Smith who aimed to democratize honor: they argued honor should motivate a broad swath of individuals to act bravely, upholding justice while avoiding injustice in the process. The prospect of honor is integral to civic flourishing, they said, because it spurs citizens to do what is best and right for the common good.

Among contemporaneous political philosophers, Sharon Krause has offered the most compelling argument for honor's role and its necessity in a liberal democracy. She aims to reconcile the best of honor from before the Age of Revolutions with the best of honor from after. Honor from the Old World, Krause writes, "reminds us of the aristocratic capacities in ourselves that have survived the advent of the modern man and calls us to confront liberal democracy's need for them."[31] These capacities, which include "courage, pride, high and principled ambition, [and] the sense of duty to oneself," are "irreducibly aristocratic if only in the sense that they are not commonly held, although anyone may hold them and in democratic societies all of us can reach for them."[32] She suggests democracies permit, if not encourage, all persons to tap their aristocratic aspects for the betterment of their polities.

For Krause, the US's founding generation is exemplary in this regard. She cites the founders' "love of fame" as essential to the formation of the American Republic, albeit tempered by "nascent patriotism" and a "genuine desire to serve the public good."[33] What emerges is "democratic honor," which is "tied to universal principles of right rather than to concrete codes of conduct applicable only to a particular group."[34] Democratic honor might not be born of slave morality, but it aims to remove vice and brutality from forms of honor that derive from the morality of the rulers.

Krause acknowledges the problematics of establishing a theory of democratic honor in American history. The most obvious is the development of "southern honor," which "combined the sense of duty to oneself and the desire for self-respect with the quest for public recognition" but "coalesced around the defining ideology of a slaveholding society."[35] One way Krause attempts to solve this problem is by disarticulating "southern honor" from "honor among the founders." Building on Bertram Wyatt-Brown's groundbreaking historiography of antebellum southern life, she writes: "In direct contrast to the honor of men like Washington, Hamilton, Jefferson, and Madison, southern honor was based upon 'faithfulness to a particular place and people and their past, not upon some abstract idea such as "freedom" and "democracy."'"[36] Krause's circumscription of the founding generation is puzzling, though: Southerners, too, were founders. Indeed, most signers of the Declaration of Independence were slaveholders, as were almost half of the delegates to the Constitutional Convention. (It bears noting, too, that three of the men she lists were slaveholding Virginians, the seat of American slaveocracy before the nineteenth century; the other, Hamilton, participated in slave markets and probably used the labor of enslaved persons in his household; and there is little evidence that any believed non-white persons should be equal beneficiaries of freedom, democracy, and honor in the newly formed US.) Krause's attempt to dissociate southern honor from a normative theory of democratic honor derived from the American political cultures belies the complex historicity of those cultures. While she admits that honor was far more determinative to life in the South than it was in the North, geographic bifurcation is analytically nugatory because it obscures how white supremacy was a "defining ideology" of all American society, slaveholding or otherwise. Put simply, honor was grounded in politico-intellectual formations of antiblackness.

Because of the racialization of chattel slavery, one cannot wrest antiblackness from honor in American political thought, let alone American sociality. Orlando Patterson has established the inextricability of honor to slavery across epochs and locations. "In all slave societies," he writes, "the slave was considered a degraded person ... the honor of the master was enhanced by the subjection of his slave ... and wherever slavery became structurally important, the whole tone of the slaveholders' culture tended to be highly honorific."[37] Blackness marked the slave in early America; persons racialized as such, enslaved or otherwise, were precluded from attaining honor because the broader polity did not recognize them as worthy of it. Even where chattel slavery was abolished or not practiced, underlying racial logics that stigmatized blackness obtained. Patterson posits the "ideology of the 'Sambo,' the degraded man-child" as the dominant racial logic through which Southerners regarded black subjectivity. He reads their abiding investment in the Sambo, a figure he locates in "all other slave systems," as "further proof ... that slaves are universally treated as dishonored persons."[38] While Sambo remained omnipresent in the North, the social dynamics that stemmed from the gradual end of slavery in the region sparked the advent of a sort of post-slavery Sambo figure to grapple with those changes: Zip Coon.

The name "Zip Coon" comes from the popular blackface character of 1830s and 1840s American theatre culture. But Zip Coon ideology, the notion that black persons' efforts toward intellectual attainment and cultural sophistication always already fail and are thereby apt for ridicule, predates this era. It furnished the humor for several of the most popular eighteenth-century Anglo-American dramatic comedies; it also animates the racist chauvinism of observational accounts of black public and private life such as Mordecai Noah's articles on the black dandys and dandizettes of New York City. The most striking renderings of the Zip Coon figure *avant la lettre* took shape in the visual arts that coalesced in anticipation of and immediately after emancipation decrees, especially in cities like Boston, London, and Philadelphia. Artists such as George Cruikshank, Edward Williams Clay, and Gabriel Shear Tregear developed visual lexicons that helped reify notions of blackness-as-abjection. Their cartoons and paintings, always intricate in detail and arresting in grandiloquence, visualize the purported inanities that black freedom was sure to occasion; ghastly black political leadership, social graces gone awry, and horrors of miscegenation are their most common themes. Editors and illustrators regularly appropriated these works' distinguishing aesthetics, figures, and templates, often lifting them entirely without attribution. A sort of visual *lingua franca* of the Zip Coon figure surfaced: it said free black life without strict white supervision is inevitably bound for dissolution and destruction.

Edward Williams Clay's Zip Coon oeuvre and approach was the most influential in the US. His most famous work, the *Life in Philadelphia* series (1825–1830), inspired copycat artists on both sides of the Atlantic. Homemakers used its images for wallpaper patterning and other décor. The fourteen-plate series lampooned the personal ostentation, bourgeois norms, and sartorial excesses Clay saw on the streets of Philadelphia. Although *Life in Philadelphia* included white figures, the notability it earned stemmed from its depictions of black men and women. Their simian visages, disproportionately grotesque corporeality, and lurid racial colorations complement the malaprop-riddled, nonsensical captions. Low-quality versions of these figures are ubiquitous in contemporaneous broadsides, magazines, newspapers, and books. For example, the celebrated British humorist Thomas Hood, best known for his contributions to *Punch* magazine, published his own "Sketches of Life in Philadelphia" for his *New Comic Annual of 1831* (1830). Hood used Clay's visual templates but removed the bits of local specificity that anchor them to Philadelphia. (Over the course of the 1830s and 1840s, London-based artists like Hood who engaged Clay's work abstracted and exaggerated his black figures; that this was the period that commenced the abolition of slavery in the United Kingdom suggests they did so in response to black freedom throughout the empire.) The circulation of these images in cheap print culture formats like *The New Comic Annual of 1831* extended the reach of Zip Coon ideology to more generable readerships, especially those in more isolated areas outside urban centers. The emergence of Zip Coon as one of the two primary blackface characters on the global minstrel stage endowed that ideology with a theatricalized and thus reifying phenomenalism that captivated white audiences. Sheet music for "Zip Coon" (c. 1834) featured a Clay-like image on the cover. Such print-to-professional performance-to-print-to-amateur and home performance cycles reinforced the "truth" of Zip Coon even further. The "truth" of Zip Coon ideology is that blackness marks those persons, free or enslaved, whom nature made for social degradation: to be black is to be excluded from the category of "the good," in Nietzsche's sense of the term. Thus, honor is always beyond the grasp of black people, regardless of any actions they might perform.

Krause identifies politics as an arena within which all individuals in liberal-democratic societies might achieve honor, but Zip Coon insists otherwise. The fatuity of black political actors is an abiding theme of the figure's aesthetic and ideological interventions. The stump speech delivered by a Zip Coon-like political character was a mainstay of the blackface minstrel stage. Animating the humor of these linguistically nonsensical set pieces was the very idea of black political subjecthood. The most popular stump speeches drew on current events and political movements. For example, the famed blackface minstrel Charley White delighted audiences time and again with his "Burlesque Lecture on Women's Rights." Its mockery of the mid-century women's rights movement guilefully takes aim at early black feminism. "I tell you now, aforehand, I is goin' right into dis subjec' like a hungry nigger into a bowl ob clam soup, by simply axin' you dese 'stounding questions: Who am woman? Whar did she came from? Who does she belong to, and which way are she gwine to? Now a good many common-taters, and mighty common-taters dey am too, at dat, hab tried to make out dat da first woe was brought on de human race by *Eve* trying to coax *Adam* to climb de apple tree and steal de apple."[39] Although there is no evidence White performed this "lecture" as a black woman, his allusions to Sojourner Truth and her famed "Ain't I a Woman?" (1851) speech are clear. Besides the succession of questions that mirrors the rhetorical structure of Truth's speech, White's references to the Biblical creation myth recall the feminist hermeneutics that shaped "Ain't I a Woman?" and, more broadly, the thrust of black women's activism in the era. Regardless of its gendered manifestations, figurations of Zip Coon posited all black persons as constitutionality deficient political actors.

As Zip Coon began to predominate in the American cultural imaginary, a vibrant and powerful black political sphere materialized in cities and towns across the country, especially in the Northeast.[40] Its most conspicuous manifestations were the first black-owned newspapers and the Colored Conventions Movement.[41] These efforts projected a collective consciousness among black persons across regions and locations, a consciousness that fostered the emergence of a corporate identity that we often call "blackness." An American isonomy free of chattel slavery was their chief objective, but more local institutions and organizations were the engines that powered the struggles against the daily obstacles that beset black populations. How these bodies developed and served their communities has become a central subject in the historiography of African American politics. But we have too seldom considered their intellectual foundations, the distinctive theoretical elaborations of the political concepts that animated abolitionism and other black political ventures. The deep disputes that shaped black politics in antebellum New York that the rest of this chapter takes up, for instance, reflect astute notions of respectability as vital to, if not the lifeblood of, democratic forms of life. What I aim to illuminate about respectability is how it is a philosophically complex and politically disruptive ethic, something far more dynamic than the flattened notion, the "outwardly focused symbolic politics" grounded in pious capitulations, than it is regularly taken to be.[42] Respectability of this sort threatens Zip Coon ideologies because of its universal attainability: it never requires persons to be something other than what they are but reaffirms them as they are.

MORAL ELEVATION AND THE POLITICS OF BLACK LABOR

The labor activism of Peter Paul Simons offers one of the richest elaborations of this form of respectability. Simons was a porter who probably worked in luxurious hotels like the Astor House that were located near black enclaves in what is now lower Manhattan. He was born sometime in the 1810s. The exact year is virtually impossible to determine because of irregularities in his recorded age across several censuses. Problems with age and related data in nineteenth-century government records are common, especially for black persons, but the variance in Simons's age is egregious.[43] There is a very strong possibility that Simons did not know his birth year because he was born into indentured servitude as the child of an enslaved woman. New York's Act for the Gradual Emancipation of Slavery of 1799 freed enslaved women's children who were born after July 4, 1799, as Simons was, but mandated that they serve their mothers' owners as indentured servants for twenty-eight years if male or twenty-five years if female. The law did not free the mothers themselves; unless manumitted, they and other enslaved persons born before that date did not become free until July 4, 1827, as the Act Relative to Slaves and Servants of 1817 decreed. Simons's mother, Phebe, was almost certainly born in the late 1760s or early 1770s as part of the lot of enslaved persons in and around the city, which vastly exceeded the number of free African Americans in the area.[44] She first appears on a federal census in 1840 as head of household but becomes part of Simons's household in subsequent censuses. Neither one of them is on a census before 1840, which could very well mean they were bound to a white master and lived in his or her household.[45] The evidence thus suggests Simons was reared as an indentured servant, with at least one enslaved parent nearby, amid New York's tumultuous transition from a state with slavery to a free state.

Simons emerged from this milieu with a deep appreciation for the potentialities of the black laboring classes, and he dedicated his political life to the eradication of their exploitation. With the ratification of a new state constitution in 1821, he witnessed the revocation of the franchise from virtually all black men, large numbers of whom were artisans and journeymen, when the state raised property requirements for every "man of colour" to a level only a few dozen African Americans could meet. (The law enfranchised most white men; in 1826, the state removed the few remaining barriers to universal white male suffrage.[46]) Some Federalist delegates to the constitutional convention argued this proviso should hold for all prospective voters. Among the most outspoken was Jonas Platt of Poughkeepsie, who served in federal and state governments and on the New York State Supreme Court. On the convention floor, Platt opened with all the familiar tenets of Zip Coon ideology: "I admit, that most of the free negroes in our state, are unfit to be entrusted with the right of suffrage; they have neither sufficient intelligence, nor a sufficient degree of independence, to exercise that right in a safe and proper manner." But he went on to argue that any race-based conditions for the franchise violated the republicanism that animated their entire political enterprise. Were the "proviso [to] be ingrafted into our constitutions, the practical commentary will be, that a portion of our free citizens shall not enjoy equal rights with their fellow citizens. All freeman, of African parentage, are to be constitutionally degraded: no matter how virtuous or intelligent."[47] Platt lost the debate, and the proviso stood in New York for the next half century until the Fifteenth Amendment to the US Constitution (1870) nullified it.

Simons was one of the black New Yorkers who came of age in this political landscape and marshaled the "practical commentary" against black disenfranchisement Platt foresaw. In 1837, several of them (including Simons) formed a committee and began to institutionalize their efforts to overturn the 1821 law. With a base of operation in New York City, they sent the proprietor of the *Colored American* newspaper, Phillip Bell, on a "political tour through the [Hudson] River Counties of the State, with a view to excite an INTEREST among our brethren of the towns and villages of the Hudson border, in regard to their political rights." Bell's objective was to motivate these "young colored men" to "DELUGE the Legislative Hall . . . with PETITIONS, praying the Legislature to grant the colored citizens" the right to vote—a "right which they had enjoyed uninterruptedly for 40 years."[48] The committee organized the logistics for the petition drive and boosted the campaign with public meetings. A year later the committee became the New York Association for the Political Elevation and Improvement of the People of Color (NYPE).

The NYPE's primary objective was to "obtain the erasure of that antirepublican and odious clause from our State Constitution, by which a large portion of true and loyal inhabitants of the State, are disenfranchised."[49] Such political efforts complemented the work of organizations such as the New York Committee of Vigilance, which provided legal defense for free and enslaved black persons in New York City. Under the leadership of David Ruggles, who was also part of the NYPE, the Committee of Vigilance also aided fugitives from slavery. There is no record Simons was part of the Committee of Vigilance, but their extralegal actions and "cross-class unity and participation from members [throughout] the black community" appealed to his labor-based egalitarianism: these were the sorts of associations that recognized all black persons as worthy political actors.[50] The voice of even the most menial worker was vital, Simons argued, because it spoke to the conditions of his or her oppression with the greatest clarity and urgency. His experiences with slavery, indentured servitude, and freedom proved to him the criticality of perspectival specificity to black politics and its struggle for a genuine American democracy.

Simons knew that a major rationale against black suffrage that emerged from the 1821 constitutional convention was that the property requirement proviso would inspire black workers to elevate themselves morally and financially. Simons found such arguments more than disingenuous: they powered antidemocratic forms of oppression to which black politics must strive to put an end. He abhorred the ways in which the proviso encouraged bourgeois reformers to double down on their calls for personal austerity and collective rectitude. Their watchword was "moral elevation," and there was no political ethos Simons censured more. In an 1839 address before the African Clarkson Association, he called moral elevation the "discording tone" that is "trumpet sound from the pulpit," "thundered from the press," and "now the topic of our common arguments."[51] By 1840, black reformers who championed moral means as the most advantageous modality of black politics began to dominate African Americans' political associations in New York. The most striking example of their dominance was the Committee for Vigilance's removal of Ruggles from his leadership post in 1839, but Simons's refusal to serve as an elected delegate to represent New York City at the state Colored Convention of 1840 is just as telling.[52] It seems the shift to moral elevation over and above other forms of political action vexed Simons to such a degree that he refused to take any visible role in black politics from this period until the Civil War, when he recruited soldiers for the Union Army and worked against colonizers' efforts to send newly free black persons away from the US.[53]

One of the features of moral elevation that galled Simons, at least as he saw it, was that its advocates were supercilious prigs who demeaned anyone who questioned their campaigns. Moral elevation "is sounded to be the prolific parent of all virtue," he told the African Clarkson Association, and "he who would dare whisper in the faintest breath against it, is thought no less than the parent of all vice, crime, and degradation, that possibly could afflict humanity."[54] Simons claimed proponents of moral elevation drowned out anyone who proposed a different course of action (e.g., strikes and other forms of labor protest; public demonstrations; petitions to legislatures; violence) by claiming the high ground. Even worse, moral elevation was self-defeating and only compounded blacks' oppression because it "carrie[s] along with it blind submission." Simons said: "Yes brothers, our soft manners when particularly addressing those of pale complexions, this very great respect which is particularly shown to them also, moral elevation carries these which are roots of degradation with it."[55] His gendered appeal to his "Brother Clarksons" suggests moral elevation enervates manhood; more broadly, it instantiates an abiding claim in modern black thought that any politics grounded in moral suasion upholds a morality of the rulers that positions black persons as always and forever at the bottom strata of the American polity.

As Simons found himself increasingly alienated by the ascendancy of moral elevation in the late 1830s, he continued to acclaim benevolent societies such as the African Clarkson Association that maintained egalitarian collectivism as its ethos. Such organizations, Craig Steven Wilder explains, have "been misconstrued as the arrogant stamp of a tiny, elite class, when in reality African societies were quite varied and their charges included the impoverished, fugitives, and orphans."[56] The African Clarkson Association was founded in 1829 as a "charitable society of African descent to afford mutual means of education to the members thereof and relief to their families in cases of sickness or death."[57] Historians of antebellum black institutions regularly label the Clarkson Association a "literary society," and in large part it was. But the prevailing connotation of "literary society" as a relatively rarefied, bourgeois entity does not pertain here: its members included men from across the demographic spectrum, from freeborn and well-off to formerly enslaved and indigent. Simons upheld these societies as paradigmatic of the best of black politics: "Unity alone has elevated us to our present stand, and benevolent societies was the father of it; some thirty years back there was nothing to guide us but discord and enmity, but with the introduction of institutions, came virtue, benevolence, sympathy, brotherly affection, unity."[58] This full-throated embrace of early black nationalist institutions deems racial solidarism, what he calls "unity," the linchpin of the best forms of African Americans' political culture.

Simons embraced racial solidarism as a normative virtue with a practical instrumentality: it blunts the antagonisms that economic, occupational, or social distinctions foster. He shared this outlook with the political philosopher Maria W. Stewart, who almost certainly knew him.[59] Both took aim at the ways "classes of distinction" among African Americans hampered black freedom struggles.[60] Stewart blamed personal jealousies as the primary hindrance to racial solidarism, whereas Simons singled out moral elevation. He said, "yes it's nothing but this moral elevation that causes us to have so little confidence in one another.... Yes Brothers, this moral elevation of our people is but a mere song, it is nothing but a conspicuous scarecrow designed expressly, I may safely say, to hinder our people from acting collectively for themselves. For long as it continues we will have a lack of confidence in one another, and if we suspect each other, how can we act together?"[61] He suggests the reason moral elevation precludes racial solidarism among black persons is that it "degrades" the lifeworlds of everyday working people as pitiably abject and epistemologically nugatory; hence, they can offer nothing culturally rich or intellectually generative for the polity.[62] The political implication is that the masses of black people, those most in need of moral elevation, must have no say in the decision-making processes and institutions that regulate their lives. Simons deemed the "false philanthropy" of moral elevation a "means for to hinder [black people] from acting in another way to obtain their rights."[63]

At the core of Simons's notion of "acting in another way" is what I understand as respectability. Respectability here describes acts of self-imposition that refuse to degrade others as less deserving of a voice in the polity's affairs, regardless of their positionality. To function otherwise, to capitulate to the demands of one's economic or social superiors, is to subscribe to a politics of *uplift*. Uplift projects based on behavioral reform toward individual abstemiousness were ubiquitous in antebellum America. Social reformers pressed campaigns such as temperance as nostrums to remedy all sorts of ills that beset black communities. Simons flatly rejected their efforts as futile: "There is no such thing as elevating a nation of people by good morals."[64] Moreover, he argued that moral elevation reinforces hierarchies that position black and working-class populations as never deserving of full political autonomy and civic participation. His notion of respectability rejects uplift's underlying social value theories as inherently antidemocratic. The two constituencies Simons homed in on to develop these claims were black women and the black laboring classes.

Proponents of moral uplift believed it was necessary to establish gendered divisions of labor for black women and men that never really obtained in American chattel slavery.[65] Their social models projected thriving black families if black women preoccupied themselves with the affairs of the hearth above all else; if they must work for income, women should limit themselves to domestic labor. Politics and other public matters were for men, although reformers did support the activities of women's benevolent societies and volunteer work as valuable ancillaries to the political efforts men carried out. Simons knew "such ideals bore little resemblance to lives of black women," and he adduced bourgeois reformers' prescriptions of spurious gender roles as further evidence that moral elevation was a sociological project designed to fail and thus to exacerbate black oppression.[66]

Simons condemned any effort to restrict black women's full and unfettered participation in the public sphere. He called out the general misogyny that deemed black women deficient political actors and thought producers, and singled out women who perpetuated such notions. Of those women "who consider their [judgments] less" deserving of a public hearing than men's, he said they "ought to be outcasts of all popular societies: for their influence might excite the same opinion, of self[-]incapability in many a promising damsel, and I sincerely contend that, that where a female feels this inferiority she is but a dead member to the intellectual and cultivated society of mankind."[67] One rarely finds such unrestrained calls for black women as full participants, indeed leaders, in the intellectual and political cultures of antebellum America. In the 1830s Maria Stewart was probably the only member of the black intelligentsia to match Simons's advocacy in this regard. Although Stewart's Christian hermeneutics disposed her to recognize traditional gender roles as largely meritorious, she called for businesses and schools with black women at the head because the historical failings of the American polity (and black men) left them no other option for personal fulfillment and collective achievement.[68] Unlike Stewart's, Simons's claims were more philosophical than historiographical: even though black women were confined to the lowliest segments of the American polity, as *persons* they warranted whatever form of social and political inclusion they desired.

Simons's (gender) politics stemmed from his relationships and interactions with black women whose physical and intellectual labors were crucial to the development of free black communities in post-slavery New York. These were women who built institutions that mitigated the effects of black privations. They were women such as Simons's mother, sister, and common-law wife whose drudgery made black life possible. As he put it, "it has been those who toil daily at the rough and most laborous work that has accumulated that the means to benefit them while living, then to bequeath a legacy when dead." Labor was at the core of Simons's political philosophy because labor was the foundation of black sociality. "Seek for means first, all, or principal part of the means that is among us, you will find among the laboring classes," he declared. Labor was productive action, and black workers proved they had the wherewithal to perform the "physical and political efforts" necessary to quash slavery and achieve full citizenship.[69] These were politics that must be superintended by black persons relegated to the peripheries of their own communities and the broader American polity.

Simons's insistence that the black laboring classes, especially black women workers, deserved to be respected as political actors instantiated the judgment that drudgery was not something one should be ashamed of—a judgment very few members of the African American intelligentsia shared. Disputes over the social and political ramifications of black menial labor began to dominate the black public sphere in the late 1820s, culminating in the mid-1850s with condemnations such as Frederick Douglass's that scorned defenses of what he called the "contented degradation" of black toilers.[70] Douglass and similarly minded critics wanted to disassociate blackness from American chattel slavery. For them, images of exhausted black menials were too redolent of enslavement and therefore worked against abolitionism and the struggle for full citizenship. Simons regarded such critiques of black labor and calls for "higher attainments" in employment as slights to the realities of black life and, worse, concomitants of moral elevation.[71] As the mainstream of the antebellum black sphere would have it, the physical labor by which African Americans sustained themselves was a source of incredible *shame*.

Those who denigrated black toilers curiously overlooked the hyperracialization of labor fields in Northern cities, especially considering the immigration boom from northern and western Europe. These snubs reinforced the notion that blackness itself was the mark of shame. In a sort of Lockean syllogism, they deduced that because the labor black people perform is shameful and labor is a property of the body, black embodiment itself is always already shameful. The practices that consigned African Americans to drudgery were no matter to their racial calculus. Respectability aims to countervail such judgments of black embodiment by acts of self-affirmation that esteem the totality of persons, from their identities to their labor: there is no need to position persons as better than the work they do because each form of work is as legitimate in its contributions to the polity as any other.

No writer rendered the political-philosophical significance of respectability with more perspicuity and beauty than the era's most eminent black intellectual, James McCune Smith. McCune Smith was born in

New York City to a woman who was enslaved in and around Manhattan. He was almost certainly an indentured servant bound to his mother's owner, whom he believed was his father.[72] McCune Smith was educated at the city's Free African Schools, which the New York Manumission established in the 1790s to educate free black children and the children of enslaved persons. He excelled there and hoped to study medicine in New York, but several institutions refused him admission on account of his race. He landed at the University of Glasgow, where he took a medical degree, the first on record for an African American. McCune Smith drew deeply on his medical education and practice to refute the racist demography and biologism that defined so much of American social thought. Yet his political thought derived from his early years with his mother, whose menial labor made his academics possible.

In the prefatory essay to Frederick Douglass's *My Bondage and My Freedom* (1855), McCune Smith calls himself the "son of a self-emancipated bond-woman."[73] His immediate task here is to offer some context for who he is, the man honored with introducing Douglass's magisterial second autobiography. But its more generative and incisive critical function is to fold unknown enslaved persons, especially black women, into the history of fugitivity that Douglass's narrativized escape both exemplifies and overshadows. Their stories did not capture the Anglo-American cultural imagination the way Douglass's narratives did, yet these nameless "self-emancipated" persons were no less imaginative and mettlesome in their flights to freedom and lives after. Like Simons, McCune Smith grounded his politics in the efforts of unknown black persons whose lives did not comport with the behavioral models that more bourgeois moral reformers, including Douglass, preferred.

A few years before he enshrined his mother's fugitive heroism as commensurate to Douglass's, McCune Smith had done the same with that of a black washerwoman. She is the subject of one of the literary sketches of his series on black working persons, *Heads of the Colored People, Done with A Whitewash Brush* (1852–1854). "The Washerwoman" typifies the formal experimentation and narrative ironies that distinguished McCune Smith as one of the most daring and innovative essayists in nineteenth-century American letters. It relies on a kind of textualized theatricality to detail her labor and home life. The refrain "Dunk! Dunk!!" evokes her incredible work ethic to complement the *mise-en-scène* of her "small [apartment], hot as an oven, the air in it thick and misty with the steam rising from the ironing table." Pictures of abolitionists and famous black activists hang on the walls, and religious literature and popular fiction are strewn on a "newly varnished mahogany table."[74] Out of these cramped quarters emerges a grace and resiliency that its trappings might not otherwise signify. At the center of it all is the washerwoman whose personal story parallels the most famous episode in Douglass's life story: his clash with the notorious slave breaker Edward Covey.

Douglass identified his battle with Covey as the existential turning point in his "humble history." As he put it in the great chiasmus of American literature, "you have seen how a man was made a slave; you shall see how a slave was made a man."[75] Douglass's tale of his defeat of Covey in *Narrative of the Life of Frederick Douglass, An American Slave. Written by Himself* (1845) is the critical intertext for McCune Smith's description of the washerwoman's triumph over her former owner. He writes:

> Each one of her three sisters had been brought North with the white family, and went back for the children's sake into bondage. [The washerwoman] alone had remained North from her girlhood as a slave, until one day, when she had reached woman's years, her so-called master, with much bustle, with whip in hand, had called her upstairs for punishment. The scene was short and decisive; the tall, stout man had raised his arm to strike—"see here!" fiercely exclaimed the frail being before him, "if you dare touch me with that lash, I will tear you to pieces!" The whipper, whipped, dropt his uplifted arm and quietly slunk downstairs.[76]

The sketch immediately turns from this story to describe the "good-for-nothing looking, quarter grown, bushy-headed boy, a shade or two lighter than his mother." Her son "had come into the world after the fashion which so stirs up Ethiop's [i.e., William J. Wilson's] pious honor"—that is, relations between powerful white men and black women subordinates.[77] Of course Douglass's parentage is an obvious allusion.[78] But considering the washerwoman's life in slavery and freedom in New York, McCune Smith might very well have been alluding to his early years with his mother. The boy in the sketch was a bookworm like the precocious McCune Smith; for both the boy in the story and the young McCune Smith there was "no evidence around the [home] that [they] called any one father . . . except the unseen, universal 'our Father, which art in Heaven!'"[79] The sketch's literary, philosophical, and autobiographical resonances instantiate the leveling so central to respectability: a social valuation of toiling single black mothers as equal to world-historical figures such as Frederick Douglass.

After McCune Smith published "The Washerwoman," which is the third installment of the series, his editor, Frederick Douglass, published a brief note in *FDP* claiming that individuals in the city who suspected they were the real-life subjects of *Heads of the Colored People* stopped into the newspaper's offices. Douglass said they were looking for McCune Smith to exact a bit of vengeance on the author: "We shall not be surprised to learn that a certain distinguished colored gentleman of New York City has come in violent contact with a *broom-stick*!" McCune Smith should remain on guard, Douglass joked, because black washerwomen unhappy with the sketch were looking to fling a "few drops of moderately hot '*suds*' upon his neatly attired person." The jocular tone of the note masks Douglass's displeasure with the series up to that point. He had hoped that McCune Smith would, "by his faithful pictures of contented degradation, rouse the colored people to seek higher, more useful and profitable employments," but he found *Heads of the Colored People* to be too celebratory of African Americans' lowly employments and too cynical regarding black possibility for higher achievements.[80] Despite these misgivings, Douglass allowed his New York correspondent to continue with the series.

A little less than a year later, and after McCune Smith published three more installments, Douglass had had enough. He published his own piece saluting the black New Yorkers whom he deemed most estimable and worthy of literary memorialization. The piece opens with a rebuke of the dominant view of black persons in American culture and thought. Douglass writes:

> The opinion of the public, concerning them, is generally made up with very insufficient means. They see them either in rags and idleness, or dressed up in the gaudy trappings of waiters and flunkeys, dancing attendance behind their chairs at table, in hotels or steamboats, or forming a part of their grand equipages, (the ebony to se[e] off ivory,) rolling down the life-thronged Broadway. Hence the popular verdict respecting them is, that they are a shallow, frivolous, and servile race, to be pitied, perhaps, but wholly destitute of those qualities which command respect.[81]

Without naming him, Douglass indicts McCune Smith for fueling black derogation with *Heads of the Colored People*. Even though they were confined to drudgery and menial labor, black workingmen and workingwomen projected images of servility and cultural inadequacy onto the race that leave African Americans as a whole appearing unworthy of respect from themselves and others, Douglass claimed. He was stupefied that McCune Smith would perpetuate such racist judgments with his singular intellectual gifts and dazzling literary talents.

Douglass then rendered his own "heads of the colored people" in direct response to *Heads of the Colored People*, albeit in just this one piece. His portraits focus on black persons and institutions that comport to the supposed virtues of bourgeois capitalism and middle-class decorum.

> But not only have I seen much that is cheering in the way of churches, Sunday Schools, Literary Societies, intelligent ministers and respectable congregations among our people in New York. In a single morning, I visited six establishments belonging to, and under management of colored men, bearing all the marks of material prosperity. Two of these were druggists, (a somewhat out of the way business for ignorant people.) Well stocked and are mainly patronized by the white people in their neighborhood. In the very center of business, I found a colored gentleman keeping a large clothing store, apparently doing a good business. Next door to him, I saw watches, clocks, gold pens, pencils, and all sorts of jewelry; and on going into this place, I found it belonged to, and was managed by a colored gentleman. In another part of the city, I walked into a wholesale china store, on Pearl Street, found it large and reaching far back from the street; it was densely packed. This store is the property of a colored man, who twenty years ago, went to New York as common porter.—One of the most splendidly furnished dining saloons, on Broadway, is kept by a colored man. But in this line we have never been very far behind-hand. In respect to talents and real ability, I believe there is enough among the colored citizens of New York, to give wise and wholesome laws to an empire.[82]

That Douglass lands on the prospect of a black empire explains why none of his subjects are women. The "heads" he exhibits are meant to typify those black men who have achieved cultural refinement and intellectual merit and who thus embody the feasibility of black (self-) government:

these are the *representative men* he wanted McCune Smith to focus on.[83] Douglass ends the essay by asking, "why will not my able New York correspondent bring some of the real '*heads of the colored people*' before our readers?"[84]

McCune Smith did not give in to his editor's acerbic prodding, let alone the threats he might have received from washerwomen in the city. He rejected Douglass's claim that African Americans should showcase their most decorous and accomplished fellows as representatives of the race for a general audience. To do so was not only a misapprehension of history and a foolish capitulation to American bigotry, McCune Smith suggested, but more importantly it was a refusal to embrace those persons whom he declared "the last hope" for the American polity: *Heads of the Colored People* was his "salvific" project, as Derrick Spires calls it. "Through these installments," Spires writes, McCune Smith "rethinks the relation of [black workingmen and workingwomen] to the civic community, repositioning some of [the] most vilified laborers as representative citizens based on their ideals, not their finances, and resituating citizenship in the home and social institutions, as personal fulfillment displaces money as the ruling idea."[85] McCune Smith renders his subjects—especially those who work with their hands, who still bear the marks of enslavement on their bodies and in their employments, who are confined to the lowest strata of the polity—as the best of American democracy and its most excellent representative men and women.[86] As such, they most certainly do "command respect" and must be looked at again.

Respectability for workaday black life, free and enslaved, is the political crux of *Heads of the Colored People*. In a précis for the series, McCune Smith says he wants "to win the post of door keeper ... to the outermost enclosure leading to the Republic of Letters," which he imagines as "that glorious commonwealth, perpetually progressive, free from *caste* ... which smiles upon all her citizens, if they be but true, which holds triumphant sway and is crowned with perennial laurel in the *coming ages!*"[87] Such republics nurture respectability for all persons—at least with "door keepers" like McCune Smith. The Republic of Letters emerged in the late eighteenth century as a concept with which to understand material and philosophical relationships between literary cultures and representative governance. Thomas Paine, in *Rights of Man* (1791), offers the richest explication from the era: "As the republic of letters brings forth the best literary productions, by giving to genius a fair and universal chance; so the representative system of government is calculated to produce the wisest laws, by collecting wisdom where it can be found. I smile to myself when I contemplate the ridiculous insignificance into which literature and all the sciences would sink, were they made hereditary; and I carry the same idea into governments."[88] Be it a polity or a literary milieu, a republic should be no respecter of persons. The rubric of what Paine calls "heredity" includes gender and race, as *Heads of the Colored People* so vividly reminds us. Contempt for inheritances of all sorts as standards for political standing instantiates slave morality and its antihierarchical aims. To achieve equality in a republic or any other form of democratic governance, then, respectability must be its highest virtue.

Republicanism appealed to black thinkers such as McCune Smith because of its cardinal precept: freedom as nondomination. Melvin Rogers has demonstrated how African American political thinkers over the course of the long nineteenth century kept the "language of republicanism very much alive" as it waned elsewhere in Anglo-American political philosophy. He theorizes "two key themes that emerge" from their interventions: "what is required of civic virtue under conditions of racial domination," and "how . . . a definition of freedom as nondomination [can] be deployed to combat racial domination specifically."[89] The realization of a just, democratically robust polity motivated these queries. For McCune Smith, respectability must be at the core of any republican formation. The Republic of Letters he posits in *Heads of the Colored People* is no mere rhetorical figure (e.g., metaphor), but a textualized performative act that aims to bring about the mechanisms that produce and sustain "free institutions that secure nondomination."[90] Republics *do things*, and McCune Smith argued that respectability for society's most downtrodden must pervade the American Republic if it is to reach its most excellent ends.

One thing a republic should do is ensure that its citizens live without shame. Societies built on the principle of freedom as nondomination must ensure that all persons live without privation but have their basic needs met to stand without shame before others.[91] Nineteenth-century black thinkers were adamant in their insistence that they receive the material resources necessary to do so—resources they earned by dint of their labor and ostensible citizenship.[92] Thinkers such as McCune Smith and Simons remind us that the American polity regarded certain identities as nature's mark of inherent unworthiness, regardless of one's material conditions.[93] McCune Smith's *Heads of the Colored People* calls on its readers to grapple with this more elemental and embedded structure of shame. It does so by ceding (literary) space to the most marginalized in American society: our work is to respect such persons as political equals to all others in the polity for no reason other than their capacities as human persons.[94] Labor is one of those capacities. *Heads of the Colored People* rejects all forms of shame affixed to the work persons do, however menial.

In fact, labor becomes the means by which the series' subjects claim respectability. What McCune Smith writes about bootblacks pertains to the black laboring classes more broadly: they are "thrifty, energetic, progressive. Free muscles, steadily exercised, produce free thought, energy, progress." Such professions have made persons of "*character*, not of *wealth*."[95] The character of persons in relation to others is a main concern for black republican thinkers. "Impoverished character" is the foundational problem of the American polity, they argue, and the "resolution... depends on a characterological transformation" from a great many of its citizens.[96] *Heads of the Colored People* offers character models to guide these transformations. The series esteems black working persons and their labor as figures to be respected—to be looked at, and listened to, again—if the American Republic is ever to fulfill its greatest ideals.

5 · Care

Caroline "Caddy" Ellis toils away in Frank J. Webb's novel *The Garies and Their Friends* (1857). The middle child of a free black family in antebellum Philadelphia, she is forever tending to some domestic chore or someone else's needs. Caddy's "earthly paradise," Webb writes, would be a "place where she could [exist] in a perpetual state of house cleaning."[1] Her "shrewish disposition," incorrigible fussiness, and regular squabbles with little brother Charlie instantiate the humor the nineteenth-century novel of manners works to effect.[2] She typifies the pap that many critics argue mars Webb's novel as both literary object and political statement.[3] In his groundbreaking survey of African American literary history (1989), Blyden Jackson concludes that *The Garies* "would be at home in vulgar fiction at virtually any time and place for at least the last four hundred years" because it is full of characters like Caddy that articulate fatuous comic bits and plotlines.[4]

Jackson's dismissal reflects critical consensus. The literary history of *The Garies* sometimes prompts cursory recognition—it is the second published novel written by an African American and the first that takes up free black life as a primary subject—but sustained commentaries are scarce. Webb aimed for a serious political fiction, one that would clarify how antiblack racism and class oppression operate as mutually constitutive systems of mid-century America. The novel projects the entanglements of race and class conflict writ large when white capital foments an anti-abolitionist race riot to destroy black properties, depreciate real estate valuations, and capture the market. But critics by and large have dismissed *The Garies* as little more than assimilationist fluff because of its investments in bourgeois culture, especially the ideological functionalities of the domestic novel. Webb's painstaking attention to the inner workings of the home rather than the barbarities of chattel slavery registers as insufficiently oppositional, if not downright spineless, within a cultural matrix that fostered a minor literature of black revolt that included Frederick Douglass's "The Heroic Slave" (1853) and Martin Delany's *Blake; or, The Huts of America* (1859–1862). That Webb was a black man who eschewed blunt abolitionist agitation in favor of a tale of black domesticity made *The Garies* even more of an anomaly and, as history has had it, a novel we should feel free to ignore.

The logic guiding Webb's detractors is that the domestic and the political are discrete realms, that the former entails a set of private engagements and intimacies that have little to do with the worldmaking power of the latter. Such judgments turn on a thoroughly gendered axiology: the prioritization of domesticity in *The Garies* means it is sorely lacking in (literary) manliness, with nothing substantive to contribute to the work of black politics. No wonder there was hardly any mention of the novel in abolitionist media or the black press at the time of its publication. Frederick Douglass did reprint the lengthy *London Daily News* review in his newspaper in December 1857, but he never wrote about *The Garies* again.[5] Perhaps once he read the novel, Douglass, like many others in the era and since, deemed it too feeble a literary object to be useful in black liberation struggles.

Webb was peculiar among black male writers in the era.[6] He chose to follow the lead of that "damned mob of scribbling women" whose sentimentalist novels dominated the mid-century American literary marketplace.[7] As Robert Reid-Pharr writes, "Webb was clearly in conversation with a score of authors, mostly female, of the mid-nineteenth century whose sentimentalism and emphasis on the domestic helped shape the ideological structures of the antebellum American writing world."[8] These writers, led by Harriet Beecher Stowe, cast the home as the primary locus for the cultivation of moral character and thus civic value and political judgment. It was only in the home, they argued, that one could acquire the requisite virtues and self-discipline with which to avoid the addictions, cupidity, and materialism that social critics declared were destroying the modern world. Literary sentimentalists amplified their claims in the many reform movements that swept America. They created a discourse and a propaganda that indexed the whirlwind of antebellum sociality, even though reformers themselves were often relegated to the margins of society. Webb based *The Garies* in the rhetorical interventions women reformers spearheaded, especially the argument that the best resources for political life are created and maintained in domestic life.

The Garies follows three families navigating the social turmoil of 1830s Philadelphia and its aftereffects some twenty years later. Clarence Garie, a wealthy white Georgian planter, moves his family to the city because the mother of his children, Emily, wants them to live in a free state among enterprising African Americans. Emily is an enslaved woman of "light-brown complexion [with] the faintest tinge of carmine." Clarence purchased her at a Savannah auction for two thousand dollars, outbidding "all the young bucks in the neighborhood who had competed with him at the sale." Over the course of a decade of living together, they built a life of "tenderness and affection." They have two children who "showed no trace whatsoever of African origin," and another on the way.[9] Webb plays on the scandal of southern slavers fathering enslaved children then treating them as revenue-generating chattel, a dominant trope in abolitionist culture.[10] Yet Clarence raises his children as though they are scions of the Georgia slaveocracy. The novel's initiating event, the Garies' move to Philadelphia, instantiates his commitment to their betterment: "I'm going north, because I wish to emancipate and educate my children—you know I can't do that here" in Georgia, he says.[11]

In Philadelphia, they move into a house next door to the Stevens family. George Stevens, the novel's chief villain, is a corrupt attorney who blackmails clients, bribes public officials, and orchestrates the climactic anti-abolitionist race riot. George discovers Clarence is his long-lost first cousin and, during the riot, murders him to claim the Garie fortune as the only surviving heir. (Georgia probate courts won't recognize the half-black Garie children as heirs.) George Stevens's wife, Jule, is a rank racist who concocts a plan to get the Garie children kicked out of their school because it is the one her children attend. The teacher sees no choice but to expel the Garies to avoid the "reproach of abolitionism."[12] (In mainstream antebellum opinion, little was worse than being associated with, let alone confused for, an abolitionist.) The Stevens' racist villainy coupled with the Garies' tragic mulatta tale—Emily dies of heartbreak while hiding from the rioters and her baby is stillborn—make for very standard narrative fare in nineteenth-century American popular race fiction.

The Ellises are Webb's most significant literary invention. This "highly respectable and industrious coloured family" provides a window into the ambitions, achievements, and battles of free black populations in the decades leading up to the Civil War.[13] Charles, a carpenter, and Ellen, a seamstress, give all of themselves for family and community. For example, Charles ventures out during the riot to warn the Garies about a mob coming to attack them and their home because they are "amalgamationists"—i.e., an interracial family. A "gang of ruffians" spots Charles and chases him up a rooftop to throw him over. As he clings to a ledge, "one of the villains" strikes Charles's hands with a hatchet, "severing two fingers and severely mangling the other."[14] He falls and nearly dies. His and Ellen's daughters, Esther and Caddy, nurse him back to health and take in odd jobs to help the family make ends meet. Their younger brother Charlie is a precocious, strong-willed adolescent who takes the reins as family patriarch as soon as his age and circumstance allow. (He is away during the riot and learns of his father's condition in letters from home; his tearful response reveals the young man of deep feeling that sentimentalists acclaimed.) Charlie endures several ordeals while working for others that he otherwise would not have if not for the good of his family. The Ellises model the form of black domesticity that Webb proposes will yield the most excellent black community: intelligent in its judgments, protective and redistributive of its resources, and nurturing of its inhabitants' talents and aspirations. At the core of these communal formations is the practice of care.

This chapter theorizes how care, especially as it takes shape in and around the domestic realm, regulates the democratic vision of *The Garies*. Caring emerges from psychological attachments between persons by which the self deems the other worthy of care for no other reason than that he or she needs it. Care takes shape in acts of remediation one performs following his or her encounter with someone else's pains, aside and apart from gross self-interest. "To care for someone," Aisha K. Finch writes, "is to rethink being in relation as a form of connection that derails the needs of state and capital, producing a radical otherwise in their violations. To care is to be about the business of living with people, sharing in and amplifying their life force, recognizing their value and worth.... Most of all, it is intentional—a deliberate and purposeful creation of collective well-being."[15] Finch notes that black feminist ethics has always held the intentionality of care as foundational to black liberatory politics, not downstream of them. She goes so far as to argue that care can act "as a way to disrupt the condition of premature death, as a way to unsettle the slow violence of late colonial modernity, and as a philosophy of survival in the face of literal and psychic death."[16] *The Garies* draws from this tradition to espouse what I understand as a democratic form of care, a praxis of caring for others and being cared for by others regardless of either's station in the polity.[17] It is an embodiment of equal regard; it is the loving action of slave morality. As such, a sensuous political demand emanates from its enactments: the weak are as deserving of power as the strong because they are equally deserving of giving and receiving care.

BLACK NATIONALIST HOMEMAKING: PARLORS AND PICTURES

In her Preface to *The Garies*, Harriet Beecher Stowe commends Webb's "reliable" portrayal of African Americans in Philadelphia and the "incidents" they lived as "mostly true ones, woven together by a slight web of fiction." The "large class" of black people in the city, she writes, "constitute a peculiar society of their own, presenting many social peculiarities worthy of interest and attention."[18] More than an imprimatur of the novel's literary quality and sociological explications, Stowe's Preface primes readers for its insistence that the distinctiveness of black life, especially in the home and the family, is an historical inevitability, social necessity, and political good—that is, Webb's black nationalism. According to the reviewer for *The Athenaeum* (London), black nationalism in *The Garies* is the logical response to the antiblack animus that pervaded every aspect of American life: "The intense abhorrence of the Free States for their coloured brethren is an antipathy stronger than institutions. It is in vain that philosophical American parents give their children black dolls to give them juvenile and pleasant associations; black remains black, unpleasant to whites."[19] The reviewer scoffed at the liberal assumption that exposure to, and sympathy for, black life via cultural surrogates such as dolls and literary objects would abate racist discord because what white Americans truly disdained was the "bodily reality" of black persons.[20] This phenomenological critique of racial facticity organized the ever more radical black public sphere of the 1850s, when thinkers such as Martin Delany and Mary Ann Shadd Cary began to revolutionize black political discourse in terms that ran counter to white reformers' paternalistic logics and social philosophies. Stowe's endorsement of *The Garies* signaled to (white) readers who were apprehensive of the rising tide of radical black thought that Webb's novel is of a different order than the (sometimes violent) polemics that appealed to more and more African Americans at the time.

When Webb published *The Garies* in London in 1857, there were two primary strands of black nationalism in African American political culture. One was *chauvinism*, which drew on Euro-American race theories to claim African persons and their descendants possessed innate qualities of body, mind, and spirit that distinguished them from non-African persons. Their ethnologies, not to mention the terror they endured daily, convinced black chauvinists that racial separatism was the only way to improve their condition. Led by figures such as Delany and Alexander Crummell, they practiced forms of separatism that ranged from all-black institutions to emigration from the US to the Caribbean, Africa, and elsewhere. Black chauvinism was ascendent in the 1850s and reached its apex later in the century and in the 1920s. The other strand, which dated back to the late eighteenth century, was *assimilationism*. Black assimilationists such as David Walker and Frederick Douglass rejected racial ethnologies and regarded the idea that black persons needed total separation from white persons and institutions as illogical and self-defeating. Although these men and women did establish and take part in all-black organizations, they viewed such efforts as pragmatic stepping-stones toward full inclusion in the American polity. As Walker writes in his *Appeal to the Colored Citizens of the World* (1829): "Treat us like men, and we will be your friends. And there is not a doubt in my mind, but that the whole of the past will sink into oblivion, and we, yet under God, will become a united and happy people. The whites may say it is impossible, but remember that nothing is impossible with God."[21] Walker, who wrote the first great militant treatise in African American political thought in *The Appeal*, had more faith in the possibility of a racially inclusive America than did most of his contemporaries.

In *The Golden Age of Black Nationalism, 1850-1925*, Wilson Jeremiah Moses explains how chauvinists and assimilationists in the 1850s shared a deep commitment to Western culture and thought. He writes: "Black nationalists on the eve of the Civil War, despite their fierce rhetoric of independence, despite their declamations about God-given mandates to develop a separate destiny, were hardly eager to remove themselves from white society, and were reluctant to contemplate a future severed from the values of Anglo-American civilization."[22] Even the most fervent black chauvinists who left the US believed they should graft Euro-American ideas and procedures, of which they saw themselves as co-producers, onto native populations whom they regarded as heathen and benighted; some went so far as to call for white protectorates of independent black polities to spur "African regeneration."[23] Webb took part in these debates in abolitionist and emigrationist circles in Philadelphia, London, Kingston, and other cities across the circum-Atlantic world in which he lived. In *The Garies*, he stages the entanglements between chauvinism and assimilationism without settling on either side; instead, he urges black nationalists of all stripes to anchor their ventures in domesticity's virtues. For Webb, a caring and cared-for home must be ground zero for any form of black political struggle.

Rarely is domesticity or the home a focal point in black nationalist historiography and theory. An exception might be *fin-de-siècle* racial uplift, when Booker T. Washington spearheaded the movement for what Moses calls a "technocratic nationalism." Washingtonians aimed for a "business and industrial technocracy among black people" that responded to "the demands of the age for skilled industrial workers and competent businessmen [who] could make themselves sophisticated contributors to the new industrial revolution."[24] An army of race men and race women preached that none of this was possible if African Americans did not build the proper home lives. "The house is the greatest institution on earth for good or evil," a leading black South Carolina minister named Richard Carroll proclaimed during an Emancipation Day celebration in Sumter, South Carolina to some 8,000 attendees. "You can't make a great, good, patriotic and intelligent race if you live in low, wicked, filthy, and ungodly homes."[25] Carroll and his cohort placed great emphasis on hygiene, sexual decorum, cleanliness, ventilation, and space in the home. Less so with earlier black nationalists such as Webb and Maria Stewart, who were far more concerned with the development of virtues in the home that would regulate black politics and public conduct. For example, Stewart found African Americans wanting in racial solidarism, which she regarded as fundamental to any worthwhile political project. She blamed black parents for the poor example they set for children. Because "we and our fathers have dealt treacherously with one another, and because many of us now possess that envious and malicious disposition," she told a black women's literary society in 1832, "we had rather die than see each other rise an inch above a beggar. No gentle methods are used to promote love and friendship amongst us, but much is done to destroy it."[26] Stewart said it was only in the home where African Americans could break the cycle and cultivate the racial solidarism necessary to win "their rights and privileges" and achieve a "higher repute" in the world's eyes.[27]

Webb, too, esteemed the home as the primary crucible for the formation of political subjecthood. He did not minimize the importance of institutions—racism in Philadelphia's school systems is a major theme in *The Garies*, for instance—but deemed the care one gives and receives in the home, or the lack thereof, instrumental above all else in shaping public character. *The Garies* commends a black home life that is *sui generis* in the values and concerns that matter to its denizens *as* black persons but rejects racial separatism vis-à-vis non-black persons and entities. In fact, the novel asserts that black persons must never cede the American polity because it is as much theirs as anyone's, and the home must prepare them for participation and stewardship therein. Robert Reid-Pharr describes this position as a kind of "integrationism," or "a stance in which the cultural similarity of all American people is insisted on while racial distinctiveness is maintained. The black and the white are at once the same and different."[28] Built at once on "cultural similarity" and "racial distinctiveness," integrationism of this sort is a delicate politics. *The Garies* posits black domesticity and its care practices as the bulwark against forces that threaten integrationism's coherence, integrity, and potency.

Webb develops these arguments mainly in the Ellises' storylines. He introduces the family on a typical evening at home amid an idyllic *mis-en-scène* of china dishes, copper kettle, and soft butter for a smoking hot corn cake. "I wish Charlie would come with that tea," Mrs. Ellis says as she waits to begin their nightly ritual.[29] Once he arrives, everyone settles in to reflect on the day. The women perform small chores, Charlie does his homework, and Mr. Ellis reads newspapers and makes small repairs around the house. Here are all the trappings of a typical middle-class parlor scene in mid-century American fiction—except, of course, that the Ellises are a black family. For Webb, the parlor is a crucial site of encounter where African Americans engage and (re)fashion a wide range of public discourses. He deemed the black parlor what we now call a counterpublic, a space where minoritarian subjects, always conscious of their minoritarian status, formulate discourse for themselves and for strangers beyond their immediate settings. Counterpublics are usually understood as the product of institutions, but state impositions and other forms of suppression have undermined black institutions' ability to create and sustain their counterpublics.[30] The parlor is less susceptible to these vicissitudes because of its relative autonomy as part of the home.

The parlor's atmospheric niceties conceal the lifeworlds that engender the structures of thought that have been codified as "black politics," especially black nationalism. These lifeworlds are customarily narrated in settings of extreme physical labor (e.g., the plantation), of shattered innocence and dreams (e.g., the schoolhouse), and of quotidian indignity (e.g., public streets). In the normative logics of black nationalism, the parlor is a site of capitulation and surrender to white bourgeois norms; put bluntly, it is a place of and for racial sellouts. Jasmine Nichole Cobb finds that the historicity of the black parlor tells a much different story. She argues that in nineteenth-century black parlors "diverse conceptions of Black freedom" emerged because they were "place[s] for dissimilar groups of people and cultural producers to convene around visions of Blackness separated from slavery." There they devised "projects of domesticity and domestication" mediated by "pictures of freedom as tools of sense making that helped orient parlor dwellers to changing conceptions of the nation and the Atlantic world, each as representative of home."[31] Parlors were especially generative domains for the evolution of black women's intellectual and cultural work because the patriarchal strictures that regulated other black counterpublics in the era were often held at bay.[32] The feminization of the parlor is precisely what rendered its activities and networks mere trivialities within the masculinist imagination and therefore within prevailing historiographies of black nationalism.

In *The Garies*, the making of black political selves in the parlor begins with the careful curation and maintenance of the space. After Clarence Garie arrives in Philadelphia, for example, he visits the home of the wealthy African American real estate magnate Mr. Walters, who is a sort of social sponsor for the Garie family in the city. Webb's punctilious rendering of "the elegance of the room" details "not only great wealth, but cultivated taste and refined habits." Swept up in the parlor's careful urbanity, Clarence's attention becomes fixed on a portrait of "a black man in the uniform of a general officer." The painting is of Toussaint Louverture, leader of the Haitian revolution. "Looks like a man of intelligence. It is entirely different from any likeness I ever saw of him," Mr. Walters says. "The portraits generally represent him as a monkey-faced person, with a handkerchief about his head."[33] As Clarence grapples with the "novelty" of the portrait's sublimity and its subject's grandeur, he encounters the facticity of Mr. Walters's body in the parlor space. Webb delineates a sort of physiognomic symmetry between Mr. Walters and Louverture in the portrait. He writes:

> Mr. Walters was above six feet in height, and exceedingly well-proportioned; of jet-black complexion, and smooth glossy skin. His head was covered with a quantity of wooly hair, which was combed back from a broad but not very high forehead. His eyes were small, black, and piercing, and set deep in his head. His aquiline nose, thin lips, and broad chin, were the very reverse of African in their shape, and gave his face a very singular appearance. In repose, his countenance was severe in its express; but were engaged in agreeable conversation, the thin sarcastic-looking lips would part, displaying a set of dazzlingly white teeth, and the small black eyes would sparkle with animation.[34]

Webb's phenomenological sketch evokes phrenology and other antebellum racialist discourses by merging the political with the aesthetic. His aim is to demonstrate how the political derives from how we regard and thus value persons alongside whom we live, that a polity's cultural formations are the constitutive architectonics of its political formations. *The Garies* is Webb's demand for what one critic describes as a "revolution in aesthetic representation" as the means to instigate a "revolution in political representation."[35]

The scene thus models a reading practice in which the beholder *absorbs* himself in the world around him. The goal is to suspend bias so that one becomes vulnerable to the production of new affective and intellectual epiphanies. Clarence becomes so "absorbed" in the parlor, especially in "the likeness of [the] negro officer," that he does not notice when Mr. Walters enters.[36] Through the mediation of his absorption, Mr. Walters's mien comes to signify the Louverture-like revolutionary potentiality that courses throughout black populations. This view of the black masses was common among black political thinkers, even though they regarded Louverture as a mythic, almost godlike figure with superlative intellectual might, physical prowess, and political genius. William Wells Brown offered a typical portrait in an 1854 lecture at St. Thomas's Church in Philadelphia, which Webb very likely attended. Wells Brown said: "Toussaint was a man of a prepossessing appearance, of middle stature, and possessed an iron fame. . . . His private virtues were many, and he had a deep and pervading sense of religion, and in the camp, carried it even as far as Oliver Cromwell. It might be said that an inward and prophetic genius revealed to him the omnipotence of a firm and unwearied adherence to a principle."[37] Wells Brown went on to ask: "Who knows [but] a Toussaint . . . may someday appear in the Southern States of this Union? That they are there, no one will doubt. That their souls are thirsty for liberty, all will admit. . . . [T]he day is not far distant when the revolution of St. Domingo will be reënacted in South Carolina and Louisiana. The Haytian revolution was not unlike that which liberated the slaves of Sparta."[38] Clarence's absorption in the Toussaint portrait generates new ways of imagining black revolutionary possibility, nation-building, and personhood.

The parlor space makes these revelations possible. The care that characters exhibit toward the parlor's upkeep and layout underscores the novel's insistence on its import to the work of liberation and democratic socialization. For example, the Ellises are a neat and tidy family, but Caddy makes sure their parlor stays pristine for visitors. Early in the novel, the family receives short notice that old friends plan to stop by and Caddy springs into action. Webb writes, "Caddy seemed quite put out by the announcement of the intended visit. She declared that nothing was fit to be seen, that the house was in a state of disorder shocking to behold, and that there was scarce a place in it fit to sit down in; and she forthwith began to prepare for an afternoon's vigorous scrubbing and cleaning."[39] Once her family leaves the parlor, Caddy gets to work: "Caddy took undivided possession of the little parlour, which she soon brought into an astonishing state of cleanliness. The ornaments were arranged at exact distances from the corners of the mantelpiece, the looking-glass was polished, until it appeared to be without spot or blemish, and its gilt frame was newly adorned with cut paper to protect it from the flies. The best china was brought out, carefully dusted, and set upon the waiter, and all things with doors placed in a state of forwardness to receive their expected guest."[40] Her care for the space instantiates her care for those who will inhabit it and the work they do for others. Caddy's obsession with order and cleanliness is not only her recognition of others' "value and worth," but also her contribution to the "creation of collective well-being."[41] However obliquely, Webb calls on readers to honor the ways black women's quotidian (domestic) labors have been the backbone of African American political life. Their labors have furnished the spaces, finances, and repose necessary for undertaking those actions we recognize as political and celebrate as such: black politics cannot exist without black women's caring efforts in and around the home. Forgoing scenes of pamphleteering, or high-flown abolitionist oratory, or activist social campaigns such as the free-produce movement, all of which were popular among antebellum black Philadelphians, Webb homes in on what he regards as domesticity's singular offerings to African American political life.

Samuel Otter argues that Webb undermines his effort to acclaim black women's workaday labors with a character such as Caddy because of the kind of comedy she enacts. Otter writes, "Caddy's dignity is often undercut by the slapstick comedy that accompanies her efforts."[42] After she prepares the parlor for the unexpected and soon-to-arrive visitors, for example, she notices a "beggar boy" drawing on the recently scrubbed front doorsteps with charcoal. "Choked with wrath at the sight of the steps," she chases after the boy with a broom but ends up knocking one of the visitors in the head instead. Otter reads these sorts of encounters, which recur in the novel, as Webb's staging of the "thin line between decorum and pratfall."[43] Notwithstanding the fragility of bourgeois social graces and all of Caddy's slapstick, her care practice is never disparaged but always deemed essential and generative. Her investments in others' personal needs and the common good provide refuge from a brutal world while making space for them to reimagine that world anew. Comedy, silliness, laughing, and other forms of pleasure are not inherently impediments to the creation of a new and better world but can help make it possible.

During the anti-abolitionist riot, Caddy uses her domestic savvy to save the lives of her family and friends. They had taken refuge in Mr. Walters's home to escape the mob and its weaponry, which included gunfire. At one point some rioters use "axes [to] work upon the door";

"if they are not dislodged, they'll cut their way in," exclaimed one of the young men inside. "The stones are exhausted," he continued, "and I don't know what we shall do" to keep them out.[44] With no way to slow down the intruders, Caddy comes to the rescue. Webb writes:

> Just then a splash a water was heard, followed by shrieks of agony. "Oh, God! I'm scalded! I'm scalded!" cried one of the men upon the steps. "Take me away! take me away!" In the midst of his cries another volume of scalding water came pouring down upon the group at the door, which was followed by a rush from the premises. "What is that—who could have that—where has that water come from?" asked Mr. Walters [an Ellis family friend], as he saw the seething shower pass the window, and fall upon the heads below. "I must go and see." He ran upstairs, and found [Charlie's best friend] Kinch and Caddy busy putting on more water, they having exhausted one kettle-full—into which they had put two or three pounds of cayenne pepper—on the heads of the crowd below. "We gave 'em a settler, didn't we, Mr. Walters?" asked Caddy, as he entered the room. "It takes us; we fight with hot water. This," said she, holding up a dipper, "is my gun. I guess we made 'em squeal."[45]

Basic objects for the home stave off the mob; hot water was the basis for all sorts of healing and cleansing activities, and cayenne pepper was used for poultices and to treat all sorts of internal ailments, especially stomach pains. Where the "hard" stones fail, the "soft" objects of domestic care succeed. Caddy's heroics amid the gravity of the riot scene undermine Otter's claim that slapstick "undercuts" her dignity. Otter never explains how comedy, physical or otherwise, attenuates or lessens one's value as a political actor.

Neither Caddy nor any other black character in *The Garies* comports to the minstrel form or its logics, as one would expect given the popular cultural contexts of the late 1850s. Blackface minstrelsy haunted all forms of African American public culture in the era, especially objects and texts like *The Garies* that dealt with social manners.[46] The closest intimation of minstrelsy in a black character is the mischievous and always "dirty" Kinch, who spends much of the novel looking to play marbles or to get into some sort of adolescent rogueries. Even then, his ingenuity is what keeps the mob from breaching Mr. Walters's home. He devises and rigs the mechanism that delivers the cayenne-pepper-infused hot water on the invaders' heads: "'Look at this,' replied Caddy, fitting a broom handle into the end of a very large tin dipper. 'Kinch cut this to fit; so we have nothing to do but to stand back here, dip up the water, and let them have it; the length of the handle keeps us from being seen from the street. That was Kinch's plan.'" Kinch invents Caddy's water dipper "gun," as she calls it.[47] Their homespun contraption made of everyday objects signifies Webb's insistence that the caring home, more so than the revolutionary's battlefield or the orator's platform, is ground zero for the realization of black self-determination and democratic forms of life.

In the novel's dénouement, we learn that Mrs. Walters restored the room in which they "made so brave a defense" against the rioters. There are "no reminiscences of that desperate attack ... save that bullet-hole in the ceiling, which Mr. Walters declares shall remain unfilled as an evidence of the marked attention he has received at the hands of his fellow-citizens."[48] Handsome new furniture, children's clothing, and a grand piano adorn the space. On the wall there are now two paintings. Next to Louverture's is the new portrait, "which no doubt holds a higher position in the regard of the owner of the mansion than the African warrior aforesaid."[49] It depicts "a likeness of the lady who is sitting at the window,—Mrs. Esther Walters, *nee* Ellis. The brown baby in the picture is the little girl at her side,—the elder sister of the other brown baby who is doing its best to pull from its mother's lap the doll's dress upon which she is sewing."[50] The political drive of the novel culminates in this reveal: revolutionary violence must be complemented and ultimately supplanted with caring home lives to achieve lasting freedom and self-government, especially for minoritarian populations. Like other nineteenth-century black nationalists, Webb believed that domestic behaviors, habits, and proprieties determined racial destiny. He championed careful family planning as the lodestar of African American political life: physical force (figured as masculine in Louverture's portrait) without domesticity (figured as feminine in the Walters family portrait) is counterproductive and self-defeating.

The most common way critics have dealt with Webb's refusal to esteem armed struggle is to claim the novel posits financial power as African Americans' base for achieving their political objectives. They adduce the relative power Mr. Walters wields as one of the wealthiest men in the city. He is "worth half a million of dollars," owns some "one hundred brick houses," and holds "ten thousand dollars' worth of stock" in a railroad company.[51] His wealth along with the novel's affirming scenes of middle-class lifeways has prompted many critics to judge *The Garies* as an early apologia for a black American bourgeoisie, a Talented Tenth *avant la lettre* whose money and behavioral codes of conduct will lead the masses of African Americans to freedom and citizenship. Writing a few years after the novel's 1969 re-release and first publication in the US, amid the headiness of the Black Power/Black Arts Era, Addison Gayle called *The Garies* a "manifesto for the Black middle class." He describes Webb's novel as a reflection of "too many Afro-Americans" who aimed "to become white by one formula or another." In his reading *The Garies* prefigured a doomed project—as he put it, "Black man can never approach the image vouchsafed by white Americans"—that culminated in an "impasse of division and internecine warfare and prevented us from embarking upon a truly revolutionary course."[52] Gayle's argument exemplifies this still dominant critical view that *The Garies* espouses capitalist assimilationism as the cure for American racism.

This argument is not an altogether untenable one, especially by way of Black Power-era interpretative protocols. George Stevens seems to say so plainly in the novel when he tells his wife, "I tell you what, Jule, if I was a black ... living in a country like this, I'd sacrifice conscience and everything else to the acquisition of wealth."[53] But he is the main villain of *The Garies*: why would Webb express one of the novel's main political arguments in Stevens's voice? Further, the pursuit of financial accumulation is the source of the characters' greatest calamities, especially the anti-abolitionist race riot and the deaths of Clarence and Emily Garie and their unborn child. Russell Sbriglia reads these events as narrative figures of "the novel's Marxian preoccupation with exposing racial prejudice as little more than the ideological mystification of class conflict within an allegedly classless society—a preoccupation that renders it a prescient work of ideology critique."[54] I argue that Webb regarded African Americans' distinctiveness as black persons as their greatest weapon in class conflict because they are treated as a class ("niggers") regardless of whatever economic goods they hold. *The Garies* does not champion "green power" or money but deems it a chimera for African Americans and shaky political ground upon which to build a politics.[55] Rather, the novel champions forms of black power that emerge from practices of loving care that extends across lines of difference, economic or otherwise, *within* the race. Bell, Gayle, and similarly minded critics do not recognize this sort of black power because it is never bellicose but deeply tender, never vanguardist but thoroughly relational.

THE "FATAL OBJECTION": WORK, EDUCATION, AND BLACKNESS

Relationality, the notion that what happens to one person in a group shapes what happens to the many in that group, has been a longstanding tenet of black feminist political philosophy. In its most democratic formulations, relationality rejects crude identitarianism in favor of structures of belonging that embrace differences of all sorts. Intragroup difference and care defines black life in *The Garies*. At every turn and from every direction African Americans come to each other's aid. The ingenuity of the urchin Kinch and the fussy Caddy saves the wealthy aesthete Mr. Walters and his home; Charles Ellis nearly loses his life to rescue the Garies whom he had just met; and Mr. Walters works to restore the legacies of the orphaned Garie children. In such moments there are no stipulations that the party who receives aid must sacrifice or compromise his or her particularity to receive it. For Webb, a liberatory relationality must stand on reciprocities of care that respect difference in all its strangeness, entanglements, and intensities. This is a form of political life that, as Jack Turner writes, "figures the self as relational, as individualized through complex, dialogical interaction" that can only be called "democratic."[56] This way of living with others in public is equality embodied, a collapsing of the gap between the weak and the strong by way of loving attachments of care that are without condition, treachery, or self-interest.

Relationality is the most enduring paradigmatic touchstone critics use to gauge black life, albeit most often in the concept's negative formulation: one bad apple spoils the bunch. Crime, vagrancy, "broken families," and other so-called social pathologies traditionally regarded as endemic to black culture are what commonly frame condemnations of black people *en masse* in mainstream American discourse. Within the nineteenth-century black public sphere, African Americans' menial employments were regularly scorned for how they reflected poorly on the group. The problem was less the nature of a job *per se* than one's seeming contentedness with it. In his *Appeal to the Colored Citizens of the World*

(1829), David Walker blasted such complacency in a vignette about a bootblack he met in the street. He writes:

> I said to him, what a miserable set of people we are! He asked, why?—Said I, we are so subjected under the whites, that we cannot obtain the comforts of life, but by cleaning their boots and shoes, old clothes, waiting on them, shaving them &c. Said he, (with the boots on his shoulders) "I am completely happy!!! I never want to live any better or happier than when I can get a plenty of boots and shoes to clean!!!" Oh! how can those who are actuated by avarice only, but think, that our Creator made us to be an inheritance to them forever, when they see that our greatest glory is centered in such mean and low objects? Understand me, brethren, I do not mean to speak against the occupations by which we acquire enough and sometimes scarcely that, to render ourselves and families comfortable through life. I am subjected to the same inconvenience, as you all.—My objections are, to our *glorying* and being *happy* in such low employments; for if we are men, we ought to be thankful to the Lord for the past, and for the future. Be looking forward with thankful hearts to higher attainments than *wielding the razor* and *cleaning boots and shoes*. The man whose aspirations are not *above*, and even *below* these, is indeed, ignorant and wretched enough.[57]

At the time of Walker's writing, chattel slavery was virtually nonexistent in Northern states because of a spate of gradual emancipation measures enacted in the late eighteenth century. Yet formerly enslaved persons and their descendants had few prospects for work outside the drudgery and service they performed while enslaved. Walker recognized the realities of racialized American labor markets, admitting he was subject "to the same inconvenience," but decried any lack of interest in "higher attainments" among black persons. He deemed this mentality a relic of slavery and a hindrance to black liberation and human flourishing—and African Americans were the ones responsible for its destruction. He argued that the bootblack's state of mind had not only economic consequences but also psychological and corporeal ramifications for black persons: their "greatest happiness" will stem from destroying that mindset and will lead to the "salvation of our whole body."[58]

Walker also denounced black persons who were satisfied with receiving the most meager education. He follows his anecdote about the bootblack with another about a conversation he had with an "elderly coloured man on the topics of education, and of the great prevalency [sic] of ignorance among us."[59] According to Walker, the man said

> "I know that our people are very ignorant but my son has a good education: I spent a great deal of money on his education: he can write as well as any white man, and I assure you that no one can fool him," &c. Said I, what else can your son do, besides writing a good hand? Can he post a set of books in a mercantile manner? Can he write a neat piece of composition in prose or in verse? To these interogations [sic] he answered in the negative. Said I, did your son learn, while he was at school, the width and depth of English Grammar? To which he also replied in the negative, telling me his son did not learn those things. Your son, said I, then, has hardly any learning at all—he is almost as ignorant, and more so, than many of those who never went to school one day in all their lives. . . . Most of the coloured people, when they speak of the education of one among us who can write a neat hand, and who perhaps knows nothing but to scribble and puff pretty fair on a small scrap of paper, immaterial whether his words are grammatical, or spelt correctly, or not; if it only looks beautiful, they say he has as good an education as any white man—he can write as well as any white man . . . I pray that the Lord may undeceive my ignorant brethren, and permit them to throw away pretensions, and seek after the substance of learning.[60]

Walker was ruthless in his rebukes of African Americans whom he deemed too pleased with bare minimums, especially in education. He was a leading proponent of the view that education was more than an avenue toward personal fulfillment: it was a weapon against the intellectual and cultural habits that fueled chattel slavery and its regimes in post-slavery societies. "For colored people to acquire learning in this country, makes tyrants quake and tremble on their sandy foundation," he writes. "Why, what is the matter? Why, they know that their infernal deeds of cruelty will be made known to the world."[61] Walker argued that an educated black populace would develop the discursive protocols to unmask the sophistry that bolsters white supremacist violence and hegemonies.

In the 1850s, education and work were two of the most pressing matters for black nationalists and political thinkers. Their convention minutes, newspapers, literature, and oratory form a robust archive on the perplexities of African Americans' aspirations for higher education and better employment in a world that afforded them virtually no opportunity to cultivate a life of the mind or earn what we now call a living wage. Webb narrativized this predicament in *The Garies* in Charlie Ellis's storyline. Early in the novel, we learn that Charlie is a "bright-faced pretty boy" who is a "favourite with both tutors and scholars." He is thirteen years old, on the brink of high school. His father "intends [on] sending him to another school ... where they teach Latin and Greek, and a number of other branches."[62] When Charlie's mother relates this plan to Mrs. Thomas, a wealthy white scion of one of the city's most famous families for whom she does sewing jobs, Mrs. Thomas scoffs: "What use can Latin or Greek be to a coloured boy? None in the world—he'll have to be a common mechanic, or, perhaps, a servant, or barber, or something of that kind, and then what use would all his fine education be to him?" She then goes on to say that Charlie should "come and live with [me] awhile" to work as a servant. Not only will the Ellises get the extra income, but Charlie will "be learning something," Mrs. Thomas explains, "good manners, &c.... [T]here is something everyone learns by coming in daily contact with reined and educated people that cannot but be beneficial." Both strands of David Walker's critique regarding black education and employment are represented here in her call for Charlie to end his studies to serve her household as a degraded factotum.

Much to Charlie's disgust, his parents agree to the arrangement. "I won't live at service—I'd rather be a sweep, or sell apples on the dock," he says. "I'm not going to be stuck up behind their carriage, dressed up like a monkey in a tailcoat—I'll cut off my own head first."[63] Charlie's indignation marks Webb's critique of African Americans who suppressed their intellectual prospects for work, money, or others' benefit. Like Walker, he placed much of the blame on a tradition of submission to white authority passed down from one generation to the next. In *The Garies*, Mrs. Ellis adduces her own service to Mrs. Thomas to justify Charlie taking the job. One of the rallying cries of antebellum black nationalism was that African Americans, especially younger ones, must end this cycle of service to white persons because it entrenches black subjection and second-class citizenship. According to Webb, ending the cycling or helping those who do is an act of radical care for oneself and the black race.

The Ellises come to understand that they must remove Charlie from Mrs. Thomas's home if they hope to nourish his talents. Proximity to white culture and acquiring civility by a kind of osmosis is not the salutary social pedagogy Mrs. Thomas promises, because it is a stifling and stultifying paternalism. A dinner party scene at her home with guests that include the Belgian chargé d'affaires and members of the First Families of Virginia dramatizes this judgment. Charlie is a waiter for the event. He becomes engrossed in the guests' "animated discussion" about "the antiquity of the use of salad." A minister "whose remarks respecting the intelligence of the children of Ham had been particularly disparaging" claims that "nowhere in Chaucer, Spencer, nor any of the old English poets could anything relating to it be found." Charlie knows that is wrong, so he retrieves a collection of Chaucer's poetry. He shows them where the poem "The Flower and the Leaf" mentions salad, humiliating the "reverend gentleman" much to everyone else's delight. Amid the laughter the Belgian minister says, "Ah . . . the child of Ham know more than the child of Shem, dis time."[64] His minstrelization, which marks the global traffics of blackface minstrelsy in the era, obscures Charlie's learning and intellect: it is an insult. The Belgian diplomat's racist quip turns Charlie into a curiosity, a human party trick, that restores the racial hierarchy that Charlie dared to topple by correcting the minister's literary error. For black knowledge production to be anything other than a divertissement, the scene suggests, black persons must hone their capacities within social settings among interlocutors that respect their capacities as equal to those of all others.

If one reads *The Garies* as a manifesto of black capitalism, the novel's portrayal of Charlie's service to Mrs. Thomas gives the impression that there are employments so beneath contempt that African Americans must reject them out of hand. But Webb is quite careful not to denigrate black labor of any sort. The problem that he (and black nationalists generally) saw were the relationships that black workers had to endure as workers, that they had to tolerate some of the same abuses and exploitations to which they were subjected while enslaved. These relationships invigorated those structures of feeling that bolstered the prevailing proposition that black inferiority is constitutive of the American project. In *The Garies*, Mr. Walters lays out this view in his response to Charlie's service to Mrs. Thomas: "Well, don't let him stay there. A great many white people think that we are only fit for servants, and I must confess we do much to strengthen the opinion by permitting our children to occupy such situations when we are not in circumstances to compel us to do so.... It is impossible to have the same respect for the man who cleans your boots, that you have for the man who plans and builds your house." Charlie's work "begets a feeling of dependence," Mr. Walters says, and that "will spoil him for anything better all his days."[65] Black nationalists argued that the humiliation and dejection typical of black working conditions were violations of personal dignity that preclude individual and communal growth—and African Americans must take care to separate themselves from such conditions.

Mr. Walters wants African Americans to treat their children and young people the way white Americans do theirs. "If you can't get on without the boy's earning something, why don't you do as white women and men do? Do you ever find them sending their boys out as servants?" he asks. "No, they rather give them a stock of matches, blacking, newspapers, or apples, and start them out to sell them. What is the result? The boy that learns to sell matches soon learns to sell other things; he learns to make bargains, he becomes a small trader, then a merchant, then a millionaire. Did you ever hear of anyone who had made a fortune at service?"[66] These sorts of contentions are fodder for critics who read *The Garies* as a call for "green power" to bring about black political power. But the novel's general critique of capital and its insistence on cross-class solidarity suggests Mr. Walters's comments are more rhetorical and suggestive than determinative and expectational. The idea is not that African Americans must strive to become millionaires, a feat all but impossible then and barely possible now, but that they should seek out pathways that allow them to be as audacious and venturesome in their pursuits as possible.

In the mid-1830s, when most of the action of *The Garies* takes place, Pennsylvania legislators limited the franchise to "white freemen" in the state constitution, citing black labor to justify the move.[67] In constitutional convention debates, proponents grounded their arguments about blacks' capacities as workers in the logics of antebellum race science:

Whether negroes are a different species from the white man, and only a link in the chain of being, connecting the white race with some one of inferior rank to themselves, has not been settled by philosophers and naturalists. The God of nature has made them a distinct, inferior caste, and placed a mark on them too visible to be disregarded. . . . We see them engaged in no business that requires even ordinary capacity; in no enterprises requiring talents to conduct them. The mass are improvident, and seek the lowest avocations, and most menial stations.[68]

These sorts of arguments left out, usually intentionally, the fact that black workers were almost always barred from acquiring skilled or professional employments and were regularly denied apprenticeships, training, and credit. Black nationalists argued the only way to disrupt this cycle was for African Americans to cultivate their own entities and institutions.

Compounding their problems was the influx of roughly five million immigrants from western and northern Europe who fought African Americans in the labor market from the 1830s through the Civil War era. The historian Leon Litwack notes that "the Irish immigrant did not immediately displace the Negro laborer" because employers continued to prefer "Negro 'humility' to Irish 'turbulence.'"[69] On one hand, black "humility" was the problem that black nationalists hoped to solve. On the other, escalating antiblack animus and terror over the course of these several decades made the Irish the preferred workforce in Northern cities for even the most menial of jobs. In the mid-1850s, Frederick Douglass pressed on the irony of these developments to appeal for new directions in black employment. In one of his most sociologically penetrating editorials of the era, "Learn Trades or Starve!" (1854), Douglass wrote:

> Employments and callings formerly monopolized by us, are so no longer. White men are becoming house-servants, cooks and stewards on vessels—at hotels.—They are becoming porters, stevedores, wood-sawyers, hod-carriers, brick-makers, white-washers and barbers, so that the blacks can scarcely find the means of subsistence—a few years ago, and a white barber would have been a curiosity—now their poles stand on every street. Formerly blacks were almost the exclusive coachmen in wealthy families: this is no longer; white men are now employed, and for aught we see, they fill their servile station with an obsequiousness as profound as that of the blacks. The readiness and ease with which they adapt themselves to these conditions ought not to be lost sight of by the colored people.[70]

As the Irish came to dominate the service industry in cities such as Philadelphia and New York, Douglass called on black people to learn trades because they will "provide the means of our elevation."[71] He closes the editorial with a plea to anti-slavery tradesmen to apprentice and train African Americans because such efforts were necessary for their survival. "One thing is certain," Douglass proclaimed, "we must find new methods of obtaining a livelihood, for the old ones are failing us very fast."[72]

In Charlie, Webb creates a character with the skills to out-compete white workers but whose blackness undercuts his qualifications. After their father's accident, Charlie and his sisters decide to get better paying work to help the family. He finds job postings in the newspapers for cooks, chambermaids, waiters, milliners, footmen, and mechanics. With none of these jobs fit for a boy his age and with his training, he finds a notice for a position that suits his talents: "Wanted, a youth of about thirteen years of age who writes a good hand, and is willing to make himself useful in an office.—Address, Box No. 77, Post-office."[73] Charlie jumps at the opportunity—"I'm their man!"—and his fine script in his application letter wins him an interview. When he arrives at the firm's offices, its owners turn skeptical that it is Charlie's handwriting and ask him to write something on the spot. Satisfied, they debate among themselves whether they can bring him on. "'Engage *him*!' exclaimed Twining [one of the owners]—'why, you surprise me, Western—the thing's absurd; engage a coloured boy as under clerk! I never heard of such a thing.'" Mr. Western, his partner from New Orleans, responds, "Well, I must say you Northern people are perfectly incompwenhensible. You pay taxes to have niggers educated, and made fit for such places—and then won't let them fill them when they are pwepared to do so."[74] He then breaks the news to Esther with Charlie standing by, "I should like to take your brother very much; but you see, in consequence of there being so much excitement just now, relative to Abolitionism and kindred subjects, that my partner and myself [feel] just now it would be rather awkward for us to receive him. We should like to take him; but his *colour*, miss—his complexion is a *fatal* objection."[75] In antebellum America race over talent and skill was the order of the day. For Webb, black people could not abolish this social practice from the inside but had to create entities and systems of their own.

Douglass came to a similar conclusion when he argued that America's racial hierarchy rendered higher education virtually worthless for

African Americans. In "Learn Trades or Starve!" he writes: "If the alternative were presented to us of learning a trade or of getting an education, we would learn the trade, for the reason, that with the trade we could get the education, while with the education we could not get the trade.... An educated colored man, in the United States, unless he has within him the heart of a hero, and is willing to engage in a life-long battle for his rights, as a man, finds few inducements to remain in this country."[76] The respective merits and comparative advantages of a technical training as opposed to a liberal education galvanized the antebellum black public sphere. Douglass believed the trades would deliver black men and women from drudgery while supplying them with the skills to build their own communities. He called on black and white anti-slavery tradesmen to hire young African Americans as apprentices to spearhead the process. "What BOSS anti-slavery mechanic will take a black boy into his wheelwright's shop, his blacksmith's shop, his joiner's shop, his cabinet shop?" Douglass asked. "Here is something *practical*; where are the whites and where are the blacks that will respond to it? Where are the anti-slavery milliners and seamstresses that will take colored girls and teach them trades, by which they can obtain an honorable living?"[77]

Webb agreed with Douglass that black tradesmen had a responsibility to take on African Americans as apprentices but doubted the viability of white tradesmen in that venture. In *The Garies*, Charlie applies to apprentice with a white bank engraver named Thomas Blatchford, a well-known abolitionist in the city. Impressed with Charlie's portfolio, Blatchford decides to hire him, but his white employees and apprentices refuse to accept it. "We won't work with niggers!" the workmen declare. "No nigger apprentices!" "Why sir," one explains, "the men and boys discovered that you intended to take a nigger apprentice, and have made up their minds if you do they will quit in a body." Blatchford tries to plea with the men by showing them Charlie's portfolio and pointing out his social temperament, but to no avail. "'Damn his behaviour and education!' responded one fellow; 'let him be a barber or shoe-black—that is all niggers are good for. If he comes, we go—that's so, ain't it, boys?'"[78] (As Douglass pointed out in "Learn Trades or Starve!" even these professions were increasingly hard for African Americans to come by.) Blatchford refuses to stand on his principles but succumbs to what is essentially mob pressure, firing Charlie. "'All because I'm coloured,' said he, bitterly, to himself—'all because I'm coloured!'"[79]

Such scenes did not discourage Webb from pushing African Americans to obtain technical skills or higher education, but they proved to him the necessity of black governance in those pursuits. When Webb published *The Garies*, Philadelphia's public schools were segregated. There were no black high schools and younger African Americans were split between nine all-black public schools and private schools run by churches and benevolent societies.[80] An African American boy like Charlie would have had to find a high school outside the city. In the novel, a white benefactor named Mrs. Bird tries to get Charlie admitted to a prestigious high school in New England. She takes an interest in him after witnessing his dazzling performance during academic exercises at his school. After an injury to Charlie's arm, Mrs. Bird invites him to convalesce at her country home. Webb's Mrs. Bird is an allusion to Mrs. Bird in Harriet Beecher Stowe's *Uncle Tom's Cabin* (1852). Stowe's Mrs. Bird helps her US senator husband to see the moral rot of the Fugitive Slave Law of 1850 and together they help Eliza and her son Harry in their flight from slavery. Both characters represent the sympathetic, virtuous white female benefactor figure around whom so much abolitionist discourse was organized. Mrs. Bird's goodwill in Stowe's novel is both morally lucid and practically triumphant: Eliza and Harry make it to freedom. But Mrs. Bird's goodwill in *The Garies* reaches its limits and fails in the face of antiblack animus. After she enlists her connections at Warmouth Academy to get Charlie admitted, the board rejects his application because no one can make Mrs. Bird's "*protégé* a shade whiter."[81] She plots to find other ways to advance Charlie's education, but the racist slights he endures and news of his father's brutal maiming during the race riot convince him to leave Warmouth for good, despite its relative comforts. "'No, no, Mrs. Bird, I mustn't stay; it wouldn't be right for me to remain here, idle and enjoying myself, and they so poor and unhappy at home. I couldn't stay,'" he says. "'I must go.'"[82] Charlie once and for all spurns white assistance because, in the political logic of the novel, it ultimately undermines black liberation. In this moment, he embraces responsibility for his personal uplift, that of his family, and that of his community: it is the climax of the political narrative that shapes *The Garies*.

The Garies argues that to care for black children is to keep them away from white supervision, especially as workers and students. Webb never doubted the structural limitations that hampered African Americans' ability to create their own organizations and institutions, but he aimed to create a world in which black people live lives of full self-determination. At the core of his aspirations, and of black nationalism generally, is the eradication of what David Walker called "our wretchedness in consequence of ignorance," which white systems and social infrastructures engender and perpetuate.[83] Everything Webb wanted African Americans to build would prioritize care for black people while spurning the vicious hierarchies that corrupted American ideals and democratic forms of life. Webb narrativizes practices of care in the home, workplace, and school that he regards as foundational to the formation of a public built on relationality and thus love for the weak, wounded, and humiliated—the only sort of public that the politics of slave morality holds is worth living in.

Epilogue: "We're Not a Democracy"

Sometime during my junior or senior year of high school, a few friends and I were debating some aspect of American political history. I cannot remember any of the specifics of our arguments, but I do recall that at an especially heated moment Lionel, the cleverest of us all, said, "We're not a democracy." His pronouncement stopped the conversation cold. He explained that the United States is not a democracy because it is a constitutional republic. Lionel's ostensible distinction impressed us, and we were not quick enough on our feet to call out the definitional conflation upon which his claim rests. He was talking about a direct democracy in which citizens vote on policy measures, but this is only one form of democratic governance; a constitutional republic such as ours is another. Whatever shape a democratic polity takes, sovereign power is vested in the people. Lionel neglected this basic fact about democracies, and I wish I had pointed it out in the moment: it would have been one of only a handful of times I outwitted him.

Over the last five years, the claim that the US is not a democracy has become ubiquitous in our political discourse. One regularly encounters it in online debate forums with everyday citizens, or in conservative think pieces, or in official pronouncements of elected officials in the highest ranks of government. About a month before the 2020 presidential election, for example, US Senator Mike Lee, a Republican from Utah, tweeted "We're not a democracy."[1] After backlash in legacy and social media, Lee penned a short essay explaining his tweet. He wrote:

> Insofar as "democracy" means "a political system in which government derives its powers from the consent of the governed," then of

> course that accurately describes our system. But the word conjures far more than that. It is often used to describe rule by majority, the view that it is the prerogative of government to reflexively carry out the will of the majority of its citizens.
>
> Our system of government is best described as a constitutional republic. Power is not found in mere majorities, but in carefully balanced power.... As I said in a follow-up Tweet, democracy itself is not the goal. The goal is freedom, prosperity, and human flourishing. Democratic principles have proven essential to those goals, but only as part of a system of checks and balances among the executive, legislative, and judicial branches of the federal government, as well as between the federal government and the states.

Lee reveals his hand here: he admits that the term democracy "accurately describes our system," but decides to anchor his argument on a more colloquial meaning of "rule by majority" of citizens—a meaning that all too conveniently confirms his biases. Lee extols the nation's juridical and administrative mechanisms as a "system of checks and balances" (e.g., the way the Supreme Court's role of judicial review checks the power of the other two branches), which he regards as something other than democratic. He argues that it is only because of this system that "Americans' individual rights and cultural diversity [are] given their proper position atop our political order, over and above even majority will."[2] The problem with Lee's argument is that this system, as a collection of normative entities, is in fact democratic because it operates by way of the people's consent through their elected representatives. Liberal fulminations against the current Supreme Court notwithstanding, I have yet to encounter a compelling argument that the *institution* of the high court is antidemocratic.

Why, then, is Lee so preoccupied with delineating technical distinctions built on a faulty premise? I argue that his explanations distract readers from his main objective: to besmirch democracy itself. There are two ways Lee and his conservative allies hope this effort takes shape. The first is nothing more than rank party politics. It aims to make "democracy" such a dirty word that it becomes a smear for the Democratic Party, its values, and the policies it espouses. All manner of supposedly anti-American leftist ideologies, from communism and open borders to globalism and "wokeism," fall within its semantic field. By implication, *republic* becomes the signifier for all that is good in the American project, and the Republican Party becomes the conduit and protector of those goods. By virtue of this word game and its twisted logics, Lee and his fellow Republican officials become a chosen people tasked with leading the nation and the only legitimate keepers of the American polity.

The other outcome conservatives seek when they stigmatize democracy is a public rejection of equitable distribution of power across the polity, especially among minoritarian subjects such as the descendants of enslaved persons. This project coalesced in the mid-1950s, when antidemocratic discourse began to structure protestations against communism, integration, secularity, and civil rights for African Americans. Herman Talmadge, the segregationist governor and US senator from Georgia, instantiated this rhetoric in his 1955 screed, *You and Segregation*. He writes:

> Could it be possible that these Americans, who talk and write so much about "our democracy" do not know that this nation is a republic and not a democracy?
>
> Could it be that they desire a gradual overthrow of our republic and the establishment of a "democracy" as is advocated by the Communists and fellow-travelers?
>
> Could it be that these groups desire a "democracy" here in the United States where they will be only one race, one religion and one state?
>
> It is evident that many of this group believe only in one mixed, amalgamated race; the anti-God Marxist religion; and one all-powerful central government not segregated by state lines or Constitutional barriers. This is obviously the "true democracy" they talk, write about and proclaim so brashly.[3]

Talmadge's greatest fear regarding democracy is that it might cripple white supremacy, notwithstanding his Red-Scare-laced Christian nationalism. Nothing concerned him more than democracy's ability to hinder the entrenchment and expansion of Jim Crowism in American life.

A few years after Talmadge published *You and Segregation*, the notorious far right-wing John Birch Society (JBS) was founded on the principle that democracy is the "footstool of tyrants."[4] JBS regarded the acclaim for democracy in postwar liberal discourse a telltale sign of an insidious, anti-American ruse aimed at destroying the country, plotted by enemies from within.

> Liberals have been working so long and so hard to convert our republic into a democracy, and to make the American people believe that it is <u>supposed to be a democracy</u>.... Our founding fathers knew a great deal about history and government, and they had very nearly a clean slate on which to write the blueprint for our own. They gave us a republic because they considered it the best of all forms of government. They visibly spurned a democracy as probably the worst of all forms of government. But our past history and our present danger indicate that they were right in both particulars.[5]

JBS inspired conservatives to organize their politics around the notion that democracy violates the American credo. Its crafty rhetoric about the American founding, democracy, and republicanism subsumed the Jim Crowism of more outspoken segregationists: that is, they aimed to undermine the democratic aims of African Americans' struggle for citizenship, social inclusion, and the end of race-based domination.[6]

The "we're a republic, not a democracy" mantra from right-wing organizations and thinkers in the second half of the 1950s reached an apotheosis with Arizona Senator Barry Goldwater's ascent to the top of the Republican Party in 1964. Goldwater was the intellectual godhead who resuscitated the conservative movement in the early 1960s. In his *The Conscience of a Conservative* (1960), the single most important text for right-wing activists and intelligentsia over the second half of the twentieth century, Goldwater writes that the system the "framers created" is "hardly" a democracy. Adducing Alexis de Tocqueville's political sociology, he argues that collective "decay" is more assured for those societies that "tended to put more emphasis on its democracy than on its republicanism."[7] Goldwater won the Republican nomination for the presidency in 1964, running on a platform that called for rolling back the landmark Civil Rights Act that became law earlier that year. "While not himself a racist," Martin Luther King Jr. said, "Mr. Goldwater articulates a philosophy which gives aid and comfort to the racists."[8] At his nominating convention, "Republic, not a Democracy!" was a constant refrain among the delegates. This chant reflected King's assessment of Goldwater's political thought, especially the senator's views on democracy.

As the calamities of the war in Vietnam multiplied and the Cold War intensified, conservative thinkers came to embrace democracy as the watchword of American ideals on the global stage. President Ronald Reagan extolled democracy to vilify communism and the Soviet Union, and President George W. Bush touted exporting democracy to nations in the Middle East as a major plank of the so-called War on Terror. Yet over the past decade there has been a resurgence of antidemocratic discourse in conservative thought. Some of this change is internal to the Right's intellectual currents and foreign policies; the steady marginalization of the Reagan (i.e., Russophobia) and Bush (i.e., neoconservative adventurism) doctrines has rendered democratic talk largely nugatory in how conservatives approach global affairs. Yet I understand the reemergence of "we're a republic, not a democracy" in both elite and common parlance on the American right as more of a response to something external: recent protest movements against police brutality and other manifestations of our so-called "racial reckoning." Thus when Senator Lee tweeted "we're not a democracy" in October 2020, I read his statement in the context of the deeply contentious battle for the meaning of American history in that moment that continues to play out today.

One of the most curious, often frustrating fronts in that battle concerns the condition and quality of black American life during Jim Crow. There has been a marked rise in sentiment among African Americans, especially on social media in right-wing enclaves, that their ancestors' lives were better under Jim Crow than black life is today. They cite racial solidarity, group economics among African Americans, and stronger familial structures—colloquially, the black community was "on code" in the period. One of their most common refrains is that during Jim Crow the black family was more intact because there were higher marriage rates and fewer black children were born to single mothers. They believe that a return to the black family structure under Jim Crow is the first step toward solving the ills of black America. All data concerning the material conditions of African Americans, let alone the regime of terror they endured and the exigencies it occasioned, barely moderates what one sociologist calls "Jim Crow nostalgia."[9]

Byron Donalds, the black Republican congressman from Florida, has been the most prominent advocate of this call to return to the black family of the Jim Crow era. Donalds argues that African Americans must embrace conservatism to make this return because he views conservativism as their natural political-philosophical orientation. During a 2024 campaign stop he said, "You see, during Jim Crow, the black family was together. During Jim Crow, more black people were not just conservative—black people have always been conservative-minded, more black people voted conservatively."[10] The backlash to Donalds's comments was fierce, causing him to make clear that he does not in any way support Jim Crow regimes. But his citation of the black familial life and black political conservatism during Jim Crow—and it bears noting that Donalds' understanding of the history of black families is simplistic and he is flat out wrong about African Americans' electoral history—throws another of his favorite mantras into relief: "We're a republic, not a democracy."

Donalds's rhetoric recalls the antidemocratic discourse and the segregationist ideology at the core of modern conservatism. Such discourse registers the most recent attempt to blunt the diffusion of power across the polity, especially to the weak and the most vulnerable. "We're a republic, not a democracy" marks obstructions to the legacy that the primary subjects of this book embodied, espoused, and passed on to their descendants. Their commitment to polities organized by democratic cultures threatens conservatism. Although conservatives home in on the technicalities of democracies vs. republics and the "tyranny" of majority rule, their discourse is born of, and perpetuates, efforts to keep political power out of the hands of the powerless. When one hears "we're a republic, not a democracy," he or she should always know that this is the project afoot: to quash slave morality once and for all.

Acknowledgments

I thank my editor, Alan Thomas, and his assistant, Randolph Petilos, of the University of Chicago Press. At every stage of this project, Alan's stewardship and Randy's support were vital.

*

Portions of the introduction appeared as "Pragmatics of Democracy: A Political Theory of African American Literature before Emancipation," *American Literary History* 33, no. 3 (2021): 498–509, © Douglas A. Jones 2021, published by Oxford University Press, all rights reserved (https://doi.org/10.1093/alh/ajab046). Portions of chapter 1 were adapted from "Slave Evangelicalism, Shouting, and the Beginning of African American Writing," *Early American Literature* 51, no. 3 (2018): 69–85, used by permission of the University of North Carolina Press (www.uncpress.org). Portions of chapter 2 were adapted from "Douglass' Impersonal," *ESQ: A Journal of Nineteenth-Century Literature and Culture* 61, no. 1 (2015): 1–35, © 2024 by the Board of Regents of Washington State University.

Notes

INTRODUCTION

1. Richard Price, *Observations on the Nature of Civil Liberty, the Principles of Government, and the Justice and Policy of the War with America* (1776), https://catalog.hathitrust.org/Record/002379668.
2. Declaratory Act, 1766, 6 Geo. 3, c. 12. Price does not quote the language of the act exactly, but adds or loses nothing in doing so.
3. Richard Price, *Observations on the Nature of Civil Liberty, the Principles of Government, and the Justice and Policy of the War with America* (London: T. Cadell, 1776), 34.
4. Price, 19.
5. "The Petition of a great number of Negroes who are detained in a state of Slavery" (1777), in James G. Basker, ed., *Black Writers of the Founding Era* (New York: Library of America, 2023), 153. This petition was one of several that enslaved and free black persons in Massachusetts sent to their legislature in the 1770s. It was also the first such petition to any state (or rather, colonial) government in America. These petitions and cognate texts in the era initiated a discourse against the idea that nature fits some persons to be enslaved. Although Americans rarely cited or even alluded to Aristotle, they did formulate versions of his idea that natural slaves are persons who lack the capacity for reason; in the pro-slavery logics of the New World, blackness was the mark of those persons.
6. "The Petition of a great number of Negroes."
7. After Emancipation, African Americans' relationship to the other persons, each other, and the state as citizens became the dominant theme of their literature.
8. Sheldon Wolin, "Hannah Arendt: Democracy and the Political," *Salmagundi* 60 (Spring-Summer 1983): 3–19.

9. I do not mean to suggest that African Americans were uninterested in the law or in using legal mechanisms to achieve political aims; they most certainly were. Indeed, in no way should this inquiry be read as an affirmation of the opposition between dominant legal discourse and black politics, as if the latter is removed from the former. It is simply that my interest in this book is political philosophy in/as literary culture, and law is beyond its scope.
10. Jacques Rancière, *The Politics of Aesthetics: The Distribution of the Sensible*, ed. and trans. Gabriel Rockhill (London: Bloomsbury, 2005), 8.
11. Jacques Rancière, "Does Democracy Mean Something?," in *Dissensus: On Politics and Aesthetics*, ed. and trans. Steven Corcoran (London: Bloomsbury, 2010), 61.
12. David Waldstreicher, "The Wheatleyan Moment," *Early American Studies* 9, no. 3 (2011): 522–27.
13. Phyllis Wheatley, "The Right Honourable William, Earl of Dartmouth" (1772), in James G. Basker, ed., *Black Writers of the Founding Era* (New York: Library of America, 2023), 35.
14. Wheatley, 36.
15. Paul Gilroy, *The Black Atlantic: Modernity and Double Consciousness* (London: Verso Books, 1993), 79. See also Virginia Jackson, *Before Modernism: Inventing American Lyric* (Princeton, NJ: Princeton University Press, 2023), 110–11.
16. Lewis Gordon, *Existentia Africana: Understanding Africana Existential Thought* (London: Routledge, 2000), 24.
17. Jacques Rancière, "The Politics of Literature," in *Dissensus: On Politics and Aesthetics*, ed. and trans. Steven Corcoran (London: Bloomsbury, 2010), 160.
18. Derrick Spires, *The Practice of Citizenship: Black Politics and Print Culture in the Early United States* (Philadelphia: University of Pennsylvania Press, 2019), 4.
19. Judith Shklar, *American Citizenship: The Quest for Inclusion* (Cambridge, MA: Harvard University Press), 36.
20. Kenneth Warren, *What Was African American Literature?* (Cambridge, MA: Harvard University Press, 2012), 7.
21. Warren, 12.
22. Pierre Bourdieu, *Outline of a Theory of Practice*, trans. Richard Nice (Cambridge: Cambridge University Press, 1977), 169.
23. Thomas Paine, *Thomas Paine: Collected Writings* (New York: Library of America, 1995), 864–65.
24. Of course, a republic is a form of democratic governance in which sovereignty abides in the people. In the late colonial and early national eras, however, democracy usually signified majority rule and representative government. In Federalist No. 10 (1787) Madison famously described it this way: "The two great points of difference between a democracy and a republic are: first, the delegation of the government, in the latter, to a small number of citizens elected by the rest; secondly, the greater number of citizens, and greater sphere of country, over which the latter may be extended." Madison argued that prudence

and practicality favored a republican form for the United States federal government, which he and the other Founders enshrined in Article IV, Section 4 of the Constitution.
25. William A. Preston, "Nietzsche on Blacks," in *Existence in Black: An Anthology of Black Existential Philosophy*, ed. Lewis R. Gordon (London: Routledge, 1997), 170.
26. This project began with Jacqueline Scott and A. Todd Franklin, eds., *Critical Affinities: Nietzsche and African American Thought* (Albany: SUNY Press, 2006).
27. Friedrich Nietzsche, *On the Genealogy of Morality*, ed. Keith Ansell-Pearson and trans. Carol Diethe (Cambridge: Cambridge University Press, 1989), 17.
28. Nietzsche, 18.
29. Nietzsche, 33.
30. George Kateb, *The Inner Ocean: Individualism and Democratic Culture* (Ithaca, NY: Cornell University Press, 2006), 17.
31. Lemuel Haynes, "Liberty Extended" (1776), in James G. Basker, ed., *Black Writers of the Founding Era* (New York: Library of America, 2023), 133.
32. Haynes, 132–33.
33. Nietzsche, *On the Genealogy of Morality*, 22.
34. Hannah Arendt, *On Revolution* (New York: Penguin, 1990), 45.
35. Anna Julia Cooper, "Woman Versus the Indian," in *A Voice from the South by a Black Woman from the South* (Xenia, OH: Aldine Printing House, 1892), 117.
36. Melvin L Rogers, *The Darkened Light of Faith: Race, Democracy, and Freedom in African American Political Thought* (Princeton, NJ: Princeton University Press, 2023), 1.
37. Rogers, 11.
38. Rogers, 9.
39. An exception is Rogers's analysis of affect and embodiment in the anti-lynching activism of Ida B. Wells-Barnett and Billie Holiday. See Rogers, 176–205.
40. I begin in the mid-eighteenth century and end in the mid-nineteenth, while Rogers begins with David Walker in the 1820s and ends with James Baldwin.
41. Bourdieu, 85.
42. Charles Mills, *Black Rights/Write Wrongs: The Critique of Racial Liberalism* (Oxford: Oxford University Press, 2017), 75, 77.
43. Ralph Waldo Emerson, *Emerson: Essays and Lectures*, ed. Joel Porte (New York: Library of America, 1983), 406.
44. Frederick Douglass, *The Claims of the Negro, Ethnologically Considered* (Rochester: Lee, Mann, & Co, 1854), 34, 36.
45. Hannah Arendt, "Reflections on Violence," *Journal of International Affairs* 23, no. 1 (1969): 11.
46. John Keane, *Violence and Democracy* (Cambridge: Cambridge University Press, 2004), 1.

47. Citations of this work will be to Harriet E. Wilson, *Our Nig; or, Sketches from the Life of a Free Black* (New York: Penguin, 2009).
48. Orlando Patterson, *Slavery and Social Death: A Comparative Study* (Cambridge, MA: Harvard University Press, 1982), 79.
49. Tavia Nyong'o, *The Amalgamation Waltz: Race, Performance, and the Ruses of Memory* (Minneapolis: University of Minnesota Press, 2009), 118.
50. Oliver Sensen, *Kant of Human Dignity* (Berlin: De Gruyter, 2011), 2.
51. Mills, *Black Rights/Write Wrongs*, 112.
52. Mills.
53. Sharon Krause, "Bodies in Action: Corporeal Agency and Democratic Politics," *Political Theory* 39, no. 3 (2011): 300.

CHAPTER ONE

1. "Act III" in William Waller Hening, ed., *The Statutes at Large; Being A Collection of all the Law of Virginia, From the First Session of the Legislature in the Year 1619* (New York: Bartow, 1823), 260; Cotton Mather, *The Negro Christianized* (Boston: B. Green, 1706), 13, 4.
2. Edmund Gibson, *A Letter of the Lord Bishop of London to the Masters and Mistresses of Families in the English Colonies Abroad; Exhorting Them to Encourage and Promote the Instruction of Their Negroes in the Christian Faith* (London, 1727), 4.
3. Francis Le Jau, *The Carolina Chronicle, 1706-1717*, ed. Frank J. Kilingberg (Berkeley: University of California Press, 1956), 60-62.
4. Le Jau, 69-74.
5. Sylvia R. Frey and Betty Wood, *Come Shouting to Zion: African American Protestantism in the American South and British Caribbean to 1830* (Chapel Hill: University of North Carolina Press, 1998), 66.
6. Friedrich Nietzsche, *On the Genealogy of Morality*, ed. Keith Ansell-Pearson, trans. Carol Diethe (Cambridge: Cambridge University Press, 2007), 53.
7. Davies began converting and ministering to enslaved persons, masters, and non-slaveholding whites in Hanover, Virginia in 1748. Although he made great headway appealing to their emotions, he also concentrated on developing general literacy because reading the scriptures is of utmost importance in Presbyterianism. See Jeffrey H. Richards, "Samuel Davies and the Transatlantic Campaign for Slave Literacy in Virginia," *Virginia Magazine of History and Biography* 111, no. 4 (2003): 333-78.
8. Samuel Davies, *Letters from the Reverend Samuel Davies, &c. Shewing the State of Religion (Particularly among the Negroes) in Virginia* (London, 1757), 4-5.
9. Davies, 12.
10. Richards, "Samuel Davies and the Transatlantic Campaign," 358.
11. Joseph Roach, *Cities of the Dead: Circum-Atlantic Performance* (New York: Columbia University Press, 1996), 11-12.

12. Evangelical orature instantiates what Sandra Gustafson expounds as the general "performance semiotic of speech and text" that prevailed in eighteenth-century America, a system in which "claims to authenticity and relations of power were given form and meaning through the reliance on or freedom from text in oral performance" (Gustafson, *Eloquence Is Power: Oratory and Performance in Early America* [Chapel Hill: Omohundro Institute of Early American History and Culture and University of North Carolina Press, 2000], xvi–xvii). The performance semiotic was animated by the ongoing ascendency of verbal arts across cultures (elite, folk, or otherwise), and (depending on the circumstances) dictated the degree to which one grounded one's assertions in terms of the embodied or the literary-textual. Whereas Gustafson concentrates on the ways African American ministers successfully exploited the performance semiotic and swayed culturally distinct audiences by reconfiguring Christian narratives and tropes, my concern is how enslaved evangelicals came to recognize the discursive, literary, and performative models of the American performance semiotic as usable in the first place.
13. W. E. B. Du Bois, *The Oxford W. E. B. Du Bois Reader*, ed. Eric J. Sundquist (Oxford: Oxford University Press, 1996), 199.
14. Edward W. Said, *Beginnings: Intention and Method* (New York: Basic Books, 1975), 50. Said defines transitive beginnings as a "problem- or projected-directed beginning.... A transitive beginning assumes the following circumstance: an individual mind wishes to intervene in a field of rational activity" (p. 50).
15. George Kateb, *The Inner Ocean: Individualism and Democratic Culture* (Ithaca, NY: Cornell University Press, 1992), 241.
16. Nancy Ruttenburg, *Democratic Personality: Popular Voice and the Trial of American Authorship* (Palo Alto, CA: Stanford University Press, 1998), 3–4.
17. Ruttenburg, 17–18.
18. Historiographical contentions regarding processes of creolization and concomitant questions of survivals, transformations, and severances are long-standing. For a fine overview of the deep and contested fault lines that organize this historiography and the creolization models therein, see Richard Price, "The Miracle of Creolization: A Retrospective," *NWIG: New West Indian Guide / Nieuwe West-Indische Gids* 75, no. 1–2 (2001): 35–64.
19. Willem Bosmen, *A New and Accurate Description of the Coast of Guinea, Divided into the Gold, the Slave, and the Ivory Coasts* (London, 1705), 368.
20. Diana Taylor, *The Archive and the Repertoire: Performing Cultural Memory in the Americas* (Durham, NC: Duke University Press, 2003), 13.
21. Albert J. Raboteau, *Slave Religion: The "Invisible Institution" in the Antebellum South* (1978; Oxford: Oxford University Press, 2004), 43–93.
22. John Wesley, *Sermons on Several Occasions*, vol. 1 (London, 1829), v.
23. Roach, *Cities of the Dead*, 28.
24. For enslaved persons, the most powerful of these forms was that of Jesus. His story captivated them above all others because they understood him as one

of them: an outsider, man of the poor, and target of state-sanctioned torture. As James Cone explains, their version of the Incarnation holds "God in Christ comes to the weak and the helpless, and becomes one with them, taking their condition of oppression as his own and thus transforming their slave-existence into a liberated existence" (James H. Cone, *God of the Oppressed* [Maryknoll, NY: Orbis, 1997], 71).

25. Charles Chauncy, *Seasonable Thoughts on the State of Religion in New England, a Treatise in Five Parts* (Boston, 1743), 239.
26. Roach, *Cities of the Dead*, 28.
27. James Baldwin, *The Fire Next Time* (New York: Dial Press, 1963), 47-48.
28. Richard Allen, "Spiritual Song" (1800), in *Early Negro Writing, 1760-1837*, ed. Dorothy Porter (Boston: Beacon Press, 1971), 559.
29. Allen.
30. Allen, 559-60.
31. "Spiritual Song" never appeared in any edition of Allen's pioneering *A Collection of Spiritual Songs and Hymns, Selected from Various Authors by Richard Allen, African Minister*, which he first published in 1801. *A Collection* excludes musical notation or even suggested melodies with which to sing each song, yet it innovates in that, as Eileen Southern writes, it "seems to have been the earliest [hymnal] to include hymns to which 'wandering' refrains and choruses are attached; that is, refrains freely used with any hymn rather than affixed permanently to specific hymns." Because of such formal-lyrical innovations, Allen's hymns became a "primary source for the worship song later to be called the 'camp-meeting hymn' and the progenitor of the nineteenth-century gospel hymn," both of which are related to, though different from, slave spirituals (Eileen Southern, "Hymnals of the Black Church," *Black Perspective in Music* 17, no. 1-2 [1989]: 155). Despite its title, "Spiritual Song" does not share the formal qualities that typify Allen's hymns, and thus it reads most like a poem, which is how I treat it.
32. Porter, *Early Negro Writing, 1760-1837*, 521.
33. Allen, 560.
34. Allen.
35. Allen, 561.
36. Allen.
37. Allen.
38. Paul Gilroy, *The Black Atlantic: Modernity and Double Consciousness* (London: Verso Books, 1993), 37-38.
39. Gene Andrew Jarrett, "'To Refute Mr. Jefferson's Arguments Respecting Us': Thomas Jefferson, David Walker, and the Politics of Early African American Literature," *Early American Literature* 46, no. 2 (2011): 295.
40. Jarrett, 314-15.
41. Gilroy, *The Black Atlantic*, 37-38.

42. Elizabeth Maddock Dillon, "John Marrant Blows the French Horn: Print, Performance, and the Making of Publics in Early African American Literature," *Early African American Print Culture*, ed. Lara Langer Cohen and Jordan Alexander Stein (Philadelphia: University of Pennsylvania Press, 2012), 320.
43. Dillon, 339.
44. In 2020, Preservation Long Island launched the Jupiter Hammon project, a series of public events, exhibitions, lectures, and study groups dedicated to Hammon's life and work. The project is based at Joseph Lloyd Manor, where Hammon lived for most of his life.
45. For a major counterexample to this critical proclivity in African American literary studies, see Joanna Brooks, "Our Phillis, Ourselves," *American Literature* 82, no. 1 (2010): 1–28.
46. Cedrick May, *Evangelism and Resistance in the Black Atlantic, 1760–1835* (Athens: University of Georgia Press, 2008), 25.
47. Jupiter Hammon, "An Address to the Negroes in the State of New-York" (New York, 1787), 12.
48. Hammon.
49. Hammon's "An Essay on Slavery," a recently discovered unpublished poem, suggests he may have become more responsive to anti-slavery thought late in his life. See Cedrick May and Julie McCown, "'An Essay on Slavery': An Unpublished Poem by Jupiter Hammon," *Early American Literature* 48, no. 2 (2013): 457–71.
50. Craig Steven Wilder offers an overly sanguine reading of the reception of Hammon's performance of the "Address": "The 'Address to the Negroes' had an obvious appeal: Hammon appreciated Africans as people and parents and siblings and spouses and friends and families and communities. He understood the complexity of their personal and social ties, realities that typically determined the priority of physical freedom in an individual life. Hammon emphasized the humanity of the enslaved" (Wilder, *In the Company of Black Men: The African Influence on African American Culture in New York City* [New York: New York University Press, 2001], 71). While the African Society certainly valued Hammon's recognition of the full humanity of black persons, its charge as an association dedicated to ending chattel slavery and the amelioration of the plight of free black people living in and around New York City conflicted with the pro-slavery drift that runs throughout the entirety of the "Address." Despite their deep disagreements, Hammon and his audiences still engaged each other in person and in print deliberately and in good faith; ideological consensus was not required to receive a fair hearing. My point here is that early African American writing evinces an incredibly diverse, often conflicting range of ideas, and those of us who study this discursive field must resist homogenizing impulses if we are to grasp its profound depth.
51. Hammon, "An Address to the Negroes in the State of New-York," 5.
52. Hammon, 6.

53. Jupiter Hammon, *America's First Negro Poet: The Complete Works of Jupiter Hammon of Long Island*, ed. Stanley Austin Ransom Jr. (Port Washington, NY: Kennikat Press, 1970), 62.
54. Hammon, 63.
55. While religion was Hammon's dominant ideological guiding force, the divisions within his owner's family might also in part account for the poem's striking disinterestedness in the war as a politico-geographic conflict. Most of the Lloyds were Loyalist, but Hammon's owner and family patriarch Joseph Lloyd was not (Hammon, 64).
56. Hammon, 63-64.
57. Alexis de Tocqueville, *Democracy in America; and Two Essays on America*, trans. Gerald E. Bevan (New York: Penguin, 2003), 21.
58. Tocqueville, 13-14.

CHAPTER TWO

1. Frederick Douglass, "Is It Right and Wise to Kill a Kidnapper?" (1854), in Frederick Douglass, Philip S. Foner, and Yuval Taylor, *Frederick Douglass: Selected Speeches and Writings* (Chicago: Lawrence Hill Books, 1999), 279. In 1856 Douglass publicly welcomed the prospect of slave insurrection, proclaiming: "The slave's right to revolt is perfect. The recoil, when it comes, will be in exact proportion to the wrongs inflicted; terrible as it will be, we accept and hope for it" (Frederick Douglass, *Frederick Douglass' Paper*, November 28, 1856; hereafter this periodical is cited as *FDP*). Although he demurred when abolitionists such as John Brown laid out actual plans for slave revolts, Douglass's rhetoric signaled a constitutive shift in the anti-slavery public sphere, especially among African Americans, from a fairly steady commitment to moral suasion to whatever means might be necessary to bring about universal emancipation, citizenship, and social enfranchisement. See also David W. Blight, *Frederick Douglass' Civil War: Keeping Faith in Jubilee* (Baton Rouge: Louisiana State University Press, 1989), 88-100.
2. Douglass, "To Kill a Kidnapper," 278.
3. Ralph Waldo Emerson, "The Fugitive Slave Law," in *Emerson's Antislavery Writings*, ed. Len Gougeon and Joel Myerson (New Haven, CT: Yale University Press, 1995), 85-86. Here Emerson is quoting Aeschylus.
4. Emerson, "On the Anniversary of the Emancipation of the Negroes in the West Indies," in *Emerson's Antislavery Writings*, 33.
5. Emerson, "Compensation," in *The Collected Works of Ralph Waldo Emerson*, ed. Alfred R. Ferguson, Joseph Slater et al., 10 vols. (Cambridge, MA: Harvard University Press, 1971-2013), 2.58. Hereafter these volumes are cited as *CW*, with volume and page number.
6. Emerson, "The Fugitive Slave Law," in *Emerson's Antislavery Writings*, 87.

7. George Kateb, *Emerson and Self-Reliance* (Boston: Rowman & Littlefield, 2002), 177–78; Emerson, "Fugitive Slave," in *Emerson's Antislavery Writings*, 73.
8. Douglass, "To Kill a Kidnapper," 278.
9. Emerson, *CW*, 1.164. For Emerson the Over-Soul is not the Christian God. While Douglass is far less explicit in this regard, his notion of the All-Wise accords more with Emerson's Over-Soul than it does with the Christian God. Throughout this chapter, my discussion of the impersonal and human divinity in Douglass rests on my understanding of Douglass in the mid-1850s as an apostate of traditional Christianity but one who believes most in what Emerson in the "Divinity School Address" called "the true Christianity,—a faith in the infinitude of man" (*CW*, 1.89). Such faith is not religious in any sort of institutional or even doctrinal sense, but it is also not in any way secularism or atheism. For a similar, though slightly different conceptualization of Douglass's faith in the mid-1850s, see Jared Hickman, "Douglass Unbound," *Nineteenth-Century Literature* 68, no. 3 (December 2013): 323–62.
10. George Kateb, the most thoroughgoing elaborator of Emersonian self-reliance, has made clear that the reduction of the "biographical Ego" is essential to Emerson's theory of individualism; that is, one must cultivate "another kind of self-reliant practical activity" in service of the "grand spiritual Ego," an activity that yields a mode of thinking—which, for Emerson, is a mode of living—that is not simply "practical" but, more importantly, "philosophical" and "poetical." Kateb, *Emerson and Self-Reliance*, 33. See also George Kateb, *The Inner Ocean: Individualism and Democratic Culture* (Ithaca, NY: Cornell University Press, 1992), esp. 1–35 and 77–105.
11. Frederick Douglass, "The Lecture of Ralph Waldo Emerson," *FDP*, March 2, 1855 (emphasis in original). Douglass previewed, quoted, and reprinted Emerson as early as 1848.
12. Douglass, the educator Charlotte Forten, and the poet James Monroe Whitfield, among other nineteenth-century black intellectuals, diverge from the long-standing critical tradition that charges Emerson with advancing a mysticism in which, as George Santayana describes it, "evil is not explained, it is forgotten; it is not cured, but condoned," one in which "we have become mystics on the one subject on which, above all others, we ought to be men" (George Santayana and Martin A. Coleman, *The Essential Santayana: Selected Writings* [Bloomington: Indiana University Press, 2009], 524). Whitfield wrote a poetic homage to "Self-Reliance," and published it in Frederick Douglass's *The North Star* on December 14, 1849. And throughout her antebellum and Civil War–era journals, Forten remarks on the beauty and wisdom of Emerson's abstract teachings: he is "a man," she writes, who "make[s] us feel the utter insignificance, the great inferiority of *ourselves*. 'Tis a sad lesson, but a most *salutary* one, for who, while earnestly feeling that *he is* nothing, *knows* nothing, comparatively, will not strive with all his might to *know* and to be something?" (Charlotte Forten and Brenda Stevenson,

eds., *The Journals of Charlotte Forten Grimké* [New York: Oxford University Press, 1988], 93).

13. For over a year at least, Douglass sold "Claims," "neatly printed in pamphlet form," for "12 ½ cents" each or "per dozen, one dollar." Frederick Douglass, "The Claims of the Negro Ethnologically Considered," *FDP*, June 8, 1855.

14. Maurice S. Lee, *Uncertain Chances: Science, Skepticism, and Belief in Nineteenth-Century American Literature* (Oxford: Oxford University Press, 2012), 102. For more on the evolution of Douglass's political philosophy, see Nick Bromell, *The Powers of Dignity: The Black Political Philosophy of Frederick Douglass* (Durham, NC: Duke University Press, 2021).

15. Frederick Douglass, "The Claims of the Negro Ethnologically Considered, an Address before the Literary Societies of Western Reserve College" (Rochester: Lee, Mann & Co., 1854), 8, 34.

16. Sharon Cameron, "The Way of Life by Abandonment: Emerson's Impersonal," *Critical Inquiry* 25, no. 1 (Autumn 1998): 26, 24. In an insightful gloss of Cameron's reading of the impersonal, Branka Arsić understands Emersonian impersonality differently: "Since impersonal life traverses and inhabits us, the impersonal in Emerson does not, in my view, cancel out the personal but instead contrives it. In the same way in which the fact that we all share one universal life, as persons, we are made of experiences to which our reflexive self can attend only in retrospect" (Branka Arsić, *On Leaving: A Reading in Emerson* [Cambridge, MA: Harvard University Press, 2010], 94).

17. Branka Arsić, "Introduction," in *American Impersonal: Essays with Sharon Cameron* (New York: Bloomsbury, 2014), 8–9; Emerson, *CW*, 1.10. Douglass only appears on one page of Arsić's near 350-page edited collection, and none of the essays gives priority to non-white writers.

18. Douglass, "Claims," 6.

19. Emerson, *CW*, 2.164, 160, 175.

20. Emerson, *Emerson's Antislavery Writings*, 32.

21. Emerson, *CW*, 2.64.

22. John Carlos Rowe, *At Emerson's Tomb: The Politics of Classic American Literature* (New York: Columbia University Press, 1997), 21.

23. See the "Rethinking the Political" section of essays in Branka Arsić and Cary Wolfe, eds., *The Other Emerson* (Minneapolis: University of Minnesota Press, 2010).

24. Following M. Levine and Daniel S. Malachuk, I use the phrase "small canon" to designate the early addresses such as "The American Scholar" (1837), "The Divinity School Address" (1838), and "The Transcendentalist" (1841–42), and the books *Nature, Essays, First Series* (1841) and *Essays, Second Series* (1844). See Levine and Malachuk, "Introduction: The New History of Emerson's Politics and His Philosophy of Self-Reliance," in *A Political Companion to Ralph Waldo Emerson* (Lexington: University Press of Kentucky, 2011).

25. Cameron, "The Way of Life by Abandonment," 2–3; Emerson, *CW*, 2.182.

26. Cameron, 6n10.
27. Emerson, *CW*, 2.72.
28. Cameron, "The Way of Life by Abandonment," 10; Arsić, *On Leaving*, 94.
29. Jack Turner, *Awakening to Race: Individualism and Social Consciousness in America* (Chicago: University of Chicago Press, 2012), 27.
30. Arsić, *American Impersonal*, 76.
31. Both men also contributed to some of the same anti-slavery cultural productions, most notably Julia Griffiths's edited collection of essays, poems, portraits, sketches, and short stories, *Autographs for Freedom* (1854), copies of which Douglass gave away with new subscriptions to *FDP* as "means of extending the circulation." That volume included a poem by Emerson titled "On Freedom," and Douglass's novella "The Heroic Slave" ("A Liberal Offer to Our Subscribers," *FDP*, February 24, 1854).
32. Emerson, *The Journals and Miscellaneous Notebooks of Ralph Waldo Emerson*, ed. William H. Gilman, Ralph H. Orth et al., 16 vols. (Cambridge, MA: Harvard University Press, 1960-1982), 9.125.
33. Rowe, *At Emerson's Tomb*, 7.
34. Turner, *Awakening to Race*, 48.
35. Emerson, *CW*, 2.183.
36. In his final autobiography (1893), Douglass remembered that he "hesitated" to accept Western Reserve's invitation to deliver a commencement address since he had "never ... spoken on such an occasion, never, indeed, having been myself inside of a school-house for the purpose of an education" (Frederick Douglass, *Autobiographies* [New York: Library of America, 1994], 813).
37. Josiah C. Nott, *Two Lectures on the Natural History of the Caucasian and Negro Races* (Mobile, AL: Dade and Thompson, 1844), 28.
38. Douglass, "Claims," 14.
39. Douglass, 6.
40. Hickman, "Douglass Unbound," 326.
41. Hickman, 327.
42. Emerson, *CW*, 2.183.
43. Emerson, 2.190.
44. Maurice Lee, *Slavery, Philosophy, and American Literature, 1830-1860* (Cambridge: Cambridge University Press, 2010), 113.
45. Douglass, "Claims," 6.
46. Douglass.
47. Douglass, 6-7. Jeannine Marie DeLombard has recently argued that Douglass misread the editorial from the *Richmond Examiner* because he is relying on a misleading gloss of it from the *Thirteenth Annual Report of the American and Foreign Anti-Slavery Society* (1853). The editorial, John Moncure Daniel's "The Right of Negro Slavery," does not, in fact, "read the negro out of the human family," DeLombard writes, but "affirms [black persons'] shared humanity" with white

48. Douglass, 8–9.
49. Hickman, "Douglass Unbound," 336–37.
50. Douglass, "Claims," 36.
51. Douglass, 12.
52. Douglass, 11.
53. Douglass, 15–16, 9.
54. Douglass, 34.
55. Douglass, 35–35.
56. Western Reserve alerted the public of Douglass's participation in its commencement as early as February of that year, but in the month leading up to it, the college gave weekly notice of its order of exercises, featuring Douglass therein. The announcements, which caused some excitement but mostly trepidation and disgust, appeared in the *Daily Cleveland Herald*, the *Daily Commercial Register*, the *Ohio Observer*, and *The Portage County Democrat*, among other newspapers. One alumnus of the college called Douglass's upcoming visit "retrogression, and not progression" (Philozetian, "Western Reserve College," *Daily Cleveland Herald*, July 13, 1854). Another incensed critic, writing to the *Daily Cleveland Herald* under the pseudonym "Consistency," blasted the literary societies for welcoming Douglass, and surmised that their collective intellectual faculties must have atrophied to the point of those commonly associated with blackness. In a letter to the editor published the day before Douglass's address, Consistency wrote, "*Lo, how are thou fallen!*—It would seem as if the Society were now composed of minds whose *infantile* powers were not able to grasp a high order of speech, and sought orators whose powers and tastes assimilated to their own" (Consistency, "Editors of Herald," *Daily Cleveland Herald*, July 11, 1854).
57. Douglass, "Claims," 28, my emphasis.
58. Douglass, 19.
59. Douglass, 20.
60. Douglass, 28.
61. Josiah C. Nott and George R. Gliddon, *Types of Mankind; or, Ethnological Researches Based Upon the Ancient Monuments, Paintings, Sculptures, and Crania of Races* (Philadelphia, 1854), 458–59.
62. Douglass, "Claims," 20, 21. Douglass went on to describe how and why scientists produced such cranial models: "The European face is drawn in harmony with the highest ideals of beauty, dignity and intellect. Features regular and brow after the Websterian mold. The Negro, on the other hand, appears with features distorted,

(Note: item 47 context at top) men while insisting that, as the American "government [was] founded by and for white men, the US did not secure the rights of" African Americans (Jeannine Marie DeLombard, "The Claims of the Humanitarian, Legally Considered," *American Literary History* 35, no. 4 [2023]: 1781). Notwithstanding Douglass's mistake, this chapter tracks Douglass's arguments against "bioracism" as they unfold in "Claims."

lips exaggerated, forehead depressed—and the whole expression of the countenance made to harmonize with the popular idea of Negro imbecility and degradation. I have seen many pictures of Negroes and Europeans, in phrenological and ethnological works; and all, or nearly all ... have been more or less open to this objection. I think I have never seen a single picture in an American work, designed to give an idea of the mental endowments of the Negro, which did any thing like justice to the subject; nay, that was not infamously distorted" ("Claims," 20-21).

63. "Western Reserve College Commencement," *The Portage County Democrat*, July 26, 1854.
64. Douglass, "Claims," 21.
65. Douglass, 29.
66. Douglass, 30.
67. Frederick Douglass, "Prejudice against Color," *The North Star*, June 13, 1850.
68. Frederick Douglass, "Colored Churches," *The North Star*, February 25, 1848.
69. Douglass, "Claims," 32-33. In "Claims," Douglass even rejects the viability of Delany's black emigration schemes: "The black and the white—the negro and the European—these constitute the American people—and, in all the likelihoods of the case, they will ever remain the principal inhabitants of the United States, in some form or other" (p. 13). For more on the differences between Delany's ethnology and Douglass's, see Mia Bay, *The White Image in the Black Mind: African-American Ideas About White People, 1830-1925* (New York: Oxford University Press, 2000), 63-71.
70. Douglass, *Autobiographies*, 954.
71. Lee, *Slavery, Philosophy, and American Literature*, 112-13.
72. Emerson too scorns race pride as foolishly shortsighted and self-serving. In *English Traits* (1856), he writes: "Men hear gladly of the power of blood or race. Everybody likes to know that his advantages cannot be attributed to air, soil, sea, or to local wealth, as mines and quarries, nor to laws and traditions, nor to fortune; but to superior brain, as it makes the praise more personal to him" (*CW*, 5.25).
73. Douglass, "Claims," 33.
74. Douglass.
75. Cameron, "The Way of Life by Abandonment," 25.
76. Douglass, *Autobiographies*, 814.
77. Jason Frank, *Constituent Moments: Enacting the People in Postrevolutionary America* (Durham, NC: Duke University Press, 2010), 8, 210.
78. Frank, 210.
79. Douglass, "The Lecture of Ralph Waldo Emerson."

CHAPTER THREE

1. Harriet E. Wilson, *Our Nig; or, Sketches from the Life of a Free Black* (New York: Penguin, 2009), 3.

2. Eric Gardner argues that abolitionists "may have consciously chosen *not* to publicize" *Our Nig* and could have gone so far as to have "ruined the book's chances" in the marketplace. Eric Gardner, "'This Attempt of Their Sister': Harriet Wilson's *Our Nig* from Printers to Readers," *The New England Quarterly* 66, no. 2 (1993): 227, 245. Xiomara Santamarina reads the book's "materialist critique" of racialized drudgery as an indication that it was an "audience of black workers who would be most familiar with the racist class injustices [it] describes." Xiomara Santamarina, *Belabored Professions: Narratives of African American Working Womanhood* (Chapel Hill: University of North Carolina Press, 2005), 65–68.
3. Wilson, *Our Nig*, 18.
4. Wilson, 3.
5. Jennifer C. Nash, "Black Feminism, Love-Politics, and Post-Intersectionality," *Meridians* 11, no. 2 (2011): 15.
6. Claudia Tate, *Domestic Allegories of Political Desire: The Black Heroine's Text at the Turn of the Century* (New York: Oxford University Press, 1992), 82.
7. Wilson, *Our Nig*, 5.
8. Priscilla Wald, *Constituting Americans: Cultural Anxiety and Narrative Form* (Durham, NC: Duke University Press, 1995), 169.
9. Wilson, *Our Nig*, 9.
10. Wilson, 5.
11. Wilson, 9.
12. Wilson, 6, 10.
13. Wilson, 7.
14. Wilson, 8–10.
15. Wilson, 10.
16. Wilson, 8.
17. Lauren Berlant, *The Female Complaint: The Unfinished Business of Sentimentality in American Culture* (Durham, NC: Duke University Press, 2008), 6.
18. Wilson, *Our Nig*, 71.
19. Berlant, *The Female Complaint*, 6.
20. Thomas Jefferson, *Writings* (New York: The Library of America, 2011), 264–65.
21. Wilson, *Our Nig*, 8, 10.
22. Wilson, 12.
23. Julia Stern, "Excavating Genre in *Our Nig*," *American Literature* 67, no. 3 (September 1995): 449.
24. Stern.
25. Wilson, *Our Nig*, 22.
26. Wilson, 13, 16.
27. Orlando Patterson, *Slavery and Social Death: A Comparative Study* (Cambridge, MA: Harvard University Press, 1982), 61.
28. Wilson, *Our Nig*, 72.

29. Linda Hutcheon writes, "as form of ironic representation, parody is doubly coded in political terms: it both legitimizes and subverts that which it parodies" (Linda Hutcheon, *The Politics of Postmodernism* [London: Routledge, 2002], 97). The difficulty with reading parody in a work such as *Our Nig*, especially because of its autobiographical content, is that the legitimation of the parodied text or idea (e.g., white supremacy) could read as Wilson's positive affirmation.
30. Wilson, *Our Nig*, 8.
31. Wilson, 11.
32. Wilson, 11, 38.
33. Wilson, 39.
34. Jasmine Nichole Cobb, *New Growth: The Art and Texture of Black Hair* (Durham, NC: Duke University Press, 2022), 7.
35. Patterson, *Slavery and Social Death*, 61. This was not of course a hard and fast principle. Cobb explores how cutting black hair *qua* black hair could be a punishment for Africans and African-descended persons in the Americas. Her response to Patterson's semiotics of black hair in New World chattel slavery is well taken: "The forcible cutting of Black hair was not simply about symbolism, and hair texture was not limited to the figurative. Hair was embroiled in expressions of force and the legislation of violence against people of African descent in the United States and the Caribbean" (Cobb, *New Growth*, 44). But I find *Our Nig* hews to Patterson's claim about black hair for narrative and ideological clarity.
36. Thavolia Glymph, *Out of the House of Bondage: The Transformation of the Plantation Household* (Cambridge: Cambridge University Press, 2008), 33.
37. Wilson, *Our Nig*, 1.
38. Wilson, 3.
39. Wilson, 24.
40. Glymph, *Out of the House of Bondage*, 28.
41. Frederick Douglass, "An Address to the Colored People of the United States" (1848), in *Frederick Douglass: Selected Speeches and Writings*, ed. Philip S. Foner (Chicago: Lawrence Hill Books, 1999), 119.
42. *Proceedings of the Convention of Radical Political Abolitionists, held at Syracuse, N. Y., June 26th, 27th, and 28th, 1855* (New York: Central Abolition Board, 1855), 49.
43. Frederick Douglass, *Autobiographies* (New York: The Library of America; 1994), 54, 65, 60.
44. Douglass, 65.
45. Douglass.
46. In *The Black Atlantic: Modernity and Double Consciousness* (London: Verso Books, 1993), Paul Gilroy famously mapped the battle with Covey onto G. W. F. Hegel's allegory of lordship and bondage in *The Phenomenology of Spirit* to substantiate Orlando Patterson's notion of "social death" in *Slavery and Social Death* (1982). Gerald Aching offers a keen yet underappreciated reading of Gilroy's application of Hegel's allegory to New World chattel slavery: "Gilroy's reversal of Hegel's

resolution of the life-and-death struggle, so that the slave prefers death to a life in bondage, simplifies what is at stake in the struggle for self-consciousness and freedom. The Hegelian resolutions of the impasse in bondage describes how subjects emerge and persist in varied states of subjection and accounts for the slave's difficult but obstinate attachment to life. Consequently, by prematurely resolving the life-and-death struggle in such liberationism moments, Gilroy sets aside the question of how slaves endured their bondage in favor of an approach to modernity that privileges the symbolism of individual acts of bravery" (Gerard Aching, "The Slave's Work: Reading Slavery through Hegel's Master-Slave Dialectic," *PMLA* 127, no. 4 [2012]: 914). I quote Aching at some length here because what he diagnoses as Gilroy's simplification of Hegel's allegory is of a piece with the liberation-through-violence romance this chapter explores and *Our Nig* rejects.

47. Shatema Threadcraft, *Intimate Justice: The Black Female Body and the Body Politic* (New York: Oxford University Press, 2016), 47.
48. Threadcraft, 54.
49. Tate, *Domestic Allegories of Political Desire*, 28–29.
50. Threadcraft, *Intimate Justice*, 55.
51. James McCune Smith, "Introduction," in Douglass, *Autobiographies*, 129.
52. Smith, 137.
53. William Lloyd Garrison, "Preface," in Douglass, *Autobiographies*, 8. In his preface Garrison never mentions Covey, yet he appears in the same chapter as Douglass's apostrophe to the ships on the Chesapeake.
54. Douglass, *Autobiographies*, 273–76.
55. Douglass, 58.
56. Threadcraft, *Intimate Justice*, 50.
57. One notable exception to this claim about male writers of slave narratives is Williams Wells Brown, in whose literary and autobiographical work sexual violation of black women and the persecution of black mothers are major themes. Of course, the writers of antebellum slave narratives of any gender were working under a set of editorial demands and cultural sensibilities that restricted what they could say. As Toni Morrison writes, "over and over, [these] writers pull the narrative up short with a phrase such as, 'But let us drop a veil over these proceedings too terrible to relate.' In shaping the experience to make it palatable to those who were in a position to alleviate it, they were silent about many things, and they 'forgot' many other things. There was a careful selection of the instances that they would record and a careful rendering of those that they chose to describe" (Toni Morrison, in *Inventing the Truth: The Art and Craft of Memoir*, ed. William Zinsser, 2nd ed. [Boston: Houghton Mifflin, 1995], 90–91).
58. Douglass, *Autobiographies*, 284. See also Robert Gooding-Williams, *In the Shadow of Du Bois: Afro-Modern Political Thought in America* (Cambridge, MA: Harvard University Press, 2009), 162–209.

59. Frantz Fanon, *The Wretched of the Earth*, trans. Richard Philcox (New York: Grove Press, 2004), 51.
60. Achille Mbembe, *On the Postcolony* (Berkeley: University of California Press, 2001), 193.
61. See David Scott, *Conscripts of Modernity* (Durham, NC: Duke University Press, 2004), 58–97.
62. I borrow the formulation "reinventions" from Hortense Spillers: "Every generation of systematic readers is compelled" to "reinvent" slavery because the institution "remains one of the most textualized and discursive fields of practice that we could posit for a structure of attention" (Hortense Spillers, *Black, White, and in Color: Essays on American Literature and Culture* [Chicago: University of Chicago Press, 2003], 197).
63. G. W. F. Hegel and A. V. Miller, *Phenomenology of Spirit* (Oxford: Oxford University Press, 1977), 118.
64. Wilson, *Our Nig*, 46.
65. Wilson, 52.
66. Wilson, 43, 52.
67. Wilson, 42.
68. Frantz Fanon, *Black Skin, White Masks*, trans. Charles Lam Markmann (London: Pluto Press, 1986), 10.
69. Fanon.
70. Fanon, *The Wretched of the Earth*, 23.
71. Fanon, 44–52.
72. Wilson, *Our Nig*, 58–59.
73. Wilson, 60–61.
74. Wilson, 20.
75. P. Gabrielle Forman and Reginald H. Pitts in Wilson, 95n13.
76. Hannah Arendt, *The Human Condition* (Chicago: University of Chicago Press, 2018), 198.
77. John McGowan, "Hannah Arendt's Performative Politics," in *The Oxford Handbook of Rhetoric and Political Theory*, ed. Dilip Gaonker and Keith Topper (Oxford: Oxford University Press, 2022), n.p.
78. Hannah Arendt, "Reflections on Violence," *Journal of International Affairs* 201 (1969): 20.
79. Arendt, *The Human Condition*, 28, 46.
80. Arendt, 199.
81. Arendt, 203.
82. See Sheldon Wolin, "Hannah Arendt: Democracy and the Political," *Salmagundi* 60 (1983).
83. Wolin, 3.
84. In her controversial "Reflections of Little Rock" (1959), Arendt defended racial and other forms of discrimination as long as they were "confined within the social

sphere, where it is legitimate, and prevent its trespassing on the political and personal sphere, where it is destructive." Shortly after the essay's publication, Ralph Ellison blasted Arendt for the massive blind spot that he believed marred her views on desegregation of public accommodations and racial equality: namely, African Americans have never had the latitude to disentangle social, political, and personal realms from one another (Ralph Ellison in Robert Penn Warren, *Who Speaks for the Negro?* [New Haven, CT: Yale University Press, 2014], 343).

85. Arendt scorned slave morality and believed it had no place in the political realm. She struggled with how to incorporate the rhetorical into her normative political vision. She was certain, though, that the performative is weightier than the rhetorical. See McGowan, "Hannah Arendt's Performative Politics."

CHAPTER FOUR

1. Evelyn Brooks Higginbotham, *Righteous Discontent: The Women's Movement in the Black Baptist Church, 1880–1920* (Cambridge, MA: Harvard University Press, 1994), 207. These women also called themselves "the persevering poor," "common everyday women," and "common people of whom God made more of than the other kind" (ibid.).
2. According to census records there were a small number of enslaved persons in New York after 1827, notwithstanding the 1827 state abolition law.
3. See Antong Liu, "The Modernization of Honor in Eighteenth-Century Political Theory" (PhD diss., Duke University, 2019); Tamler Sommers, *Why Honor Matters* (New York: Basic Books, 2018).
4. William J. Wilson, "From Our Brooklyn Correspondent," *Frederick Douglass' Paper*, February 26, 1852.
5. Wilson.
6. Wilson, "From Our Brooklyn Correspondent."
7. Jane Dailey, "Deference and Violence in the Postbellum Urban South," *Journal of Southern History* 63, no. 3 (1997): 553–90.
8. Shane White, *Stories of Freedom in Black New York* (Cambridge, MA: Harvard University Press, 2002), 12. Leslie M. Harris, the preeminent historian of black New York City before 1863, also uses the figure of the shadow to express slavery's spectral-like influence on the milieu of post-1827 emancipation New York City. See her *In the Shadow of Slavery: African American in New York City, 1628–1863* (Chicago: University of Chicago Press, 2003).
9. Mordecai Noah, "Africans," *National Advocate*, August 3, 1821.
10. Noah.
11. Oliver Sense, *Kant on Human Dignity* (Berlin: De Gruyter, 2011), 2.
12. Sense, 144, 175.
13. Nick Bromell, "Democratic Indignation: Black American Thought and the Politics of Dignity," *Political Theory* 41, no. 2 (2013): 295.

14. Bromell. Vincent W. Lloyd has recently argued the opposite—that is, that dignity is quite literally the "struggle against domination" (Lloyd, *Black Dignity: The Struggle Against Domination* [New Haven, CT: Yale University Press, 2022], 15, passim).
15. Immanuel Kant, *Groundwork of the Metaphysics of Morals*, trans. Mary Gregor and Jens Timmermans (Cambridge: Cambridge University Press, 1998), 46, 47.
16. Thomas Jefferson, *Writings* (New York: The Library of America, 2011), 256.
17. Jefferson, 264.
18. Jefferson.
19. Jefferson, 269.
20. Jefferson, 266.
21. Jefferson, 268.
22. Jefferson.
23. Jefferson.
24. Richard Iton, *In Search of the Black Fantastic: Politics and Popular Culture in the Civil Rights Era* (Oxford: Oxford University Press, 2008), 17.
25. James A. Snead, "On Repetition in Black Culture," *Black American Literature Forum* 1 (Winter 1981): 46.
26. Walt Whitman, "Shut Not Your Doors," in *The Portable Walt Whitman*, ed. Michael Warner (New York: Penguin, 2004), 237.
27. Friedrich Nietzsche, *On the Genealogy of Morality*, ed. Keith Ansell-Pearson, trans. Carol Diethe (Cambridge: Cambridge University Press, 2007), 155.
28. Nietzsche, 156.
29. Marcus Cicero Tullius, *On Duties*, trans. Benjamin Patrick Newton (Ithaca, NY: Cornell University Press, 2016), 98, 100.
30. Liu, "The Modernization of Honor," 32.
31. Sharon R. Krause, *Liberalism with Honor* (Cambridge, MA: Harvard University Press, 2002), 31.
32. Krause, 14, 13.
33. Krause, 102, 103.
34. Krause, 107.
35. Krause, 121, 126.
36. Krause, 124.
37. Orlando Patterson, *Slavery and Social Death: A Comparative Study* (Cambridge, MA: Harvard University Press, 1982), 79.
38. Patterson, 96.
39. Charley White, "Burlesque Lecture on Woman's Rights," in *Brudder Bones' Book of Stump Speeches and Burlesque Orations*, ed. John F. Scott (New York: Dick & Fitzgerald, 1868), 155.
40. These "cuts and placards descriptive of the negro's deformity are everywhere ... with corresponding broken lingo," Hosea Easton wrote in his 1837 *Treatise* (Hosea Easton, *A Treatise on the Intellectual Character and Civil and Political Condition of*

the Colored People of the U. States and the Prejudice Exercised Towards Them: With a Sermon on the Duty of the Church to Them [Boston: Knapp, 1837], 41).

41. For more on the convention movement, see the groundbreaking work of the Colored Conventions Project at https://coloredconventions.org/.
42. Derrick R. Spires, *The Practice of Citizenship: Black Politics and Print Culture in the Early United States* (Philadelphia: University of Pennsylvania Press, 2019), 128.
43. The problems with Simons's age across federal censuses from 1840 to 1870 are matched by similar inconsistencies by Margaret Smith, with whom he lived and who was probably his common-law wife. Smith might also have been born into indentured servitude.
44. There is a possibility that Phebe was Simons's grandmother. In either case, the effects on Simons of the dynamics of New York's gradual emancipation were the same.
45. Enslaved persons, the indentured servants, and free live-in workers were often left off censuses. The most important point here is that black persons like Simons and his family were caught in the crucible of enslavement, indenture, and freedom in New York during the first two decades of the nineteenth century.
46. Article II of the 1821 constitution lays out citizenship, state residency, and age requirements for the franchise.
47. Nathanial B. Carter and William L. Stone, *Reports of the Proceedings and Debates of the Convention of 1821, Assembled for the Purpose of Amending the Constitution of the State of New York: Containing All the Official Documents, Relating to the Subject, and Other Valuable Matter* (Albany, NY: Horsford, 1821), 374.
48. "A Call to Colored Young Men," *Colored American*, August 19, 1837.
49. "Important Meeting," *Colored American*, September 2, 1837.
50. Harris, *In the Shadow of Slavery*, 210.
51. Peter Paul Simons, "Delivered before the African Clarkson Association" (1839), in C. Peter Ripley et al., eds., *Black Abolitionist Papers*, vol. 3 (Chapel Hill: University of North Carolina Press, 1985), 288.
52. Harris, *In the Shadow of Slavery*, 210; "Public Meeting," *Colored American*, August 15, 1840.
53. "The Colored Citizens of New York and the African Civilization Society," *The Weekly Anglo-African*, April 21, 1860.
54. Simons, "Delivered before the African Clarkson Association," 288.
55. Simons, 289.
56. Craig Steven Wilder, *In the Company of Black Men: The African Influence on African American Culture in New York City* (New York: NYU Press, 2001), 81.
57. Quoted in Daniel Perlman, "Organizations of the Free Negro in New York City, 1800–1860," *The Journal of Negro History* 56, no. 3 (1971): 186.
58. Simons, "Delivered before the African Clarkson Association," 288.
59. See Maria W. Stewart, *Maria W. Stewart: Essential Writings of Nineteenth-Century Political Philosopher*, ed. Douglas A. Jones (Oxford: Oxford University Press, 2024), xxix–xxxiv.

60. Simons, "Delivered before the African Clarkson Association," 291.
61. Simons, 289.
62. Simons, 290.
63. Simons, 289.
64. Simons, 289.
65. As Leslie Harris writes, "slave owners blurred blacks' gender roles by forcing women to do men's work, such as fieldwork, and men to perform domestic service.... In New York City, such blurring or eliminating of traditional gender roles continued under freedom." Harris, *In the Shadow of Slavery*, 204.
66. Harris.
67. Simons, "Wicked Conspiracy," *Colored American*, December 30, 1837.
68. See Stewart, *Maria W. Stewart: Essential Writings*, 81–86, 180–87.
69. Simons, "Delivered before the African Clarkson Association," 291.
70. Frederick Douglass, "Communipaw," *Frederick Douglass' Paper*, June 17, 1852.
71. David Walker and Peter P. Hinks, eds., *Appeal to the Coloured Citizens of the World* (University Park: The Penn State University Press, 2000), 31.
72. Thomas M. Morgan, "The Education and Medical Practice of Dr. James McCune Smith (1813-1865), First Black American to Hold a Medical Degree," *Journal of the National Medical Association* 95, no. 7 (2003): 605.
73. Frederick Douglass, *Autobiographies* (New York: The Library of America, 1994), 137.
74. James McCune Smith, *The Works of James McCune Smith*, ed. John Stauffer (Oxford: Oxford University Press, 2006), 201.
75. Douglass, *Autobiographies*, 60.
76. McCune Smith, *The Works of James McCune Smith*, 202.
77. McCune Smith.
78. In *My Bondage and My Freedom*, Douglass wrote: "My mother died without leaving me a single intimation of *who* my father was. There was a whisper, that my master was my father; yet it was only a whisper, and I cannot say that I ever gave it credence"—Douglass, *Autobiographies*, 156.
79. Douglass, 202.
80. Douglass, "Communipaw."
81. Frederick Douglass, "Letter from the Editor," *Frederick Douglass' Paper*, May 15, 1853.
82. Douglass.
83. William J. Wilson, writing under the pseudonym "Ethiop" for *FDP*, wrote about the development of a black "aristocracy" that aligned with Douglass's notion here. In an 1852 column for *FDP*, Wilson (as Ethiop) wrote about the "necessity of a [sophisticated] and monied class among us here, who, feeling their true position would stoutly maintain their ground" and govern the collective of African Americans ("From Our Brooklyn Correspondent," *FDP*, April 8, 1852). Radiclani Clytus notes that Ethiop's idea for a black aristocracy, which

anticipated W. E. B Du Bois's theory of the Talented Tenth (1903), has "its roots in Nathaniel Parker Willis's contemporary notion of the 'Upper Ten Thousand' or the 'Upper Ten,' an idiom that Willis coined to refer to New York's hereditary gentry, and a usage that clearly predates and is etymologically relevant to W. E. B. Du Bois's own frame of reference" for his philosophy of racial uplift of similar name. "Visualizing in Black Print: The Brooklyn Correspondence of William J. Wilson aka 'Ethiop,'" *J19: The Journal of Nineteenth-Century Americanists* 6, no. 1 (2018): 65n85.

84. Douglass, "Letter from the Editor."
85. Spires, *The Practice of Citizenship*, 147.
86. An ostensibly different understanding of "representative men" emerges in *Representative Men*, in which Emerson writes about great men such as Plato, William Shakespeare, and Napoleon Bonaparte whose works and actions, their genius, reveal features of a "general mind" that courses throughout all of humanity (*Representative Men: Seven Lectures* [Boston: Phillips, Sampson, and Company, 1849], 15). For McCune Smith, representative men and women also demonstrate more familiar aspects of humanity—e.g., grit, ingenuity, creativity, and persistence in the face of unthinkable odds—but these aspects are more actionable for the creation of democratic forms of life.
87. McCune Smith, *The Works of James McCune Smith*, 190.
88. Thomas Paine, *Collected Writings* (New York: The Library of America, 1995), 563.
89. Melvin Rogers, "Race, Domination, and Republicanism," in *Difference without Domination*, ed. Danielle Allen and Rohini Somanathan (Chicago: University of Chicago Press, 2020), 61, 62.
90. Rogers, 60.
91. Philip Petit, "Republicanism across Cultures," in *Republicanism in Northeast Asia*, ed. Jun-Hyeok Kwak and Leigh Jenco (London: Routledge, 2015), 18.
92. Jack Turner calls this "duty to help one's fellow citizens secure the material minimums" the "*democratic egalitarian obligation.*" Turner, *Awakening to Race: Individualism and Social Consciousness in America* (Chicago: University of Chicago Press, 2012), 47.
93. Nothing captures this dynamic with greater trenchancy than an old black American riddle:
    Q: "What does America call an educated and successful black American?"
    A: "A nigger."
94. Disability is another marginalized identity that *Heads* esteems. In "The News-Vender" sketch, for instance, the titular protagonist had been "razed to the knees" (McCune Smith, *The Works of James McCune Smith*, 191) and serves as a model of industry, creativity, and civic excellence.
95. McCune Smith, 199.
96. Rogers, "Race, Domination, and Republicanism," 69.

CHAPTER FIVE

1. Frank J. Webb, *The Garies and Their Friends* (Baltimore, MD: Johns Hopkins University Press, 1997), 16.
2. Webb. *The Garies* is the first novel of manners in the African American letters, and one of only a relative few.
3. The criticism on *The Garies* and Caddy is barely an afterthought therein. An exception is Samuel Otter's readings of her housecleaning in "Frank Webb's Still Life: Rethinking Literature and Politics through *The Garies and Their Friends*," *American Literary History* 20, no. 4 (Winter 2008): 732–36.
4. Blyden Jackson, *A History of Afro-American Literature, Volume 1: The Long Beginning, 1746–1895* (Baton Rouge: Louisiana State University Press, 1989), 344. Jackson never finished the *History*, but drafts and notes of subsequent volumes are available in his papers at the University of North Carolina at Chapel Hill.
5. *Frederick Douglass' Paper*, "Literature," December 4, 1857.
6. Webb's writings do share some ideological and tonal affinities with William Wells Brown's corpus, especially the novel *Clotel; or, The President's Daughter* (London: Partridge and Oakley, 1853).
7. This is Nathaniel Hawthorne's epithet. He called these women's novels "trash," singling out Maria Susan Cummins's runaway bestseller *The Lamplighter* (1854) as the most baneful of the lot. See William Charvat et al., eds., *The Centenary Edition of the Works of Nathaniel Hawthorne*, vol. 17 (Columbus: Ohio State University Press, 1988), 304.
8. Robert Reid-Pharr, "Introduction," in Webb, *The Garies*, xviii.
9. Webb, *The Garies*, 2.
10. Abolitionists were successful in turning individuals against the institution of chattel slavery by railing against this practice. See Fanny Kemble's *Journal of a Residence on a Georgian Plantation in 1838–1839* (New York, 1863), *passim* for a representative anti-slavery denunciation of slaveowners fathering enslaved children.
11. Webb, *The Garies*, 100. Clarence Garie owns dozens of other enslaved persons and leaves them on the plantation when he moves to Philadelphia. Webb describes him as a "very kind master" and says "his slaves were as happy as slaves can be under any circumstances" (p. 58). When the Garies left Georgia, "many of the slaves were in tears, and all deeply lamented the departure" of the family (p. 105). Webb adopts the trope of the kind master that Stowe made famous in the character of St. Clare, but he offers little critique of it and never addresses the enslaved population on the Garie plantation after this scene.
12. Webb, 159.
13. Webb, 16.
14. Webb, 216–19.

15. Aisha K. Finch, "Black Feminism and the Practice of Care," *Palimpsest: A Journal of Women, Gender, and the Black International* 11, no. 1 (2022): 2.
16. Finch. Of course care can be something other than beneficence and can take negative forms (e.g., condescension, paternalism), thus reinforcing oppressive power imbalances.
17. Joan Tronto offers a definition of democracy that turns on care: "Democracy is the allocation of caring responsibilities and assuring that everyone can participate in those allocations of care as completely as possible" (*Who Cares? How to Reshape a Democratic Politics* [Ithaca, NY: Cornell University Press, 2015], 15).
18. Webb, *The Garies*, xix.
19. "The Garies and Their Friends," *The Athenaeum* 1565, October 24, 1857.
20. "The Garies and Their Friends."
21. David Walker, *Appeal to the Coloured Citizens of the World*, ed. Peter P. Hinks (University Park: The Penn State University Press, 2000), 73.
22. Wilson Jeremiah Moses, *The Golden Age of Black Nationalism, 1850-1925* (New York: Oxford University Press, 1978), 45-46.
23. In an 1863 sermon to Barbadian emigrants to Monrovia, Liberia, called "Emigration, an Aid to the Evangelization of Africa," Alexander Crummell said: "A portion of them [natives] have already been brought into compliance with these manifest providential arrangements. By a most singular and favoring providence, thousands of American emigrants have crossed the wide ocean, and taken up their residence in this Republic. Here we are touching and influencing, in divers ways, thousands of heathen natives. *Our mission is evidently to organize the native labor all around us; to introduce regulating and controlling law among them; to gather their children into schools, in order to train their intellects; to make these people civilized and Christian people; and to incorporate them into our Republic as citizens, and into the Church of God as brethren!*" (Alex Crummell, *Africa and America: Addresses and Discourses* [Springfield, MA: Willey & Co., 1891], 422). Crummell and Edward Blyden, another black nationalist and founding figure of Pan-Africanism, called for American and British protectorates, respectively, over parts of West Africa.
24. Moses, *The Golden Age of Black Nationalism*, 28.
25. "Carrol[l] Advises the Race," *The Gazette* (Raleigh, NC), January 15, 1898.
26. Maria W. Stewart, *Maria W. Stewart: Essential Writings of Nineteenth-Century Political Philosopher*, ed. Douglas A. Jones (Oxford: Oxford University Press, 2024), 91.
27. Stewart.
28. Webb, *The Garies*, viii.
29. Webb, 15.
30. Michael C. Dawson, "A Black Counterpublic? Economic Earthquakes, Racial Agenda(s), and Black Politics," *Public Culture* 7 (1994): 207.
31. Jasmine Nichole Cobb, *Picturing Freedom: Remaking Black Visuality in the Early Nineteenth Century* (New York: New York University Press, 2015), 13, 16.

32. Dawson, "A Black Counterpublic?," 197–211.
33. Webb, *The Garies*, 123.
34. Webb, 121–22.
35. Russell Sbriglia, "Specters of Marx in Frank J. Webb's *The Garies and Their Friends*: Class, Race, and the Critique of Ideology," *ESQ: A Journal of Nineteenth-Century American Literature and Culture* 64, no. 4 (2018): 588.
36. Webb, *The Garies*, 121.
37. William Wells Brown, "St. Domingo: Its Revolutions and its Patriots. A Lecture" (Philadelphia, 1855), 12–13.
38. Brown, 32.
39. Webb, *The Garies*, 45.
40. Webb.
41. Aisha K. Finch, "Black Feminism and the Practice of Care," *Palimpsest* 11, no. 1 (2022): 2.
42. Otter, "Frank Webb's Still Life," 737.
43. Otter.
44. Webb, *The Garies*, 214.
45. Webb.
46. Zip Coon ideology, which I explore in chapter 4, is absent in *The Garies*. Given the novel's focus on free black life, especially in Philadelphia where Edward Clay and other illustrators and writers set their lampoons of African Americans' aspirations and expressive cultures, it is remarkable how carefully Webb avoided reproducing any element of Zip Coon ideology, if even to rebut it.
47. Webb, *The Garies*, 215.
48. Webb, 33.
49. Webb, 345.
50. Webb, 333.
51. Webb, 50.
52. Addison Gayle, "The Politics of Revolution: Afro-American Literature" (1972), in Nathaniel Norment Jr., ed., *The Addison Gayle Jr. Reader* (Champaign: University of Illinois Press, 2009), 134–35.
53. Webb, *The Garies*, 127.
54. Sbriglia, "Specters of Marx," 567.
55. Bernard Bell, *The Afro-American Novel and Its Traditions* (Amherst: University of Massachusetts Press, 1987), 42–45.
56. Jack Turner, "Audre Lorde's Politics of Difference," in *African American Political Thought: A Collective History*, ed. Melvin L. Rogers and Jack Turner (Chicago: University of Chicago Press, 2021), 586.
57. Walker, *Appeal to the Coloured Citizens of the World*, 32.
58. Walker.
59. Walker, 33.
60. Walker, 34.

61. Walker, 34.
62. Webb, *The Garies*, 25.
63. Webb, 27.
64. Webb, 6. Chaucer did not in fact write this poem, but Webb would not have known that. Later in the nineteenth century scholars discovered *The Floure and the Leafe* was written by someone else; the author remains anonymous.
65. Webb, 63.
66. Webb.
67. *Constitutions of Pennsylvania* (Harrisburg, PA: Wm. Stanley Ray, State Printer, 1916), 139. It reads: "Every white freeman of the age of twenty-one years, having resided in the State one year, and in the election-district where he offers to vote ten days immediately preceding such election, and within two years paid a State or county tax, which shall have been assessed at least ten days before the election, shall enjoy the rights of an elector."
68. *Proceedings and Debates of the Convention of the Commonwealth of Pennsylvania, to Propose Amendments to the Constitution*, vol. ix (Harrisburg, PA: Packer, Barrett, and Parke, 1838), 364.
69. Leon F. Litwack, *North of Slavery: The Negro in the Free States, 1790–1860* (Chicago: University of Chicago Press, 1961), 163.
70. Frederick Douglass, "Learn Trades or Starve!" *Frederick Douglas's Paper*, March 4, 1853.
71. Douglass.
72. Douglass.
73. Webb, *The Garies*, 287.
74. Webb, 291–92.
75. Webb, 292.
76. Douglass, "Learn Trades or Starve!"
77. Douglass.
78. Webb, *The Garies*, 298.
79. Webb, 299.
80. Gary B. Nash, *First City: Philadelphia and the Forging of Historical Memory* (Philadelphia: University of Pennsylvania Press, 2006), 180–81.
81. Webb, *The Garies*, 243.
82. Webb, 265–66.
83. See "Article II" in Walker, *Appeal to the Colored Citizens of the World*.

EPILOGUE

1. https://x.com/SenMikeLee/status/1314016169993670656.
2. https://www.lee.senate.gov/2020/10/of-course-we-re-not-a-democracy.
3. Herman E. Talmadge, *You and Segregation* (Birmingham, AL: Vulcan Press, 1955), 15.

4. *The Blue Book of the John Birch Society* (Boston: Western Islands, 1961), 100.
5. *Blue Book of the John Birch Society*, 161. See also JBS founder Robert Welch's "Republics and Democracies," September 17, 1961.
6. Quote from *Partisans*.
7. Barry Goldwater, *The Conscience of a Conservative* (Shepherdsville, KY: Victor Publishing Company, 1960), 18, 22.
8. "Negro Spokesman Bitter on Goldwater Nomination, Saying It Will Aid Racists," *New York Times*, July 17, 1964.
9. See Michelle R. Boyd, *Jim Crow Nostalgia: Reconstructing Race in Bronzeville* (Minneapolis: University of Minnesota Press, 2008).
10. https://www.nbcnews.com/politics/congress/byron-donalds-defends-comments-jim-crow-fiery-exchange-joy-reid-rcna155969.

Index

abolitionism, 45; political parties of, 77, 79; Transcendentalism and, 52; Webb on, 127; Wilson on, 74, 85
Aching, Gerald, 173n46
aestheticism, 36-37, 101, 134
African Clarkson Association, 112-14
African Colonization Society, 99, 182n23
African Society, 40-41
Allen, Richard, 15, 23; "Spiritual Song," 32-37, 164n31
amalgamation, 70, 128. *See also* miscegenation
American School of Ethnology, 46, 48, 53, 56, 59-61
Anglican Church, 15, 23-24, 28
Arendt, Hannah, 88; on discrimination, 175n84; on slave morality, 176n85; on violence, 16, 17, 87
aristocratic value equation, 10-11
Arsić, Branka, 49, 52, 168nn16-17
assimilationism, 91, 125-26, 130-31, 139

Bacon's Rebellion (1676), 16
Baldwin, James, 31
Bell, Phillip, 111, 140
Berlant, Lauren, 72
black feminism, 19, 68, 108, 140
Black Lives Matter movement, 95
black nationalism, 89, 129-40
Black Power movement, 68, 139

blackface minstrelsy, 107-8, 137, 144
black-owned newspapers, 108-9, 111
Bloom, Harold, 51
Blue Laws, 95
Blyden, Edward, 182n23
body politics, 20, 60; Douglass and, 52-65, 81; laborers and, 116-21; violence and, 16. *See also* habitus
Bourdieu, Pierre, 9, 14
Bromell, Nick, 97-98
Brown, John, 77, 166n1
Bush, George W., 155

Cameron, Sharon, 49-51, 63
care, 19-20, 125-29, 136, 140
Carroll, Richard, 131
Cary, Mary Ann Shadd, 81, 129-30
Chaucer, Geoffrey, 144, 184n64
Chauncy, Charles, 30
chauvinism, 130, 131
Christian nationalism, 153
Christianity, 10-13, 26-27, 33, 44, 104
Cicero, 103-4
Civil Rights movement, 95, 154
Clay, Edward Williams, 106-7, 183n46
Clytus, Radiclani, 179n83
Cobb, Jasmine Nichole, 133, 173n35
Colored Convention movement, 108-9, 112, 178n41
colorism, 74-76

Committee for Vigilance, 112
community versus individual slaves, 76–77
Cone, James, 164n24
Cooper, Anna Julia, 12–13
counterpublics, 133
creolization, 163n18
Cruikshank, George, 106–7
Crummell, Alexander, 130, 182n23
Cummins, Maria Susan, 181n7
Curran, John Philpot, 58

dandies, 96–98, 101–2, 106
Daniel, John Moncure, 169n47
Dartmouth, Earl of (William Legge), 5–6
Darwinism, 56, 64
Davies, Samuel, 23–24, 162n7
Declaration of the Rights of Man and of the Citizen (1789), 3
Delany, Martin R., 61, 80–81, 126, 129–30, 171n69
DeLombard, Jeannine Marie, 169n47
democracy, 88, 151–56; evangelicalism and, 23–27; honor in, 93, 103–5; Protestantism and, 11–13, 26–27; republicanism versus, 9, 151–56, 160n24; as slave morality, 10–13, 44; Tronto on, 182n17
Democratic Party, 9
democratic personality, 14, 27
democratic subjectivization, 13–20
demos, 5
Dickens, Charles, 94
Dickinson, Emily, 63
Dillon, Elizabeth Maddock, 39
domestic violence, 17
domesticity, 131–34
Donalds, Byron, 155–56
Douglass, Frederick, 15–16, 179n78; assimilationism of, 130; body politics of, 52–65, 81; Emerson and, 52–53; gender issues of, 78–79, 81–82; on human rights, 58; on impersonality, 45–46, 48–49, 55, 58; on individual versus community slaves, 76–77; on individualism, 52–53; McCune Smith and, 117–21; on racial theories, 53–60, 170n47; on respectability, 18; on slave catchers, 46, 47, 48; on slave insurrection, 166n1; on US Constitution, 77; on violence, 77; Webb and, 126, 148; Wilson and, 77
Douglass, Frederick, works of: autobiographies, 63, 77–81, 169n36; "Claims of the Negro, Ethnologically Considered," 46, 48–49, 53–65; "The Heroic Slave," 77, 126; "Learn Trades or Starve!," 146–47; "Prejudice against Color," 61
doxa, 9
Dred Scott decision (1857), 45
Du Bois, W. E. B., 25, 139, 180n83

Easton, Hosea, 177n40
ecstasy, 14–15, 21–23
Ellis, Caroline "Caddy," 125
Ellison, Ralph, 176n84
emancipation, gradual, 109–10, 141, 178n44
Emerson, Ralph Waldo: on democratic individuality, 47; Douglass and, 52–53; on Fugitive Slave Act, 46, 50; on impersonality, 47, 49–52, 63, 168n16; on individualism, 52–53, 167n9; McCune Smith and, 180n86; on "Over-Soul," 47, 49–51, 167n9; on racism, 50, 52, 171n72; Santayana on, 167n12; on self-reliance, 51–53, 167n10; on slavery, 46–47, 64–65
Emerson, Ralph Waldo, works of: "Circles," 15, 51, 53, 54–55; "Compensation," 46–47, 51; "Emancipation in the British West Indies," 50; "The Fugitive Slave Law," 46; *Representative Men*, 180n86
Enlightenment philosophy, 37–39, 104
Equiano, Olaudah, 37
"Ethiop." *See* Wilson, William J. "Ethiop"
ethnology, 57–59, 61–62. *See also* American School of Ethnology
evangelicalism, 15, 18, 23–27
evolutionism, 56, 64

Index

Fanon, Frantz, 82, 84–85, 89
Federalist Papers, 160n24
feminism, 108; Jacobs and, 78–79; Wilson and, 74. *See also* gender
Finch, Aisha K., 128–29
Foster, George, 94
Frank, Jason, 63–64
Franklin, Benjamin, 53
Fugitive Slave Act (1850), 45, 46, 50, 149

Gardner, Eric, 172n2
Garner, Margaret, 85
Garnet, Henry Highland, 77, 80–81
Garrison, William Lloyd, 77, 79, 80
Gates, Henry Louis, Jr., 67
Gayle, Addison, 139, 140
gender, 17, 78–79, 81–82, 108, 115–16. *See also* feminism
Gibson, Edmund, 162n2
Gilroy, Paul, 6–7, 36, 173n46
Gliddon, George R., 59
Glymph, Thavolia, 76
Goldwater, Barry, 154
Gordon, Lewis, 7
gospel hymns, 164n31
Great Awakening, 11, 26
Great Chain of Being, 70, 145–46
Green, Joshua, 70
Griffith, Julia, 169n31
Grimké, Charlotte Forten, 167n12
Gustafson, Sandra, 163n12

Habermas, Jürgen, 39
habituation procedures, 13–20
habitus, 14
hair style, 74–77, 173n35
Haitian revolution, 134–35
Hammon, Jupiter, 15, 23, 40–44, 165n44
Hammon, Jupiter, works of: "An Address to the Negroes in the State of New-York," 40, 165n50; "An Essay on Slavery," 165n49; "An Evening's Improvement," 43; "The Kind Master and Dutiful Servant," 41–43
Harris, Leslie M., 176n8, 179n65
Harris, Samuel, 81

Hawthorne, Nathaniel, 181n7
Haynes, Lemuel, 11–12
Hegel, G. W. F., 82–83, 173n46
Hickman, Jared, 54, 56
Higginbotham, Evelyn Brooks, 91
Holiday, Billie, 161n39
honor, 17–18; aristocratic, 104–5; Cicero on, 103–4; in democracy, 93, 103–5; democratization of, 104; problem of, 102–9; southern, 105–6
Hood, Thomas, 107
"hush harbors," 29
Hutcheon, Linda, 173n29
hymns, 164n31

Iliad, 104
impersonality, 15–16; Douglass on, 45–46, 48–49, 55, 58; Emerson on, 47, 49–52, 63, 168n16
indentured servants, 11, 16–17, 109–10, 117, 178n45
individualism, 25, 39, 47; Douglass on, 52–53; Emerson on, 52–53, 167n10
individuation, 36–44; revivalists and, 25, 30; Ruttenburg on, 27
integrationism, 132
Irish immigrants, 146–47
Iton, Richard, 100–101

Jackson, Andrew, 9
Jackson, Blyden, 125, 181n4
Jacobs, Harriet, 78–79
Jarrett, Gene Andrew, 37–38
Jefferson, Thomas, 37, 105; on racial differences, 72, 98–101; on Wheatley, 100
jeremiad, 31, 43
Jim Crowism, 8–9, 91, 153–56
John Birch Society (JBS), 153–54
Jones, Absalom, 36, 37

Kansas-Nebraska Act (1854), 45
Kant, Immanuel, 7, 18–19, 97, 98
Kateb, George, 11, 47, 167n10
King, Martin Luther, Jr., 154
Krause, Sharon, 20, 104–6, 108

INDEX

"ladder of infamy" (Wilson), 70, 72
Lee, Maurice S., 62
Lee, Mike, 151-52, 155
liberalism, 74; "compassionate," 72, 73
liberation-through-violence model, 68, 77-83, 86, 174n46
Liberia, 182n23
literacy, 24-27
literary individuation, 36-44
literary societies, 113, 132
Litwack, Leon, 146
Liu, Antong, 104
Lloyd, Joseph, 166n55
Lloyd, Vincent W., 177n14
lynchings, 91, 161n39

Madison, James, 105, 160n24
May, Cedrick, 40
Mbembe, Achille, 83
McCune Smith, James, 79-81, 93, 116-23; Douglass and, 117-21; Emerson and, 180n86; *Heads of the Colored People, Done with a Whitewash Brush*, 18, 92, 117-23; medical degree of, 117; Paine and, 121; Simons and, 18, 117
Melville, Herman, 63
Mills, Charles, 14, 19
minstrel shows, 107-8, 144
miscegenation, 70-72, 74-75, 107, 127-28
Montesquieu, 104
"moral elevation" campaigns, 112-14
Morrison, Toni, 174n57
Morton, Samuel G., 53
Moses, Wilson Jeremiah, 130-31

Nash, Jennifer, 68
nationalism: black, 89, 129-40; Christian, 153; "technocratic," 131
natural rights, 2-3
neoconservatism, 155
Neoplatonism, 51
New Light ministers, 23-24, 28
New York Association for the Political Elevation and Improvement of the People of Color (NYPE), 111
Nietzsche, Friedrich, 10-12, 102-3, 108

Noah, Mordecai, 96-97, 106
Nott, Josiah C., 59
novels, 67, 126, 181n7; of manners, 125, 181n2; of seduction, 69-70
Nyong'o, Tavia, 18

orature, 23-27
Otter, Samuel, 136, 137, 181n3

Packer, Barbara, 51
Paine, Thomas, 9, 119-21
Parmenides, 101
parody, 73, 173n29
Patterson, Orlando, 17, 74, 106, 173n46
Paul, Saint (the apostle), 33
Pentecost, 34-35
perfectionism, 13
performance theory, 24, 29, 163n12
Peter, Saint (the apostle), 31-32, 34-35
Platt, Jonas, 110, 111
Poirier, Richard, 51
Porter, Dorothy, 34
Pragmatism, 64
Preston, William A., 10
Price, Richard, 1

Raboteau, Albert J., 29
racial biologism, 46
racial differences, 60, 74-77, 173n35; Jefferson on, 72, 98-101; Webb on, 134
racial solidarism, 113-14, 131-32
racial theories, 50, 53-60, 130, 170n47
racism, 59-61, 97, 125; Emerson on, 171n72; internalized, 71; stereotypes and, 106-10, 183n46; Webb on, 147-48
Radical Political Abolition Party, 77, 79
Rancière, Jacques, 4, 8
Reagan, Ronald, 155
Reid-Pharr, Robert, 126, 132
Remond, Charles Lenox, 77
republicanism, 9, 151-56, 160n24
respectability, 18-19, 91-93, 109-23; Douglass on, 18; Simons on, 109-10; slave morality and, 102; theory of, 93-102

Roach, Joseph, 29, 31
Rogers, Melvin, 13-14, 122
Rousseau, Jean-Jacques, 104
Rowe, John Carlos, 50
Ruggles, David, 111, 112
Ruttenburg, Nancy, 27

Said, Edward W., 163n14
Santamarina, Xiomara, 172n2
Santayana, George, 167n12
Sbriglia, Russell, 139
segregation, 9, 127, 132, 139, 153-56
self-reliance, 52-53, 167n10
Sensen, Oliver, 18-19, 97
sentimentalism, 71-72, 126-28
separatism, 36, 130
sexual assault, 68, 78-79, 81-82, 98, 174n57
Simons, Peter Paul, 18, 92, 93, 109-16; McCune Smith and, 18, 117, 122-23; spouse of, 178n43
skin color, 74-77
slave catchers, 46, 47, 48
slave insurrection, 166n1
slave morality, 68-69, 156; Arendt on, 176n85; democracy and, 10-13, 44, 47-48; performativity of, 83-89; respectability and, 102
slavery, 17-18, 29; civil, 1-2; Emerson on, 46-47, 64-65; Hegel on, 82-83; indentured servants and, 16; individual versus community, 76-77
Smith, Adam, 104
Snead, James, 101
social death, 173n46
Society for Promoting Religious Knowledge among the Poor, 23
Southern, Eileen, 164n31
speech acts, 68-69, 87-89
Spillers, Hortense, 175n62
Spires, Derrick, 8, 121
spirit possession, 15, 27-32
spirituals, 164n31
Stewart, Maria W., 113, 115, 131-32
Stowe, Harriet Beecher, 67, 129, 130, 149, 181n11

"Talented Tenth" (Du Bois), 139, 180n83
Talmadge, Herman, 153
Tate, Claudia, 78-80
Taylor, Diana, 29
temperance movement, 74
Thoreau, Henry David, 63
Threadcraft, Shatema, 78, 81
Tocqueville, Alexis de, 44, 154
Toussaint Louverture, 134-35
Transcendentalism, 15-16, 18, 101; Douglass and, 45, 47-49, 55; Emerson and, 46-52
"transitive beginnings" (Said), 163n14
Tregear, Gabriel Shear, 106-7
Tronto, Joan, 182n17
Truth, Sojourner, 108
Turner, Jack, 51-52, 53, 140, 180n92

US Constitution, 77, 161n24; Thirteenth Amendment, 3; Fifteenth Amendment, 110

violence, 16-18, 67-69; Arendt on, 16, 17, 87; Douglass on, 77; Fanon on, 82, 85; Glymph on, 76; liberation through, 68, 77-83, 86, 174n46
voting rights, 9, 110-11, 151, 184n67

Wald, Priscilla, 69
Walker, David, 77, 150; *Appeal to the Colored Citizens of the World*, 37, 44, 68, 89; on assimilationism, 130; on complacency, 141; Jefferson and, 99
Warren, Kenneth, 8-9
Washington, Booker T., 131
Watts, Isaac, 23
Webb, Frank J.: on domesticity, 131-34; Douglass and, 126; *The Garies and Their Friends*, 19-20, 125-50; sentimentalism of, 126-27; Stowe on, 129
Wells Brown, William, 135, 174n57, 181n4, 181n6
Wells-Barnett, Ida B., 161n39
West African religions, 28-29

Wheatley, Phyllis, 5–7, 36–37, 101; evangelicalism of, 15, 23; Gilroy on, 6–7; Jefferson on, 100
White, Charley, 108
white supremacists, 19, 52, 171n72; Krause on, 106; Wilson on, 85
Whitfield, James Monroe, 167n12
Whitman, Walt, 63, 101
Wilder, Craig Steven, 39, 113, 165n50
Willis, Nathaniel Parker, 180n83

Wilson, Harriet E.: Douglass and, 77; on hair styles, 74–77; *Our Nig*, 16–17, 67–77, 83–89; on skin color, 74–77
Wilson, William J. "Ethiop," 93–94, 118, 179n83
women's rights movement, 108, 115–16
Wyatt-Brown, Bertram, 105

Zip Coon ideology, 106–10, 183n46
"zone of non-being" (Fanon), 84

www.ingramcontent.com/pod-product-compliance
Lightning Source LLC
Chambersburg PA
CBHW022011290426
44109CB00015B/1138